Writing Motivation Research, Measurement and Pedagogy

This book provides a unique reference and comprehensive overview of the issues pertinent to conceptualizing, measuring, researching, and nurturing writing motivation.

Abdel Latif covers these theoretical, practical, and research issues by drawing on the literature related to the eight main constructs of writing motivation: writing apprehension, attitude, anxiety, self-efficacy, self-concept, learning goals, perceived value of writing, and motivational regulation. Specifically, the book covers the historical research developments of the field, the measures of the main writing motivation constructs, the correlates and sources of writing motivation, and profiles of motivated and demotivated writers. The book also describes the types of the instructional research of writing motivation, provides pedagogical guidelines and procedures for motivating students to write, and presents suggestions for advancing writing motivation research, measurement, and pedagogy.

Detailed, up-to-date, and with a glossary which includes definitions of the main terms used in the six chapters, this book will be of great interest to academics, researchers, and post-graduate students in the fields of language education, applied linguistics, psycholinguistics, and educational psychology.

Muhammad M. M. Abdel Latif teaches English language education/TESOL at Cairo University, Egypt. His main research interests include writing motivation and written text production processes, and he has widely published in international journals.

Routledge Research in Language Education

This series aims to present the latest research from right across the field of education. It is not confined to any particular area or school of thought and seeks to provide coverage of a broad range of topics, theories and issues from around the world.

Integrative and Interdisciplinary Curriculum in the Middle School
Integrated Approaches in Teacher Preparation and Practice.
Edited by Lisa M Harrison, Ellis Hurd, and Kathleen Brinegar

Curriculum and the Generation of Utopia
Interrogating the Current State of Critical Curriculum Theory
João M. Paraskeva

Sport, Physical Education, and Social Justice
Religious, Sociological, Psychological, and Capability Perspectives
Edited by Nick J. Watson, Grant Jarvie and Andrew Parker

Quality and Equity in Education
Revisiting Theory and Research on Educational Effectiveness and Improvement
Leonidas Kyriakides, Bert P.M. Creemers, Anastasia Panayiotou, & Evi Charalambous

Creative Learning in Digital and Virtual Environments
Opportunities and Challenges of Technology-Enabled Learning and Creativity
Edited by Vlad P. Glăveanu, Ingunn Johanne Ness, and Constance de Saint Laurent

Reconceptualizing the Role of Critical Dialogue in American Classrooms
Promoting Equity through Dialogic Education
Edited by Amanda Kibler, Guadalupe Valdés and Aída Walqui

Towards Rational Education
A Social Framework of Moral Values and Practices
Demetris Katsikis

Schooling and Social Change Since 1760
Creating Inequalities through Education
Roy Lowe

For a complete list of titles in this series, please visit www.routledge.com/Routledge-Research-in-Education/book-series/SE0393

Writing Motivation Research, Measurement and Pedagogy

Muhammad M. M. Abdel Latif

LONDON AND NEW YORK

First published 2021
by Routledge
2 Park Square, Milton Park, Abingdon, Oxon OX14 4RN

and by Routledge
52 Vanderbilt Avenue, New York, NY 10017

Routledge is an imprint of the Taylor & Francis Group, an informa business

© 2021 Muhammad M. M. Abdel Latif

The right of Muhammad M. M. Abdel Latif to be identified as author of this work has been asserted by him in accordance with sections 77 and 78 of the Copyright, Designs and Patents Act 1988.

All rights reserved. No part of this book may be reprinted or reproduced or utilised in any form or by any electronic, mechanical, or other means, now known or hereafter invented, including photocopying and recording, or in any information storage or retrieval system, without permission in writing from the publishers.

Trademark notice: Product or corporate names may be trademarks or registered trademarks, and are used only for identification and explanation without intent to infringe.

British Library Cataloguing-in-Publication Data
A catalogue record for this book is available from the British Library

Library of Congress Cataloging-in-Publication Data

Names: Abdel Latif, Muhammad M. M., author.
Title: Writing motivation research, measurement and pedagogy / Muhammad M.M. Abdel Latif.
Identifiers: LCCN 2020027903 (print) | LCCN 2020027904 (ebook) | ISBN 9780367856274 (hardback) | ISBN 9781003013976 (ebook)
Subjects: LCSH: Composition (Language arts)--Psychological aspects. | Authorship--Psychological aspects. | Motivation in education. | Motivation (Psychology)
Classification: LCC PN181 .A34 2021 (print) | LCC PN181 (ebook) | DDC 808.02--dc23
LC record available at https://lccn.loc.gov/2020027903
LC ebook record available at https://lccn.loc.gov/2020027904

ISBN: 978-0-367-85627-4 (hbk)
ISBN: 978-1-003-01397-6 (ebk)

Typeset in in Times New Roman
by KnowledgeWorks Global Ltd.

To Dalia (my wife), and to Ayten and Adam (my children)

Contents

List of Tables   *x*
Introduction   *xi*

1 Writing motivation research: Historical developments and conceptualisations of the constructs   1

Introduction 1
Writing Motivation: Definition and importance 1
*Motivational constructs researched in writing studies:
    Historical roots and developments 4*
*Defining writing motivation constructs: Resolving
    problematic conceptualization issues 7*
Conclusion 20
References 22

2 Measuring writing motivation   33

Introduction 33
Measures of attitudinal/dispositional constructs 33
Measures of situational constructs 41
Measures of writing ability belief constructs 45
Measures of writing learning goal constructs 56
Measurers of writing motivation sources 59
The qualitative approach to assessing writers' motivation 60
*Guidelines for developing and validating writing
    motivation measures 64*
Conclusion 66
References 67

3 Profiling motivated and demotivated writers   75

Introduction 75
The role of personal variables in writing motivation 75

Performance, belief, and behaviour correlates
of writing motivation 79
Learning and instructional practices as sources
of writing motivation 90
Characteristics of demotivated and motivated writers 96
Conclusion 98
References 99

4 Instructional research of writing motivation   110

Introduction 110
Technology-supported instruction 111
Strategy instruction 114
Feedback instructional treatments 117
Genre-based instruction 122
Task interest-based instruction 124
Therapeutic training 125
Conclusion 128
References 130

5 Motivating students to write: Some research-driven guidelines   137

Introduction 137
Nurturing and fostering students' writing motivational
    perceptions, beliefs, and goals 139
Using appropriate teaching materials and writing tasks 141
Meeting students' language and writing
    performance needs 143
Integrating technological tools into writing instruction 145
Optimizing teacher feedback 146
Orchestrating peer assessment activities 148
Conclusion 149
References 152

**6 Advancing writing motivation measurement,
research, and pedagogy**   155

Introduction 155
Strengthening the conceptualizations and
    operationalizations of writing motivation constructs 155
Researching writing motivation correlates and sources 157

Developing writing motivation instructional research 159
*Promoting effective writing motivation
    instructional practices 161*
References 162

Glossary   166
Index   171

Tables

1.1	A framework of the types of writing motivation constructs.	21
2.1	A list of the writing apprehension and attitude scales published since the 1970s.	34
2.2	A list of the published scales assessing the situational writing motivation constructs (writing anxiety and the motivational regulation of writing).	41
2.3	A list of the published writing self-efficacy scales and their types.	46
2.4	A list of the scales assessing writing self-concept and related constructs.	53
4.1	A summary of the main types of writing motivation instructional studies.	129
5.1	Main guidelines and specific pedagogical procedures for motivating students to write.	150

Introduction

My interest in the writing motivation area has grown since 2005 when I started doing my PhD research at the University of Essex, UK. In my PhD research, I looked at the influence of L2 learners' writing apprehension and self-efficacy (two motivational constructs) on their text production processes. For more than one and a half decades, I have developed an increasing interest in reading writing motivation literature and writing about the area. I can say two factors have fostered my continuous interest in writers' motivation. First, the developments this research area has witnessed since the turn of the century. Second, the increasing recognition of the influential role motivation plays in students' writing learning and performance. This recognition is based on what has been observed in the many university writing courses I have taught in the Arab world. With these developments and observations in mind, I have found a pressing need for synthesizing the accumulated writing motivation literature in one volume.

Due to the important role of writing motivation plays in shaping learners' writing learning experiences, researchers and teachers need to be aware of the key issues pertinent to its research, measurement, and pedagogy. Previous writings on the area occurred normally in the form of either a journal article or a book chapter. Books addressing writing motivation issues seem to be very scarce. Despite the 4.5-decade-old research on writing motivation, no single book has yet comprehensively discussed the research, measurement, and pedagogy issues in this area. To the best of my knowledge, Hidi and Boscolo's (2007) work is perhaps the only book published to date on writing motivation. It is mainly an edited volume which includes a number of chapters, most of which are reports of empirical studies on writing motivation. That is why researchers and teachers interested in the area still need a single resource that covers the updated perspectives related to the research, measurement, and pedagogy of the multiple writing motivation constructs.

This book tries to fill in this important gap in writing psychology literature in particular and language learning psychology in general. The updated and more comprehensive coverage of the relevant issues makes the book a very important and unique reference for researchers interested in writing motivation and language learning motivation/psychology. This book is also an important resource for writing teachers as it could help them understand how to properly diagnose their students' writing motivation, and tailor writing instruction to meet their motivational needs. A main merit in the book is its coverage of a wider range of writing motivational constructs as compared to the previous works. Overall, the book provides important implications to advancing the conceptualization and operationalization of writing motivation constructs, researching writers' motivation, and designing writing instruction in a way appropriate to motivating students.

The book includes six chapters covering various issues in writing motivation research, measurement and pedagogy. It starts by defining the area and its constructs, tracing the historical research trends in writing motivation studies, and discussing the conceptualizations of the main writing motivation constructs researched so far. In chapter 2, I highlight the measurement perspectives of writing motivation constructs, review the scales previously used in assessing them, and provide some guidelines for developing and validating writing motivation measures. In chapter 3, I discuss what research says about the correlates and predictors of negative and positive writing affect and the potential factors shaping writers' motivational characteristics and levels. The review and discussion given in this chapter will help in developing initial profiles delineating the characteristics of motivated and demotivated writers. In chapter 4, I highlight the types of instructional research of writing motivation, i.e., the studies examining the effectiveness of some instructional treatments in reinforcing learners' writing motivation or alleviating their negative writing affect. Based on the insights gained from the issues highlighted and discussed in chapters 3 and 4, I allocate chapter 5 to providing some instructional guidelines on how to motivate students to write and/or alleviate their negative writing affect. In the final chapter (chapter 6), I discuss the future research and practice orientations needed for advancing writing motivation measurement, studies, and pedagogy. The book ends with a glossary which includes definitions of the main terms used in the six chapters.

Taken the above-mentioned contents into account, I can say that this is perhaps the first monograph that comprehensively covers the issues related to writing motivation measurement, research, and pedagogy. The book could help readers understand the process of researching writing motivation, and develop a deep knowledge base about its measurement, characteristics, and pedagogy.

I hope the contents of the book will meet interested readers' expectations and needs.

Muhammad M. M. Abdel Latif

1 Writing motivation research

Historical developments and conceptualizations of the constructs

1.1 Introduction

Before addressing the various issues in researching, measuring, and teaching writing motivation, it is important to start with defining it and its main constructs and tracing the historical developments in this research area. Clarifying these key concepts will help readers develop deeper understanding of the relevant issues discussed in the next parts of the book. In this introductory chapter, the author highlights the role played by motivation in shaping writers' learning experiences and performance. This is followed by tracing the historical roots and developments in writing motivation research. The longest section in chapter includes a detailed discussion of the conceptualization issues of the main motivation writing constructs researched so far. Based on the conclusions drawn from discussing these issues, the author provides a framework of writing motivation constructs and their types. The framework will guide the discussion of the issues highlighted in the following chapters.

1.2 Writing motivation: Definition and importance

Motivation cannot be ignored when talking about writing. Writing motivation has been researched so far for more than four and a half decades. Though "writing motivation" has been conceptualized in a much narrower sense than the term "motivation", it remains an umbrella term characterized by its broad conceptual nature. Some other terms have been interchangeably used with "writing motivation", including writing affect (Hayes, 1996; Piazza & Siebert, 2008; Wright, Hodges, & McTigue, 2019), writers' beliefs (Hidi & Boscolo, 2007; Pajares & Valiante, 2001), and writing self-perceptions (Bottomley, Henk, & Melnick, 1997; Leggette, Redwine, & Busick, 2020; Lingwall & Kuehn, 2013). Before defining writing motivation, it is perhaps necessary to look briefly at the definitions and conceptualizations of the two broader but related constructs: general motivation and second language (L2) learning motivation.

The word motivation is derived from the Latin verb "movere" which means "to move"; thus it generally implies the psychological and emotional force that leads the individual to make specific choices, take particular actions, exert effort, and show persistence in certain situations or tasks (Dörnyei & Ushioda, 2011). Dörnyei and Ottó (1998) provide the following comprehensive definition of motivation:

> In a general sense, motivation can be defined as the dynamically changing cumulative arousal in a person that initiates, directs, coordinates, amplifies, terminates, and evaluates the cognitive and motor processes whereby initial wishes and desires are selected, prioritised, operationalised and (successfully or unsuccessfully) acted out. (p. 65)

On the other hand, L2 learning motivation has been defined in various ways. As Dörnyei and Ushioda (2011) note, the theoretical framework of L2 learning motivation has been expanded during the following three main historical periods of its research: the social psychological period (1959–1990), cognitive-situated period (the 1990s), and the process-oriented period that started at the turn of the century. For example, during the social psychological period, Gardner (1985) viewed language learning motivation as a construct composed of three components: a desire to learn the language, a positive attitude towards learning it, and an effort made to accomplish the target language learning goal. Ten years later, Tremblay and Gardner (1995) provided a more complex framework for L2 learning motivation, which includes language attitudes, motivational behaviours related to specificity of the learner's goals, L2-learning-related value, self-efficacy, and achievement sequence. A well-cited framework of L2 learning motivation is the one developed by Dörnyei (1994) and it includes three distinct levels related to the language (integrative and instrumental motivational subsystems), the learner (need for achievement and self-confidence), and the learning situation (course-specific, teacher-specific, and group-specific motivational components).

On the other hand, four types of L2 learning motivation have been identified and researched heavily; these are integrative, instrumental, intrinsic, and extrinsic motivation. The instrumental and integrative language learning motivation constructs were introduced by Gardner and Lambert in their early works (1959, 1972). While integrative motivation refers to willingness to learn a particular language to successfully interact with its valued culture and community members, instrumental motivation means learning a language for a pragmatic purpose such as getting a better job or a financial reward. The terms "intrinsic/extrinsic motivation" were coined by Deci and Ryan (1985) in their educational psychological theory of self-determination. Intrinsic motivation means learning a language as a result of internal desires such as self-enjoyment and self-satisfaction, whereas extrinsic motivation – a closely related construct to instrumental motivation – refers to learning a language due to external rewards such as obtaining grades in a course or praise from teachers (Noels, 2001).

As for writing motivation, it is viewed as a dynamic multifaceted construct that varies depending on different developmental stages, disciplines, environments, and tasks (Wright et al., 2019). Unlike the many frameworks developed for conceptualizing L2 learning motivation, very scarce attempts have been made to typologize the types of writing motivational perceptions. For example, Daly (1985) distinguishes between two types of writers' motivational perceptions and beliefs: a) the dispositional perceptions lasting consistently over time and across situations; and b) the situational feelings which are temporary and closely tied to particular situations or tasks. Daly's taxonomy seems to resemble Linnenbrink's (2006) differentiation between trait-like and state-like learning affect. While the former type mirrors a relatively stable response to learning tasks and settings, the latter reflects a less stable and situational one. On the other hand, Hidi and Boscolo (2007) also refer to the following three motivational constructs of writing: a) motives which include the writer's goal orientation, needs, values, and interests activating their behaviours; b) perceptions of one's abilities to write and perform tasks; and c) regulation of one's writing cognition and behaviours. In Wright et al.'s (2019) recent model, writing motivation is described as a construct composed of beliefs about oneself as a writer (self-concept and self-efficacy), beliefs about writing value, and attitudes towards writing.

In light of these typologies and the relevant literature, writing motivation can be defined as an umbrella term encompassing learners' liking or disliking of writing situations and perceived value of writing, the situational feelings they experience while writing and the way they regulate them, the beliefs about their writing ability and skills, and their desired goals for learning to write.

If Skehan (1989) views motivation as the second strongest predictor of L2 learning – trailing behind language aptitude, a comparable impact can also be noted for writing motivation on student writers' performance and learning habits. Writers' performance interacts with a combination of motivational, cognitive, social, and environmental variables. Motivation plays an influential role in students' writing learning, performance, and development. With the increasing recognition that writing difficulties arise from demotivation, the motivation/affect component was included in Hayes's (1996) updated version of the Flower-Hayes (1980) writing process model. In his model, Hayes (1996) conceptualizes "motivation and affect" as a main predictor of writers' cognitive processes. Apart from the process models, some writing ability models have also emphasized the role of motivation in shaping writers' competence. For example, Sasaki and Hirose (1996) include writing confidence in their model as a potentially explanatory factor of L2 writing ability.

Research indicates that motivation greatly influences a number of dimensions related to writers' task approach behaviours (e.g., Fritzsche, Young, & Hickson, 2003; Onwuegbuzie & Collins, 2001), their composing processes (Abdel Latif, 2009; Selfe, 1984), the texts they write

4 *Writing motivation research*

(Abdel Latif, 2015), and their long-term writing experiences (Atay & Kurt, 2006). This great role is discussed in detail in chapter 3, which highlights what research says about the influence of writing motivation on learners' performance at these process and product levels. Due to the influential role of writing motivation, considerable attention should be given to researching, assessing, and teaching it. These are the three main issues this book addresses.

1.3 Motivational constructs researched in writing studies: Historical roots and developments

Very early research on writing motivation dates back to the mid-1970s when Daly and Miller (1975a) reported their seminal work on writers' apprehension. Thus, writing motivation research occurred about a decade and a half after the publication of Gardner and Lambert's (1959) early work on language learning motivation. Since the mid-1970s, the area of writing motivation research has seen major developments. During this four and a half-decade period, much literature and research have accumulated on a number of writing motivational constructs. Eight main constructs have been addressed in such accumulated research; these are: writing apprehension, attitude, anxiety, self-efficacy, self-concept, outcome expectancy/achievement goal orientation, perceived value of writing, and motivational regulation of writing. Additionally, some other writing motivational constructs have recently been coined but do not seem to be strong ones and they also overlap in one way or another with the above-mentioned constructs.

In their coinage of the larger number of writing motivation constructs, researchers were mainly influenced by educational psychology or oral language communication literature rather than language learning motivation research. A main reason for this is that these constructs were developed in first language (L1) writing environments whereas most language learning motivation research has been mainly concerned with L2 settings. Daly and Miller (1975a), for example, derived the "writing apprehension" construct from the interpersonal communication apprehension research published in the late 1960s and early 1970s (e.g., Friedrich, 1970; Giffin & Gilham, 1971; McCroskey, 1972; Phillips, 1968; Phillips & Metzger, 1973). Meanwhile, a group of educational psychologists such as Patricia McCarthy, Duane Shell, Frank Pajares, Barry Zimmerman, and Steve Graham led the early research on writing self-efficacy, self-concept, and outcome expectancy/achievement goals. In their remarkable research on writing motivation constructs, those researchers were particularly influenced by the general educational psychology literature written by Bandura (1977, 1986), Eccles (1987), and Middleton and Midgley (1997). Accordingly, the early research developments on writing motivation constructs owe much to educational psychology and oral communication literature rather than the applied linguistics and L2 learning fields. Meanwhile, the influence of L2 learning motivation research trends can be only noted in three writing motivational constructs researched for the first time during the last decade: ideal L2 writing self (Han & Hiver, 2018; Lee, Yu, & Liu, 2018), ought-to L2 writing self (Lee et al., 2018), and motivational regulation of writing (Teng & Zhang, 2016a, 2016b).

There have been major shifts in the four and a half decade-old period of writing motivation research. From the mid-1970s to the late 1980s, apprehension and attitude were the two main researched writing motivation constructs. This period was particularly characterized by the plenty of published writing apprehension research and literature. Of all the works reported on the construct during this period, John Daly and the many works he published and co-published with his colleagues remain remarkable (e.g., Daly, 1977, 1978, 1979, 1985; Daly & Hailey, 1984; Daly & Miller, 1975a, 1975b, 1975c; Daly & Shamo, 1976, 1978; Daly & Wilson, 1983; Faigley, Daly, & Witte, 1981). In addition to these works, some other few writing apprehension studies were published during this period by Burgoon and Hale (1983), Fox (1980), Richmond and Dickson-Markman (1985), Riffe and Stacks (1988), and Selfe (1984). On the other hand, a few doctoral writing apprehension studies were also completed during the 1970s and 1980s but these do not seem to have been published (e.g., Bannister, 1982; Butler, 1980; Garcia, 1977; Hadaway, 1987; Harvley-Felder, 1978).

Compared to this active writing apprehension research movement in the 1970s–1980s, scarce studies occurred during this period on the "attitude towards writing". The works reported by Blake (1976), Emig and King (1979), Hogan (1980), and Thompson (1978) are examples of such writing attitude research. Since the mid-1980s, the attitude towards writing construct has been addressed in a reasonable number of published studies. On the other hand, it can be noted in Daly and his colleagues' early works (e.g., Daly & Miller, 1975a, 1975b, 1975c; Daly & Wilson, 1983; Faigley et al., 1981) that the term "writing anxiety" was also used interchangeably with "writing apprehension" but – as will be explained in the following section – the two constructs are different. Research addressing writing anxiety has generally been scarce. Though Meier, McCarthy, and Schmeck (1984) reported an early study on writing anxiety, the few in-depth ones addressing it occurred only in the last two decades. It is worth mentioning that early published research and literature on these three motivational constructs – writing apprehension, attitude, and anxiety – originated in the US university context. The last three decades saw research addressing the three constructs in other international contexts.

The 1980s also witnessed the beginning of writing self-efficacy research. The four studies reported by Graham and Harris (1989), McCarthy, Meier, and Rinderer (1985), Meier et al. (1984), and Shell, Murphy, and Bruning (1989) are perhaps the earliest published studies on the construct. Since the early 1990s, writing self-efficacy research has grown steadily. Obviously, self-efficacy has been the most heavily researched writing motivation construct. Bruning, Dempsey, Kauffman, McKim, and Zumbrunn (2013) reviewed four waves of early writing self-efficacy research led by

McCarthy, Shell, Pajares, and Zimmerman, and their colleagues. Each stage was characterized by using a particular type of measures assessing the construct.

As for research on writing self-concept and outcome expectancy/achievement goals, it occurred in a later stage. Though Shaver (1990) made an early reference to writing self-concept through highlighting the items assessing it in Daly and Miller's (1975) Writing Apprehension Test (WAT), the research dealing with the construct was published only at the turn of the century (Pajares, Britner, & Valiante, 2000; Pajares, Miller, & Johnson, 1999; Pajares & Valiante, 1999, 2001). This early research was followed by some other scarce studies that occurred infrequently during the last two decades (Ehm, Lindberg, & Hasselhorn, 2014; Pajares & Cheong, 2003; Pajares, Valiante, & Cheong, 2007). On the other hand, the 1990s and the last decade witnessed the publication of some studies addressing four constructs which are very similar to writing self-concept but are not as broad as it. These are: the notion of writing giftedness (Charney, Newman, & Palmquist, 1995; Palmquist & Young, 1992), the implicit theories of writing (Limpo, 2018; Limpo & Alves, 2014, 2017), and the incremental and entity theories of writing intelligence (Waller & Papi, 2017). Overall, research on writing self-concept and these four similar constructs have been scarce. More than two decades ago, Pajares and Valiante (1999) noted that writing self-concept was not "as prominent in the motivation literature as other forms of self-concept" (p. 392). The scarce writing self-concept studies published in the two decades also confirm Pajares and Valiante's (1999) early note. Arguably, the scarcity of the studies published so far on writing self-concept – along with the constructs similar to it – and outcome expectancy have resulted from the influential dominance of writing self-efficacy research. This case is similar to the way extensively published writing apprehension negatively influenced the attention given to writing attitude during the 1970s–1980s period. Literature generally indicates that writers' self-concept beliefs are closely related to their self-efficacy (e.g., Bong & Clark, 1999; Zimmerman, 2000).

Another motivational construct that has received little research attention is writing outcome expectancy/achievement goal orientation. Research on the construct started in 1989 but occurred infrequently during the 1990s and the 2000s. The only four writing achievement goal orientation studies published between 1989 and 1997 were reported by Shell and Pajares, and their colleagues (Pajares & Johnson, 1994; Pajares & Valiante, 1997; Shell, Colvin, & Bruning, 1995; Shell et al., 1989). During this stage, these researchers studied the construct using the terms "writing outcome expectancy" and "writing outcome expectations". Two later waves of research on the construct occurred during the last two decades, i.e., since the beginning of the 21st century. During these two waves, the term "writing outcome expectancy" was replaced with "writing achievement goal orientation". The first wave is represented in the further writing achievement goal orientation research reported by Pajares and his colleagues (Pajares & Cheong,

2003; Pajares et al., 2000, 2007; Pajares & Valiante, 2001). The second research wave includes the writing achievement goal studies published since 2005 (Chea & Shumow, 2017; Hamilton, Nolen, & Abbott, 2013; He, 2005; Kaplan, Lichtinger, & Gorodetsky, 2009; Limpo, 2018; Limpo & Alves, 2017; MacArthur, Philippakos, & Graham, 2016; Troia, Harbaugh, Shankland, Wolbers, & Lawrence, 2013; Yilmaz Soylu et al., 2017). Meanwhile, the two studies reported by Han and Hiver (2018) and Lee et al. (2018) dealt with "ideal L2 writing self" and "ought-to L2 writing self"; two constructs which overlap with some dimensions of writers' achievement goal orientations. Overall, there has been a relative increase in the number of writing achievement goal studies published recently. That is why a considerable growth is expected to occur in this research area in the near future.

The late 1990s saw the first published studies on the perceived value of writing (Pajares & Valiante, 1999). This was followed by a few other ones dealing with the construct in the last two decades, though some of them named it differently (e.g., Behizadeh & Engelhard, 2014, 2016; Pajares & Valiante, 2001; Pajares, Valiante, & Cheong, 2007; Troia et al., 2013; Wright et al., 2019). On the other hand, research on the "motivational regulation of writing" only occurred during the second half of the last decade. The works published by Teng and her colleagues represent the early studies dealing with the construct (Teng & Zhang, 2016a, 2016b, 2018; Teng, Yuan, & Sun, 2020).

In the next section, the author discusses the conceptualizations of each of the above-mentioned eight main constructs of writing motivation and the similar ones researched. This discussion could help in resolving problematic conceptualization issues of each construct and thus defining it accurately.

1.4 Defining writing motivation constructs: Resolving problematic conceptualization issues

Understanding the nature of writing motivation requires defining its constructs accurately. The importance of reaching accurate conceptualizations of writing motivation constructs lies in helping us assess them precisely. This, in turn, will help in the appropriate diagnosis of writers' motivational perceptions and beliefs, which is an essential initial step in identifying any motivational needs they may have. Writing motivation literature is full of varied conceptualizations of a number of its constructs. In some cases, these varied definitions have caused conceptual and terminological overlaps among the constructs. In other cases, they reflect the historical changes in defining a specific construct. Additionally, there is always a mutual relationship between the way of defining a construct and the measure used for assessing it. In the next chapter, the construct validity and item type issues in the scales measuring each writing motivation construct are discussed in detail. In the following subsections, the author reviews the conceptualizations of each construct and explicates any problematic issues in defining it.

1.4.1 Writing apprehension, attitude, and anxiety

As implied above, apprehension, attitude, and anxiety were the first three writing motivation constructs researched. Some conceptual and terminological problems are found in the literature of the three constructs. On one hand, the conceptual and terminological overlaps can be easily noted in writing apprehension and anxiety literature but on the other one, another terminological problem occurs when referring to writing apprehension and attitude as different constructs.

Though much research and literature has conflated writing apprehension and anxiety (see Wynne, Guo, & Wang, 2014), they are in fact different constructs. In their seminal work, Daly and Miller (1975a) used the terms "writing apprehension" and "writing anxiety" synonymously. Despite this, their explanation of the characteristics of high apprehensive writers indicates that anxiety is a symptom of apprehension: "Individuals with high apprehension of writing would fear evaluation of their writing, for example, feeling that they will be negatively rated on it. Thus they avoid writing when possible and when forced to write exhibit high levels of anxiety" (p. 244). A gradual conceptualization change is noted in two later reports published by Daly and his colleagues (Daly & Hailey, 1984; Faigley et al., 1981), where they differentiate between two forms of the same construct. In the first report, the situational nature of writing anxiety is indicated in Faigley et al.'s (1981) description of highly apprehensive writers' behaviours:

> Highly apprehensive writers find writing unrewarding, even punishing. Consequently, they avoid, whenever possible, those situations that require writing...and when they must write they experience more than normal amounts of anxiety...Thus anxiety is reflected in the behaviours they display as they write" (p. 16).

In a later work, Daly and Hailey (1984) differentiate between two forms of writing apprehension: the trait-like dispositional form and the state-like situational one, which reflects the person's transitory feelings resulting from writing situations or tasks. According to Daly and Hailey (1984), the dispositional and situational forms of writing apprehension are distinct but complementary.

Despite Daly and his colleagues' above-noted view of anxiety as a symptom of writers' apprehension and their differentiation between the dispositional and situational forms of the construct, the problem occurs in their synonymous use or conflation of the two terms. This terminological conflation is also noted in other early studies published in the 1970s and 1980s, though the term "writing apprehension" was more commonly used. Some later studies (e.g., Huerta, Goodson, Beigi, & Chlup, 2017; Cheng, Horwitz, & Schallert, 1999) used the term "writing anxiety" but they operationalized the construct by the Daly-Miller (1975) WAT or an adapted version of it.

Besides, Cheng (2004), who depended on the term "writing anxiety" but conflated the two terms, adopted a multidimensional view of the construct by listing three types of it: a) somatic anxiety: increased physiological reactions to writing tasks; b) avoidance behaviour of writing situations; and c) cognitive anxiety: fearing negative evaluation of one's writing. Meanwhile, other researchers (e.g., Zabihi, 2008) adopted Daly and Miller's (1975a) definition of writing apprehension but labelled the construct they investigated as "writing anxiety". In the writing apprehension studies labelling the construct as "writing anxiety", researchers neither justified nor discussed the why for their terminological choice. If the two terms can be used interchangeably, the question remains: which term (witting apprehension or anxiety) is a better label for the construct and why? A further issue yet to be highlighted is whether we should conceptualize writing apprehension as a purely dispositional construct or a dispositional-situational one.

In fact, educational psychology literature indicates that anxiety is a situational construct. For example, mathematics anxiety has been defined as feelings of tension, helplessness, and mental disorganization experienced when manipulating numbers or solving math problems (Richardson & Suinn, 1972; Tobias, 1978). Test anxiety has also been viewed as encompassing four symptoms: tension, worry, irrelevant thinking, and bodily reactions (Sarason, 1984). Dictionary definitions also confirm the situational nature of anxiety. Further evidence can also be found in general psychology and language learning research, indicating that anxiety is the negative feelings associated with particular situations (e.g., Liu & Jackson, 2008; Spielberger, Gorsuch, & Lushene, 1970; Spielberger, Gorsuch, Lushene, Vagg, & Jacobs, 1983; Woodrow, 2006). According to Piniel and Csizér (2014), "language anxiety or foreign language classroom anxiety have been described as situation-specific anxiety; in other words, repeated momentary experiences of anxiety (state anxiety) linked to the context of language learning in particular" (p. 166). The American Psychological Association also defines anxiety from a situational angle as "an emotion characterized by feelings of tension, worried thoughts and physical changes like increased blood pressure" (n.d.). In many language learning studies, reading and listening anxiety have been defined from this situational perspective (e.g., Piniel, Csizér, Khudiyeva, & Gafiatulina, 2016). In light of this evidence, what Daly and Hailey (1984) regard a situational form of writing apprehension is optimally labelled as "writing anxiety".

The above-explained conceptual and terminological overlap between writing apprehension and anxiety has also been caused by the lack of studies on the latter construct. With the exception of Meier et al.'s (1984) early study in which writing anxiety was investigated peripherally as a situational construct, the negligence of researching writing anxiety lasted almost from the mid-1980s until the beginning of the 2000s. The writing anxiety studies published in the last two decades remain very scarce. A very few studies of this type were located (Cheng, 2004; Csizér & Tankó, 2015; Fritzsche,

Young, & Hickson, 2003; Han & Hiver, 2018; Piniel & Csizér, 2014; Piniel, Csizér, Khudiyeva, & Gafiatulina, 2016; Tsai, 2008; Tsao, Tseng, & Wang, 2017, Woodrow, 2011; Yao, 2019). For instance, Fritzsche et al. (2003) conceptualized anxiety as the negative feelings learners experience while performing tasks and assessed it using a measure mirroring the extent to which writers feel worried, tense, or jittery while completing their assignments. Likewise, Woodrow (2011) investigated writing anxiety as a pure situational construct through assessing it with a scale eliciting respondents' rating of how anxious they feel while completing particular writing tasks. For further information about these scales and the items included in them, see subsection 2.3.1 in the next chapter.

While writing apprehension and attitude overlap conceptually, a terminological problem occurs when naming them differently. The "attitude towards writing" appears to be an identical construct to "writing apprehension" in a number of studies. As will be explained in the next chapter (subsection 2.2.1), the statements in the previously used attitude towards writing scales (e.g., Bruning et al., 2013; Graham, Schwartz, & MacArthur, 1993; Lee, 2013) are almost the same as the ones found in the writing apprehension ones. Compare, for example, the items included in Graham et al.'s (1993) Attitudes towards Writing Scale and Bruning et al.'s (2013) Liking Writing scale to the ones in the Daly-Miller's (1975a) WAT (see the final paragraph in this subsection). The previous measures of both writing apprehension and attitude generally indicate the two constructs are identical or very similar, though writing attitude is conceptualized by some studies in a way suggesting it is not as broad as apprehension. The strong similarity between – or the identicalness of – the constructs was early noted by Shaver (1990), who states that the Daly-Miller's (1975) measure and Daly and Wilson's (1983) definition of writing apprehension match his conceptualization of the attitude towards writing.

The lack of terminological justification is also noted in writing apprehension and attitude literature. Despite the above-mentioned identicalness or similarity, the studies using the term "attitude towards writing" have neither explained the similarity and/or difference between the two terms nor justified their choice of such label. The negligence of discussing this issue in writing motivation literature has led in many cases to viewing the two constructs – contrarily to what has been indicated – as different or dissimilar. A problem resulting from this literature gap is finding the studies using the "writing apprehension" term (e.g., Britt, Pribesh, Hinton-Johnson, & Gupta, 2018; Sanders-Reio, Alexander, Reio, & Newman, 2014) or the "attitude towards writing" one (e.g., Graham, Berninger, & Fan, 2007; Lee, 2013) highlight the previous research adopting their chosen term only, despite the fact that they address identical or very similar constructs.

Based on the above discussion, we can generally conclude that writing apprehension and attitude are trait-like constructs. Examples of the items reflecting these two constructs include: "I like to write my ideas down",

"I avoid writing", "Writing is a lot of fun" (Daly & Miller, 1975a, p. 246), "I enjoy writing", "I don't like to write", and "Writing is fun" (Bruning et al., 2013, p. 32). They both share the same conceptual characteristics and that is why they reflect identical motivational perceptions (i.e., one's dis/liking of writing and writing evaluation situations), though literature generally indicates that writing apprehension has been conceptualized as a broader construct than attitude towards writing (see section 2.2.1 in the next chapter). On the other hand, writing anxiety is a state-like construct that generally means one's feeling of discomfort while performing a writing task. Examples of the items mirroring this construct include: "I often feel panic when I write English compositions under time constraint", "I tremble or perspire when I write English compositions under time pressure" (Cheng, 2004, p. 324), and "I feel jittery when I start writing an English composition" (Tsao et al., 2017, p. 226).

1.4.2 Writing self-efficacy

The writing self-efficacy construct was derived from the works of the Canadian-American psychologist Albert Bandura on the general self-efficacy and its role in human functioning. According to Bandura (1977, 1986), self-efficacy beliefs are task-specific and they act as a prerequisite for people's successful task performance because they determine their intentions and effort persistence. Writing self-efficacy has undergone some changing conceptualizations in the last three decades. Overall, there have been three major changing orientations in conceptualizing writing self-efficacy. These varied conceptualizations are particularly reflected in its measures.

The early self-efficacy studies reported in the 1980s and 1990s mostly conceptualize writing self-efficacy as writers' evaluation of their task-specific writing ability and language-specific skills. The definitions given in these early studies include: learners' evaluation of their writing skills (McCarthy et al., 1985), writers' confidence in their ability to successfully perform specific tasks, and demonstrate particular rhetorical and language skills (Shell et al., 1989), and students' confidence in possessing writing, grammar usage, and mechanics skills that match their academic level (Pajares & Valiante, 1999). Similar definitions were also adopted in some more recent studies (e.g., Csizér & Tankó, 2015; Piniel & Csizér, 2014; Woodrow, 2011). The scales representing this conceptualization orientation may include yes-no questions such as "Can you write an essay in which the ideas are expressed clearly?" and "Can you write an essay that contains no major spelling errors?", (Meier, et al., 1984, 110), or may ask respondents to rate their confidence in performing some writing skills; for example, to what extent they can "correctly punctuate a one page passage" and "organize sentences into a paragraph so as to clearly express a theme" (Pajares & Johnson, 1996, p. 166).

The second conceptualization orientation of writing self-efficacy is a cognitive one and it focuses on what can be labelled as process-focused or text composing process self-efficacy (writing self-regulatory efficacy in some researchers' terms). This orientation was commonly addressed in the works published by Zimmerman and his colleagues (e.g., Zimmerman & Bandura, 1994; Zimmerman & Kitsantas, 1999, 2002) and some other researchers (e.g., MacArthur et al., 2016). It views writers' self-efficacy as their perceived ability to regulate composing processes and activities, i.e., generate ideas and plan, execute, and regulate composing activities and strategies (Zimmerman & Bandura, 1994). It is noteworthy, however, that some studies (e.g., Csizér & Tanko, 2015; Han & Hiver, 2018; Lee et al., 2018) used different measures for assessing writing self-efficacy and self-regulation; thus they view writing self-regulation and self-efficacy as different constructs. Scale item examples representing this conceptualization trend ask respondents about the extent to which they can start the writing task easily, get and organize ideas, write fluently (Graham et al., 1993), refocus their attention on the task, find ways to overcome problems, and identify writing errors (Zimmerman & Bandura, 1994).

The third and more recent conceptualization orientation of writing self-efficacy is the multidimensional one which views it as writers' perceived ability to execute some cognitive, linguistic, self-regulatory, or learning actions. The main problem in this conceptualization trend, however, is the different writing self-efficacy dimensions researchers have focused on. Jones's (2008) study is perhaps the earliest study to view writing self-efficacy as a multidimensional construct. In this study, Jones defines writers' self-efficacy as their perceived ability to respond to writing difficulties and write different essay types and demonstrate sentence- and paragraph-level skills. On the other hand, Bruning et al.'s (2013) conceptualization focuses on writers' perceived cognitive, linguistic, and self-regulatory abilities. According to them, writers' self-efficacy is their perceived ability to: generate ideas; articulate ideas into appropriate linguistic and rhetorical written forms; and regulate their writing activities, i.e. manage, monitor, and evaluate them. Finally, Teng, Sun, and Xu (2018) view writing self-efficacy as a construct reflecting writers' perceived ability to: a) express ideas using appropriate lexical, syntactical, and rhetorical conventions (i.e., linguistic self-efficacy); b) execute planning, monitoring, and goal-setting processes (i.e., self-regulatory efficacy); and c) complete classroom tasks and understand course knowledge (i.e., performance self-efficacy).

Since writing self-efficacy is a task-specific construct, another variable that needs to be considered in conceptualizing it is the type of task(s) researched. As will be shown in the discussion of related issues in the next chapter, the previously published self-efficacy scales focused on different types of writing tasks, including paragraphs (Chea & Shumow, 2017), cloze passages and letters (Woodrow, 2011), one-page passages (Pajares & Valiante, 1997), essays (Abdel Latif, 2015), academic and scholarly writing (Kavanoz & Yüksel, 2016), papers, reports, stories (Graham et al., 1993), instructional manuals, and legal documents (Shell et al., 1989).

In accordance with the above conceptualizations and considerations, we can generally define writing self-efficacy as one's perceived ability to perform task-specific writing skills and/or operations. These above-noted varied conceptualizations, however, imply the need for viewing writing self-efficacy as a construct of various types associated with particular tasks. Overall, the following three main types can be identified in the changing conceptualizations of writing self-efficacy:

- **Product-focused writing self-efficacy (i.e. writing convention self-efficacy):** one's perceived ability to produce certain written text features (for example, writing grammatically correct sentences or good paragraphs with appropriate topic sentences).
- **Process-focused writing self-efficacy (i.e., text composing process self-efficacy):** one's perceived ability to regulate and use particular composing processes (for example, generating ideas, planning text writing, and evaluating and monitoring text production).
- **Learning writing self-efficacy:** one's perceived ability to complete specific writing classroom activities or learn particular writing course contents (for example, understanding writing course materials, doing good assignments, and performing well in writing courses).

Since writing self-efficacy is a task-specific construct, these three main types of writing self-efficacy may be also associated with the task performed. With regard to essay writing, for example, we can talk about written essay self-efficacy, essay writing process self-efficacy, and learning-to-write essay self-efficacy. This also applies to all the other writing tasks listed above, for example: written academic paper self-efficacy, academic paper composing process self-efficacy, and learning-to-write academic paper self-efficacy. Conceptualizing self-efficacy in such typology is perhaps the only way for facilitating the comparability of the findings of the much writing self-efficacy research.

1.4.3 Writing self-concept and similar constructs

As a construct, writing self-concept is close to self-efficacy and it is indeed "one of the closest constructs to self-efficacy" (Zimmerman, 2000, p. 84). Bong and Clark (1999) state that the two constructs share similar aspects despite the differences between them. Wright et al. (2019) also state that the two constructs are often referred to interchangeably because the differences between them are poorly explained. According to Bong and Skaalvik (2003), self-concept is a "composite view of oneself" (p. 2) and it is developed through personal experiences and social comparisons (i.e., comparing one's performance with peers' performances). General psychology definitions of self-concept include: "a person's perceptions of him- or herself. These perceptions are formed through experiences with and interpretations of one's environment" (Marsh & Shavelson, 1985, p. 107) and "the individual's belief about himself or herself, including the person's attributes and who and what the self is" (Baumeister, 1999, p. 247). Thus, self-concept mirrors one's general ability self-esteem and what forms it, i.e., it is not task-specific like self-efficacy. In other words, the items testing writers' self-concept may include "In writing, I make a lot of mistakes/no mistakes", and "In writing, I am not gifted/very gifted" (Ehm et al., 2014, p. 290), as compared to the following self-efficacy items: "I can write complete sentences", "I can write grammatically correct sentences", and "I can spell my words correctly" (Bruning et al., 2013, p. 30). The following supporting explanation is provided by Wright et al. (2019):

> [A] self-concept item may query: When my class is asked to write an essay, report or story, mine is one of the best. Self-efficacy, in contrast, is focused on what an individual believes he or she can achieve with the skills and abilities they currently possess. …In short, self-concept tells someone they are, in general, a good writer, whereas self-efficacy tells them they have the skill-set to successfully complete a particularly difficult essay. As such a representative self-efficacy item would be: When I get a good grade on a paper, it is because I tried very hard. (pp. 66–67)

Accordingly, self-concept refers to writers' perceived beliefs about their general writing ability. Pajares and Valiante (2001) define the construct as "the judgments of self-worth associated with one's self-perception as a writer" (p. 370).

Four other constructs similar or perhaps identical to writing self-concept have also been researched. Palmquist and Young (1992) addressed the notion of writing giftedness, i.e., the belief that one's writing ability is a gift. They operationalized the construct using a four-item scale that focuses on respondents' beliefs on the learnability and teachability of their writing skills. Research on the following three similar constructs occurred during the last decade: implicit theories of writing (Karlen & Compagnoni, 2017; Limpo, 2018; Limpo & Alves, 2014, 2017), the incremental theory, and the entity theory of writing intelligence (Waller & Papi, 2017). Implicit theories of writing are viewed as the beliefs about the malleability and improvability of one's writing ability (Limpo & Alves, 2014). Similarly, the incremental and entity theories of writing intelligence have been defined, respectively, as learners' "belief that writing intelligence is dynamic and can grow through effort and experience", and their "belief that writing intelligence is fixed and unchangeable" (Waller & Papi, 2017, 54). The three constructs and the scale items representing them were derived from Dweck's (2000) work on self-theories and motivation. The items used for assessing implicit theories of writing include: "My texts will always have the same quality, no matter how much I try to change it", and "If I write well, it's because I was born like that" (Limpo & Alves, 2014, p. 576). Similar items were also included in

Waller and Papi's (2017) scales of the entity and incremental theories of writing intelligence, for example: "You can improve your English writing skills, but you can't really change your writing talent", "No matter how hard you try, as an English language learner you can never write like a native speaker", and "No matter who you are, you can always learn to write as well as native speakers of English" (p. 58). As noted, Waller and Papi's (2017) two constructs are very identical to Limpo and Alves's (2014) "implicit theories of writing" in terms of their conceptualizations and the items of the measures. Overall, the four constructs (i.e., the notion of writing giftedness, the implicit theories of writing, and the incremental and entity theories of writing) are similar to writers' self-concept in that they are concerned with the beliefs about their general writing ability and its improvability. The main difference is that writing self-concept is a broader construct than these four ones. This conceptual overlap could have been caused by not drawing upon writing motivation literature when coining the three constructs in particular.

The above-reviewed conceptualizations of writing self-concept and similar constructs indicate the much work needed in this area. Compared to the self-concept definitions and operationalizations in general and educational psychology, many shortcomings can be noted in the little writing self-concept literature. Due to these shortcomings, writing self-concept is yet to be fully represented as a writing motivation construct. This issue is further discussed in the next chapter (subsection 2.4.2), which highlights the assessment of the construct and other related terms.

1.4.4 Writing outcome expectancy and achievement goal orientation

Both writing outcome expectancy and achievement goal orientations are goal constructs. In other words, they resemble the four types of L2 learning motivation defined in section 1.2: integrative, instrumental, intrinsic, and extrinsic motivation. That is why these two constructs overlap in one way or another. Unlike the case of the above-reviewed writing motivation constructs, no remarkable changes are noted in the conceptualizations of writers' outcome expectancy or achievement goals. This can partially be attributed to the few studies published so far on two constructs.

Outcome expectancy indicates one's beliefs about the expected outcome from completing a learning task successfully. By considering the gain obtained from successful task completion, these beliefs impact the individual's task performance (Bandura, 1986). Shell et al. (1989, 1995) define writing outcome expectancy as the perceived importance of writing for achieving some life goals. They operationalize the construct using a 20-item scale, which asks respondents to rate the importance of writing for achieving different life goals. Pajares and his colleagues followed two different approaches to researching writing outcome expectancy. In their two early studies, Pajares and Johnson (1994) and Pajares and Valiante (1997) used Shell et al.'s (1989) scale or an adapted version of it in assessing the construct. In the later studies (Pajares & Cheong, 2003; Pajares et al., 2000, 2007; Pajares & Valiante, 2001), they used a writing achievement goal orientation scale adapted from Middleton and Midgley (1997).

On the other hand, achievement goals mean learners' reasons, purposes, or desired outcomes for doing a particular academic activity (Pintrich, 2000). The motivational impact of the goals set for learning lies in stimulating learners' engagement in academic tasks. Literature implies the mutual interaction between self-efficacy beliefs and task goals (Elliot, 1999). Achievement goal orientations have been generally categorized into the following two main types: a) mastery or task goals, which mean the orientation towards learning and competence as an ultimate end through understanding materials and mastering tasks; and b) performance or ego goals concerned with demonstrating ability, receiving social recognition, and outperforming others (performance approach goals) or concealing lack of competence (performance avoidance goals) (Ames, 1992; Elliot & Church, 1997). Thus, mastery/task goals are close to intrinsic motivation, whereas performance/ego goals resemble extrinsic motivation. The items assessing these writing achievement goals include: "When I'm writing in my English, I'm trying to become a better writer" (a mastery/task goal), "When I'm writing in my English, I'm trying to impress my teacher with my writing" (a performance approach goal), and "When I'm writing in my English, I'm trying to keep people from thinking I'm a poor writer" (a performance avoidance goal) (Yilmaz Soylu et al., 2017, p. 4). It is worth noting that writers' performance avoidance goal orientation is different from their apprehension. While writing performance avoidance goals can be assessed using the items given above, the items gauging the latter include "I usually do my best to avoid writing English essays" and "I do not like my English essays to be evaluated" (Abdel Latif, 2015, p. 210).

"Ideal L2 writing self" and "ought-to L2 writing self" are two other writing achievement goal constructs addressed recently in writing research (Han & Hiver, 2018; Lee et al., 2018). "Ideal L2 writing self" is defined as "what students want to become in writing" (Lee et al., 2018, p. 180), and learners' "desired future images of themselves as competent L2 writers" (Han & Hiver, 2018, p. 48). In the reports of these two studies, the researchers included neither the scales assessing the construct nor sample items from them. However, their definitions of the construct clearly reflect it is very close to mastery achievement goals. For example, Lee et al. (2018) define ought-to L2 writing self as "what students think they ought to become in writing" (p. 180) and point out it reflects learners' extrinsic motivation but they included no items from their measure of the construct.

In light of the above-explained similarity among the four constructs (i.e., writing outcome expectancy, achievement goal orientation, ideal L2 writing self, and ought-to L2 writing self), it seems that writing achievement goal orientation is a much stronger construct than the other three. The scarce research on writing outcome expectancy in the 1980s and 1990s along with the clear lack of studies on it in the last two decades may have resulted from the weak versions in which Shell, Pajares, and their colleagues conceptualize construct. Contrarily, the relative increase in the number of writing achievement goal studies reported in the last decade may be ascribed to its robustness as a writing learning goal construct. That is why it is expected that the writing achievement goal research area will grow in the near future.

1.4.5 Perceived value of writing

Since a very few studies have addressed the "perceived value of writing" construct, it does not seem to have a clear place in writing motivation literature yet. Pajares and his colleagues researched the construct in four studies (Pajares & Cheong, 2003; 2001; Pajares, Valiante, & Cheong., 2007; Pajares & Valiante, 1999). In coining this construct, Pajares and his colleagues depended on Eccles's (1983, 1987) expectancy-value theory, which posits that one's motivation is influenced by expectancy of successful performance of a given learning activity or subject and the value given to it. Eccles and Wigfield (2002, see also Wigfield & Eccles, 1992) refer to the following four types of learning task values: importance (personal significance of the task or activity); intrinsic value (the enjoyment of doing it); utility value (the perceived usefulness of the task or activity); and cost (the perceived negative aspects of performing the task.). Task interest indicates valuing the task for "its inherent rather than its instrumental qualities in gaining other outcomes" (Zimmerman & Kitsantas, 2007, p. 55). According to Eccles (1987), expectancy beliefs and perceived task value correlate with some variables such as self-schema and task demands. The perceived value of the writing task influence learners' selection of goals and situational interest (Troia, Shankland, & Wolbers, 2012). If the task is valued, learners develop a motive to "pay greater attention, persist longer, enjoy their involvement, and acquire more knowledge" (Troia et al., 2013, p. 18).

In their four studies, Pajares and colleagues (Pajares & Cheong, 2003; 2001; Pajares, Valiante, & Cheong., 2007; Pajares & Valiante, 1999) used the terms "perceived usefulness of writing" and "value of writing" interchangeably and define the construct as learners' beliefs about importance, interest, and enjoyment of writing. This is consistent with Conradi, Jang, and McKenna's (2014) definition of task value as the belief it "is generally useful, enjoyable, or otherwise important" (p. 155). Troia et al. (2013) also used the term "task interest" to refer to learners' writing personal interest and attainment value. On the other hand, Pajares and his colleagues assessed the construct using a short scale from which they reported the following two items: "Writing is a lot of fun" and "Writing stories is interesting for me" (Pajares & Valiante, 2001, p. 370). The definitions given along with these sample items generally indicate that the "perceived value of writing" is a construct close to attitude towards writing and it reflects some aspects of intrinsic writing motivation. Thus, the construct is regarded as a dispositional one.

It is worth noting that some other writing motivation studies have addressed constructs similar to the perceived value of writing, but named them differently, including: beliefs about writing (MacArthur et al., 2016; Wright et al., 2019), writing interest, and the perceived authenticity of writing (Behizadeh & Engelhard, 2014, 2016). Wright et al. (2019) operationalize the "beliefs about writing" construct by a scale with seven items matching Conradi et al.'s (2014) above definition of task value. Besides, MacArthur et al.'s (2016) beliefs about writing scale include some items tapping learners' perceived value of writing. Behizadeh and Engelhard (2014) also used a writing interest measure and reported from it two items very similar to the above ones included in Pajares and Valiante's (2001) scale. Behizadeh and Engelhard (2014, 2016) also investigated a construct they labelled "the perceived authenticity of writing", defined as "the perception that a task is connected to a person's life" (p. 21). The scale they used to measure this construct includes some items mirroring writers' personal and academic relevance. The findings of their (2014) study indicate a close positive correlation between the students' performance on the perceived authenticity of writing and writing interest measures; this seems to suggest the similar conceptual frameworks of the two constructs.

1.4.6 Motivational regulation of writing

Teng and Zhang (2016a, 2016b) have recently researched the "motivational regulation of writing" construct. In their coinage of motivational regulation of writing, the two researchers relied mainly on the previous published educational psychology and L2 learning motivation works positing that learning self-regulation is a multifaceted construct composed of cognitive, metacognitive, social, and motivational dimensions (e.g., Dörnyei, 2001; Oxford, 2013; Pintrich et al, 1991; Wolters, 1999; Zimmerman, 2011). The works published by Teng and his colleagues (Teng & Zhang, 2016a, 2016b, 2018; Teng et al., 2020) focused specifically on measuring and researching writers' use of motivational regulation strategies. Wolters (1999) define motivational regulation strategies as the procedures or thoughts learners purposefully use to foster their engagement in a particular task. Self-regulated learners employ multiple motivational strategies to get physically and mentally ready for the task and sustain their engagement in it (Boekaerts & Cascallar, 2006). According to Teng and Zhang (2016b), writers' motivational regulation has a mediating role influencing their task performance and cognitive engagement and, in turn, their writing outcome.

The literature available generally indicates that motivational regulation of writing is a situational construct. Teng and Zhang (2016a) conceptualize it as a construct composed of the following five types of strategies: interest enhancement (e.g., bringing fun and personal interest to the task), performance self-talk (reminding oneself to outperform others in writing and get good grades in it), mastery self-talk (reminding oneself to improve their writing ability), emotional control (avoiding anxiety and frustration), and environment structuring (avoiding distraction). Abdel Latif (2009) found that L2 students use some of these motivational strategies while performing writing tasks. His think-aloud protocol data showed that writers try to avoid frustrations by performing prayers and to bring fun to the task while performing it through singing (i.e., interest enhancement).

1.4.7 Other broad and overlapping constructs

Apart from the above easily characterized writing motivational constructs, writing literature is full of other broad and overlapping ones. The broad constructs have been conceptualized as if they are pertinent to a specific writing motivational variable, but in fact these constructs reflect writing motivation as an umbrella term. On the other hand, the overlapping constructs are mainly concerned with particular writing cognitive and/or behavioural processes, but they have been operationalized by measures which include items tapping some motivational dimensions. In other words, these overlapping constructs combine some affective dimensions of writing with other behavioural and/or cognitive ones, and therefore they are not pure motivational ones.

The broadest writing motivation construct addressed in previous studies is perhaps what has been labelled as "writing self-perceptions" (Bottomley et al., 1997; Lingwall & Kuehn, 2013). Bottomley et al. (1997) describe a motivational construct they view as related to writers' self-efficacy beliefs and attitudes. However, the 38-item scale they used covers five motivational dimensions (writing general progress, specific progress, observational comparison, social feedback, and physiological states), which can be best viewed as related to learners' writing self-concept and anxiety. In the journalism and mass communication writing context, Lingwall and Kuehn (2013) also used the label "writing self-perceptions" to refer to affective, cognitive, and behavioural dimensions of writers' beliefs. They assessed the construct using a measure with a large number of items related to learners' writing self-concept and self-efficacy, and their perceived writing value and attitude, along with the cognitive and behavioural dimensions.

Writer's block, procrastination, and styles (approaches) are perhaps the most recurrent constructs overlapping with writing motivation. The term "writer's block" refers to one's inability to proceed with writing or find what to write (Boice, 1985; Rose, 1981, 1984, 1985). Though this construct is mainly a cognitive one, Rose conceptualized and measured it in a way encompassing writers' self-concept and anxiety dimensions. Another similar construct is procrastination, which has been defined as "the act of needlessly delaying tasks to the point of experiencing subjective discomfort" (Solomon & Rothblum, 1984, p. 503). In their attempt to assess PhD students' writing procrastination, Lonka et al. (2014) used a scale which includes items reflecting respondents' writing value and self-concept beliefs. Lavelle coined the term "writing styles" – labelled it as "writing approaches" in a later stage – to refer to the ways learners "think about writing as well as what they do when faced with writing tasks" (Lavelle, 2001, p. 60). Though the name given to this construct implies it is a cognitive one, in the several works reported by Lavelle and her colleagues (e.g., Lavelle, 1993, 1997; Lavelle & Bushrow, 2007; Lavelle & Guarino, 2003), it has been conceptualized and measured using items assessing respondents' composing processes along with their writing self-efficacy, self-concept, and apprehension.

Another overlapping construct that has been recently researched is writing motivation and engagement. Three studies addressing this construct (Collie, Martin, & Curwood, 2016; Yu et al., 2019; Yu, Jiang, & Zhou, 2020) depended on Martin's (2007, 2012) framework which encompasses 11 mal-/adaptive dimensions of learners' motivation and engagement. Following this framework, Collie et al. (2016) developed a scale measuring respondents' writing self-efficacy, perceived value of writing, writing mastery orientation, persistence in writing, planning writing, writing task management, writing anxiety, writing failure avoidance, uncertain control of writing outcome, self-handicapping in writing, and disengagement from writing. The same approach was followed by Yu et al. (2019) and Yu et al. (2020) in their development of the 44-item English Writing Motivation and Engagement Scale for University/College Students. They specifically conceptualize writing motivation and engagement as a construct encompassing "11 first-order factors (i.e., self-belief, valuing, learning focus, planning, task management, persistence, anxiety, failure avoidance, uncertain control, self-sabotage, and disengagement) belonging to four second-order factors (i.e., adaptive motivation, adaptive engagement, maladaptive motivation, and maladaptive engagement)" (Yu et al., 2019, p. 132). As noted in its label and conceptualization in these three studies, the writing motivation and engagement construct includes some affective dimensions but since it also encompasses other cognitive and behavioural ones, it is not a pure writing motivational construct.

1.5 Conclusion

The review and discussion given in the above sections indicate the many developments the writing motivation area has seen since the mid-1970s at the level of the constructs researched and their conceptualizations. Influenced by educational psychology and oral communication literature, writing motivation research originated in the US L1 learning environments and was mainly limited to studying writers' apprehension and attitude in the 1970s and 1980s. A shift occurred in its research orientations in the 1990s; since that time writing self-efficacy has become the most heavily researched writing motivation construct. Published research on other writing motivation constructs (writing achievement goal orientations and writing self-concept, along with their similar constructs) has particularly increased in the last two decades, but other ones (writing anxiety, perceived value of writing, and motivational regulation of writing) are still under-researched.

On the other hand, there have been overlapping aspects in conceptualization of some constructs; specifically writing apprehension versus anxiety, writing achievement goal orientations versus outcome expectancy, and writing self-concept versus the four constructs similar to it. There have also been some terminological overlap and difference problems causing conceptual gaps in writing motivation literature. Besides, research has also addressed some other constructs which are either motivationally broad (writing self-perceptions) or impure ones (writer's block, writing procrastination, styles, and writing motivation and engagement).

Taken into account all the above, it is concluded that the motivational constructs which have been researched so far can be grouped into four types related to attitudinal/dispositional perceptions, situational feelings and actions, writing ability beliefs, and writing learning goals. Table (1.1) shows the lists of the constructs belonging to each type. The second column of the table includes constructs written in non-italicized and italicized fonts. The constructs given in the non-italicized font are regarded as strong ones, whereas the italicized constructs are viewed as weak ones and normally represent some dimension of the construct given above them. That is why the italicized term is viewed as a better label for the target construct. As noted in the table, the terms "writing apprehension" and "attitude towards writing" are an exceptional case here; both constructs are very similar or identical and the frequency of using the two terms in literature is almost similar.

Writing motivation research has been concerned with three main issues: measurement of the constructs, exploring the characteristics of motivated

Table 1.1 A framework of the types of writing motivation constructs

Type	*Constructs researched*
Attitudinal/dispositional constructs	Writing apprehension/attitude towards writing Perceived value of writing
Situational constructs	Writing anxiety Motivational regulation of writing
Writing ability belief constructs	Writing self-efficacy Writing self-concept *Notion of writing giftedness* *Implicit theories of writing* *Incremental theory of writing intelligence* *Entity theory of writing intelligence*
Writing learning goal constructs	Writing achievement goal orientations *Writing outcome expectancy* *Ideal writing self* *Ought-to writing self*

and demotivated writers, and developing learners' writing motivation (i.e., instructional research). Measurement research focuses on developing and validating scales for assessing writing motivation constructs. The studies addressing the characteristics of motivated and demotivated writers usually rely on comparative, causal-comparative, correlational, or descriptive research designs to profile these characteristics and identify what may influence them. As for instructional research, it aims at testing the impact of particular teaching types on developing learners' writing motivation and/or identifying the factors influencing their effectiveness.

The issues related to the above-mentioned research types will be covered in the following three chapters. In chapter 2, the author highlights the measurement of writing motivation constructs, reviews the published scales used for assessing each construct, and discusses examples from the items included in these scales. All the measurement issues highlighted in this chapter will be linked to the construct conceptualizations discussed in the chapter 1. Chapter 3 aims at profiling the characteristics of motivated versus demotivated writers. The chapter starts by discussing how learners' personal variables (i.e., age, gender, and socio-cultural background) may influence their writing motivation. Then, the author reviews the research addressing the other correlates and sources of writers' motivational levels. In light of discussing all these issues, the author ends the chapter by summarizing what research generally says about the characteristics of motivated and demotivated writers. In chapter 4, the author reviews the previous instructional research of writing motivation. Specifically, six main types of this instructional research are described and discussed. The author describes the instructional scenarios included in each type and explains how effective these instructional types were found in motivating learners to write or alleviating their negative writing affect. Based on the issues discussed in chapters 3 and 4, the author provides in chapter 5 some research-driven guidelines for motivating learners to write and explains what each one entails. In the final chapter (chapter 6), the author highlights the main conclusions drawn from the previous chapters and presents some suggestions for advancing writing motivation measurement, research, and pedagogy. The book also ends with a glossary of the key terms in writing motivation literature.

References

Abdel Latif, M. M. M. (2009). *Egyptian EFL student teachers' writing processes and products: The role of linguistic knowledge and writing affect*. PhD thesis, University of Essex, UK.

Abdel Latif, M. M. M. (2015). Sources of L2 writing apprehension: A study of Egyptian university students. *Journal of Research in Reading*, *38*(2), 194–212. doi:10.1111/j.1467-9817.2012.01549.x

American Psychological Association. (n.d.). Anxiety. Retrieved from http://www.apa.org/topics/anxiety/

Ames, C. (1992). Classrooms: Goals, structures, and student motivation. *Journal of Educational Psychology*, *84*, 261–271. doi:10.1037/0022-0663.84.3.261

Atay, D., & Kurt, G. (2006). Prospective teachers and L2 writing anxiety. *Asian EFL Journal*, *8*(4), 100–118.

Bandura, A. (1977). Self-efficacy: Toward a unifying theory of behavioural change. *Psychological Review*, *84*(2), 191–215. doi:10.1037/0033-295X.84.2.191

Bandura, A. (1986). *Social foundations of thought and action: A social cognitive theory*. Englewood Cliffs, NJ: Prentice Hall.

Bannister, L. A. (1982). *Writing apprehension and anti-writing: A naturalistic study of composing strategies used by college freshmen*. PhD thesis, University of Southern California, USA.

Baumeister, R. F. (Ed.) (1999). *The self in social psychology*. Philadelphia: PA: Psychology Press (Taylor & Francis).

Behizadeh, N., & Engelhard, G., Jr. (2014). Development and validation of a scale to measure perceived authenticity in writing. *Assessing Writing*, *21*, 18–36. doi:10.1016/j.asw.2014.02.001

Behizadeh, N., & Engelhard, G., Jr. (2016). Examining the psychometric quality of a modified Perceived Authenticity in Writing Scale with Rasch measurement theory. In Q. Zhang (Ed.). Pacific Rim Objective Measurement Symposium (PROMS) 2015. Conference Proceedings, pp. 71–87. Singapore: Springer. doi:10.1007/978-981-10-1687-5_5

Blake, R. W. (1976). Assessing English and language arts teachers' attitudes toward writers and writing. *The English Record*, *27*, 87–97.

Boekaerts, M., & Cascallar, E. (2006). How far have we moved toward the integration of theory and practice in self-regulation? *Educational Psychology Review*, *18*, 199–210. doi:10.1007/s10648-006-9013-4

Boice, R. (1985). Cognitive components of blocking. *Written Communication*, *2*(l), 91–104. doi:10.1177/0741088385002001006

Bong, M., & Clark, R. (1999). Comparison between self-concept and self-efficacy in academic motivation research. *Educational Psychologist*, *34*(3), 139–153. doi:10.1207/s15326985ep3403_1

Bong, M., & Skaalvik, E. M. (2003). Academic self-concept and self-efficacy: How different are they really? *Educational Psychology Review*, *15*(1), 1–40. doi:10.1023/A:1021302408382

Bottomley, D. M., Henk, W. A., & Melnick, S. A. (1997). Assessing children's views about themselves as writers using the writer self-perception scale. *The Reading Teacher*, *51*, 286–296.

Britt, M., Pribesh, S., Hinton-Johnson, K., & Gupta, A. (2018). Effect of a mindful breathing intervention on community college students' writing apprehension and writing performance. *Community College Journal of Research and Practice*, *42*(10), 693–707. doi:10.1080/10668926.2017.1352545

Bruning, R., Dempsey, M., Kauffman, D., McKim, C., & Zumbrunn, S. (2013). Examining dimensions of self-efficacy for writing. *Journal of Educational Psychology*, *105*(1), 25–38. doi:10.1037/a0029692

Burgoon, J., & Hale, J. (1983). A research note on the dimensions of communication reticence. *Communication Quarterly*, *31*, 238–248. doi:10.1080/01463378309369510

Butler, D. A. (1980). *A descriptive analysis of the relationships between writing apprehension and the composing processes of selected secondary students*. PhD thesis, University of Virginia, USA.

Charney, D., Newman, J. H., & Palmquist, M. (1995). "I'm just no good at writing": Epistemological style and attitudes toward writing. *Written Communication, 12*(3), 298–329. doi:10.1177/0741088395012003004

Chea, S., & Shumow, L. (2017). The relationships among writing self-efficacy, writing goal orientation, and writing achievement. In K. Kimura and J. Middlecamp (Eds.), *Asian-focused ELT research and practice: Voices from the far edge* (pp. 169–192). Cambodia: IDP Education (Cambodia) Ltd.

Cheng, Y. S. (2004). A measure of second language writing anxiety: Scale development and preliminary validation. *Journal of Second Language Writing, 13*(4), 313–335. doi:10.1016/j.jslw.2004.07.001

Cheng, Y. S., Horwitz, E., & Schallert, D. (1999). Language anxiety: Differentiating writing and speaking components. *Language Learning, 49*(3): 417–446. doi:10.1111/0023-8333.00095

Csizér, K., & Tankó, G. (2015). English majors' self-regulatory control strategy use in academic writing and its relation to L2 motivation. *Applied Linguistics, 38*(3), 386–404. doi: 10.1093/applin/amv033

Collie, R. J., Martin, A. J., & Curwood, J. S. (2016). Multidimensional motivation and engagement for writing: Construct validation with a sample of boys. *Educational Psychology, 36*(4). 771–791. doi:10.1080/01443410.2015.1093607

Conradi, K., Jang, B. G., & McKenna, M. C. (2014). Motivation terminology in reading research: A conceptual review. *Educational Psychologist, 26*, 127–164. doi:10.1007/s10648-013-9245-z

Daly, J. A. (1977). The effects of writing apprehension on message encoding. *Journalism & Mass Communication Quarterly, 54*, 566–572. doi:10.1177/107769907705400317

Daly, J. A. (1978). Writing apprehension and writing competency. *Journal of Educational Research, 72*, 10–14.

Daly, J. A. (1979). Writing apprehension in the classroom: Teacher role expectancies of the apprehensive writer. *Research in the Teaching of English, 13*, 37–44.

Daly, J. A. (1985). Writing apprehension. In M. Rose (Ed.), *When a writer can't write: Studies in writer's block and other composing process problems* (pp. 43–82). New York, NY: Guilford Press.

Daly, J., & Miller, M. D. (1975a). The empirical development of an instrument to measure writing apprehension. *Research in the Teaching of English, 9*(3), 242–249.

Daly, J. A., & Miller, M. D. (1975b). Further attitudes in writing apprehension: SAT scores, success expectations, willingness to take advanced courses and sex differences. *Research in the Teaching of English, 9*, 250–256.

Daly, J. A., & Miller, M. D. (1975c). Apprehension of writing as a predictor of message intensity. *Journal of Psychology, 89*, 175–177. doi:10.1080/00223980.1975.9915748

Daly, J., & Hailey, J. (1984). Putting the situation into writing research: State and disposition as parameters of writing apprehension. In: R. Beach, & L. S. Bridwell (Eds.), *New directions in composition research* (pp. 259–273). New York, NY: Guilford Press.

Daly, J. A., & Shamo, W. G. (1976). Writing apprehension and occupational choice. *Journal of Occupational Psychology, 49*, 55–56. doi:10.1111/j.2044-8325.1976.tb00329.x

Daly, J. A., & Shamo, W. G. (1978). Academic decisions as a function of writing apprehension. *Research in the Teaching of English, 12*, 119–126.

Daly, J. A., & Wilson, D. (1983). Writing apprehension, self-esteem and personality. *Research in the Teaching of English, 17*, 327–342.

Deci, E. L., & Ryan, R. M. (1985). *Intrinsic motivation and self-determination in human behavior*. New York, NY: Plenum.

Dörnyei, Z. (1994). Motivation and motivating in the foreign language classroom. *Modern Language Journal,* 78(3), 273–284. https://doi.org/10.2307/330107

Dörnyei, Z. (2001). *Motivation strategies in the language classroom*. Cambridge, UK: Cambridge University Press.

Dörnyei, Z., & Ottó, I. (1998). Motivation in action: A process model of L2 motivation. *Working papers in applied linguistics* (Thames Valley University, London) 4, 43–69.

Dörnyei, Z., & Ushioda, E. (2011). *Teaching and researching motivation*. Edinburgh: Pearson Education Limited.

Dweck, C. (2000). *Self-theories: Their role in motivation, personality and development*. Philadelphia, PA: Psychology Press.

Eccles, J. (1987). Gender roles and women's achievement-related decisions. *Psychology of Women Quarterly*, 11(2), 135–172. doi:10.1111/j.1471-6402.1987.tb00781.x

Eccles, J. S. (1983). Expectancies, values, and academic behavior. In J. T. Spencer (Ed.), *Achievement and achievement motivation: Psychological and sociological approaches* (pp. 75–146). San Francisco, CA: Freeman.

Eccles, J. S., & Wigfield, A. (2002). Motivational beliefs, values, and goals. *Annual Review of Psychology*, 53, 109–132.

Ehm, J., Lindberg, S., & Hasselhorn, M. (2014). Reading, writing, and math self-concept in elementary school children: Influence of dimensional comparison processes. *European Journal of Psychology of Education*, 29(2), 277–294. doi:10.1007/s10212-013-0198-x

Emig, J., & King, B. (1979). *Emig-King attitude scale for teachers*. ERIC Document, ED 236 629.

Elliot, A. (1999). Approach and avoidance motivation and achievement goals. *Educational Psychologist*, 34, 169–179. doi:10.1207/s15326985ep3403_3

Elliot, A., & Church, M. (1997). A hierarchical model of approach and avoidance achievement motivation. *Journal of Personality and Social Psychology*, 72(1), 218–232. doi:10.1037/0022-3514.72.1.218

Faigley, L., Daly, J. A., & Witte, S. (1981). The role of writing apprehension in writing performance and competence. *Journal of Educational Research*, 75, 16–21. doi:10.1080/00220671.1981.10885348

Flower, L., & Hayes, J. R. (1980). The cognition of discovery: Defining a rhetorical problem. *College Composition and Communication*, 31(1), 21–32. doi:10.2307/356630

Fox, R. F. (1980). Treatment of writing apprehension and its effects on composition. *Research in the Teaching of English*, 14(1), 39–49.

Friedrich, G. W. (1970). An empirical exploration of a concept of self reported speech anxiety. *Speech Monographs*, 73, 67–72. doi:10.1080/03634528709378654

Fritzsche, B. A., Young, B. R., & Hickson, K. C. (2003). Individual differences in academic procrastination tendency and writing success. *Personality and Individual Differences*, 35, 1549–1557. doi:10.1016/S0191-8869(02)00369-0

Garcia, R. J. (1977). *An investigation of relationships: Writing apprehension, syntactic performance, and writing quality*. PhD thesis, Arizona State University, USA.

Gardner, R. C. (1985). *Social psychology and second language learning: The role of attitudes and motivation*. London, England: Edward Arnold.

Gardner, R. C., & Lambert, W. E. (1959). Motivational variables in second language acquisition. *Canadian Journal of Psychology*, 13, 266–72.

Gardner., R. C., & Lambert, W. E. (1972). *Attitudes and motivation in second language learning*. MA: Newbury House.

Giffin, N., & Gilham, S. M. (1971). Relationship between speech anxiety and motivation. *Speech Monographs*, 38, 70–73.

Graham, S., Berninger, V., & Fan, W. (2007). The structural relationship between writing attitude and writing achievement in first and third grade students. *Contemporary Educational Psychology*, 32, 516–536. doi:10.1016/j.cedpsych.2007.01.002

Graham, S., & Harris, K. R. (1989). Components analysis of cognitive strategy instruction: Effects on learning disabled students' compositions and self-efficacy. *Journal of Educational Psychology*, 81(3), 353–561. doi:10.1037/0022-0663.81.3.353

Graham, S., Schwartz, S., & MacArthur, C. (1993). Learning disabled and normally achieving students' knowledge of writing and the composing process, attitude toward writing, and self-efficacy. *Journal of Learning Disabilities*, 26, 237–249. doi:10.1177/002221949302600404

Han, J., & Hiver, P. (2018). Genre-based L2 writing instruction and writing-specific psychological factors: The dynamics of change. *Journal of Second Language Writing*, 40, 44–59. doi:10.1016/j.jslw.2018.03.001

Hadaway, N. L. (1987). *Writing apprehension among second language learners*. PhD thesis, Texas A & M University, USA.

Hamilton, E. W., Nolen, S., & Abbott, B. (2013). Developing measures of motivational orientation to read and write: A longitudinal study. *Learning & Individual Differences*, 28, 151–166. doi:10.1016/j.lindif.2013.04.007

Harvley-Felder, Z. C. (1978). *Some factors relating to writing apprehension: An exploratory study*. PhD thesis, University of North Carolina at Chapel Hill, USA.

Hayes, J. (1996). A new framework for understanding cognition and affect in writing. In M. Levy, & S. Ransdell (Eds.), *The science of writing: Theories, methods, individual differences, and applications* (pp. 1–27)). Mahwah, NJ: Lawrence Erlbaum Associates.

He, T. (2005). Effects of mastery and performance goals on the composition strategy use of adult EFL writers. *The Canadian Modern Language Review*, 61(3), 407–431. doi:10.3138/cmlr.61.3.407

Hogan, T. P. (1980). Students' interests in writing activities. *Research in the Teaching of English*, 14(2), 119–125.

Huerta, M., Goodson, P., Beigi, M., & Chlup, D. (2017). Graduate students as academic writers: Writing anxiety, self-efficacy and emotional intelligence. *Higher Education Research & Development*, 36(4), 716–729. doi:10.1080/07294360.2016.1238881

Hidi, S., & Boscolo, P. (2007). Motivation and writing. In C. A. MacArthur, S. Graham, & J. Fitzgerald (Eds.), *Handbook of writing research* (pp. 144–157). New York, NY: Guilford Press.

Jones, E. (2008). Predicting performance in first-semester college basic writers: Revisiting the role of self-beliefs. *Contemporary Educational Psychology*, 33, 209–238. doi:10.1016/j.cedpsych.2006.11.001

Kaplan, A., Lichtinger, E., & Gorodetsky, M. (2009). Achievement goal orientations and self-regulation in writing: An integrative perspective. *Journal of Educational Psychology*, 101(1), 51–69. doi:10.1037/a0013200

Karlen, Y., & Compagnoni, M. (2017). Implicit theory of writing ability: Relationship to metacognitive strategy knowledge and strategy use in academic writing. *Psychology Learning & Teaching*, 16, 47–63. doi:10.1177/1475725716682887

Kavanoz, S., & Yüksel, G. (2016). Developing and validating a self-efficacy scale for scholarly writing in English. *International Online Journal of Educational Sciences*, *8*(2), 71–82.

Lavelle, E. (1993). Development and validation of an inventory to assess processes in college composition. *British Journal of Educational Psychology*, *63*, 489–499. doi:10.1111/j.2044-8279.1993.tb01073.x

Lavelle, E. (1997). Writing style and the narrative essay. *British Journal of Educational Psychology*, *67*, 475–482. doi:10.1111/j.2044-8279.1997.tb01259.x

Lavelle, E. (2001) Brief report: Writing styles of college students. *Journal of College Reading and Learning*, *32*(1), 60–67. doi:10.1080/10790195.2001.10850127

Lavelle, E., & Bushrow, K. (2007). Writing approaches of graduate students. *Educational Psychology*, *27*(6), 807–822. doi:10.1080/01443410701366001

Lavelle, E., & Guarino, A. (2003). A multidimensional approach to understanding college writing processes. *Educational Psychology*, *23*(3), 295–305. doi: 10.1080/0144341032000060138

Lee, J. (2013). Can writing attitudes and learning behavior overcome gender difference in writing? Evidence from NAEP. *Written Communication*, *30*(2) 164–193. doi:10.1177/0741088313480313

Lee, I., Yu, S., & Liu, Y. (2018). Hong Kong secondary students' motivation in EFL writing: A survey study. *TESOL Quarterly*, *52*(1), 176–187. doi:10.1002/tesq.364

Leggette, H. R., Redwine, T., & Busick, B. (2020). Through reflective lenses: Enhancing students' perceptions of their media writing skills. *Journalism & Mass Communication Educator*, *75*(1) 81–97. doi:10.1177/1077695819852256

Limpo, T. (2018). Development of a short measure of writing apprehension: Validity evidence and association with writing frequency, process, and performance. *Learning and Instruction*, *58*, 115–125. doi:10.1016/j.learninstruc.2018.06.001

Limpo, T., & Alves, R. (2014). Implicit theories of writing and their impact on students' response to a SRSD intervention. *British Journal of Educational Psychology*, *84*, 571–590. doi:10.1111/bjep.12042

Limpo, T., & Alves, R. (2017). Relating beliefs in writing skill malleability to writing performance: The mediating role of achievement goals and self-efficacy. *Journal of Writing Research*, *9*(2), 97–125. doi:10.17239/jowr-2017.09.02.01

Lingwall, A., & Kuehn, S. (2013). Measuring student self-perceptions of writing skills in programs of journalism and mass communication. *Journalism & Mass Communication Educator*, *68*(4) 365–386. doi:10.1177/1077695813506991

Linnenbrink, E. (2006). Emotion research in education: Theoretical and methodological perspectives on the integration of affect, motivation, and cognition. *Educational Psychology Review*, *18*, 307–314. doi:10.1007/s10648-006-9028-x

Liu, M., & Jackson, J. (2008). An exploration of Chinese EFL learners' unwillingness to communicate and foreign language anxiety. *The Modern Language Journal*, *92*, 71–86. doi:10.1111/j.1540-4781.2008.00687.x

Lonka, K., Chow, A., Keskinen, J., Hakkarainen, K., Sandström, N., & Pyhältö, K. (2014). How to measure PhD students' conceptions of academic writing- and are they related to well-being? *Journal of Writing Research*, *5*(3), 245–269. doi:10.17239/jowr-2014.05.03.11

MacArthur, C., Philippakos, Z., & Graham, S. (2016). A multicomponent measure of writing motivation with basic college writers. *Learning Disability Quarterly*, *39*(1), 31–43. doi:10.1177/0731948715583115

Martin, A. J. (2007). Examining a multidimensional model of student motivation and engagement using a construct validation approach. *British Journal of Educational Psychology, 77*, 413–440. doi:10.1348/000709906X118036

Marsh, H. W., & Shavelson, R. J. (1985). Self-concept: Its multifaceted, hierarchical structure. *Educational Psychologist, 20*, 107–125. doi:10.1207/s15326985ep2003_1

McCarthy, P., Meier, S., & Rinderer, R. (1985). Self-efficacy and writing: A different view of self-evaluation. *College Composition and Communication, 36*, 465–471. doi:10.2307/357865

McCroskey, J. C. (1972). The implementation of a large scale program of systematic desensitization for communication apprehension. *Speech Teacher, 21*, 255–264. doi:10.1080/03634527209377961

Meier, S., McCarthy, P., & Schmeck, R. (1984). Validity of self-efficacy as a predictor of writing performance. *Cognitive Therapy and Research, 8*, 107–120.

Middleton, M., & Midgley, C. (1997). Avoiding the demonstration of lack of ability: An underexplored aspect of goal theory. *Journal of Educational Psychology, 89*(4), 710–718. doi:10.1037/0022-0663.89.4.710

Noels, K. A. (2001). New orientations in language learning motivation: Toward a contextual model of intrinsic, extrinsic, and integrative orientations and motivation. In Z. Dörnyei, & R. Schmidt (Eds.), *Motivation and second language acquisition* (pp. 43–68). Honolulu, HI: University of Hawaii Press.

Onwuegbuzie, A. J., & Collins, K. T. (2001). Writing apprehension and academic procrastination among graduate students. *Perceptual and Motor Skills, 92*(2), 560–562. doi:10.2466/pms.2001.92.2.560

Oxford, R. L. (2013). *Teaching and researching language learning strategies* (2nd ed.). Harlow, UK: Pearson.

Pajares, F., Britner, S., & Valiante, G. (2000). Relation between achievement goals and self-beliefs of middle school students in writing and science. *Contemporary Educational Psychology, 25*, 406–422. doi:10.1006/ceps.1999.1027

Pajares, F., & Cheong, Y. (2003). Achievement goal orientations in writing: A developmental perspective. *International Journal of Educational Research, 39*, 437–455. doi:10.1016/j.ijer.2004.06.008

Pajares, F., & Johnson, M. (1996). Self-efficacy beliefs and the writing performance of entering high school students. *Psychology in the Schools, 33*, 163–175. doi:10.1002/(SICI)1520-6807(199604)33:2<163::AID-PITS10>3.0.CO;2-C

Pajares, F., & Johnson, M. J. (1994). Confidence and competence in writing: The role of writing self-efficacy, outcome expectancy, and apprehension. *Research in the Teaching of English, 28*, 313–331.

Pajares, F., Johnson, J., & Usher, E. (2007). Sources of writing self-efficacy beliefs of elementary, middle, and high school students. *Research in the Teaching of English, 42*(1), 104–120.

Pajares, F., Miller, M., & Johnson, M. (1999). Gender differences in writing self-beliefs of elementary school students. *Journal of Educational Psychology, 91*, 50–61. doi:10.1006/ceps.1998.0995

Pajares, F., & Valiante, G. (1997). Influence of writing self-efficacy beliefs on the writing performance of upper elementary students. *The Journal of Educational Research, 90*, 353–360. doi:10.1080/00220671.1997.10544593

Pajares, F., & Valiante, G. (1999). Grade level and gender differences in the writing self-beliefs of middle school students. *Contemporary Educational Psychology, 24*(4), 390–405. doi:10.1006/ceps.1998.0995

Pajares, F., & Valiante, G. (2001). Gender differences in writing motivation and achievement of middle school students: A function of gender orientation? *Contemporary Educational Psychology, 26*, 366–381. doi:10.1006/ceps.2000.1069

Pajares, F., Valiante, G., & Cheong, Y. F. (2007). Writing self-efficacy and its relation to gender, writing motivation, and writing competence: A developmental perspective. In S. Hidi, & P. Boscolo (Eds.), *Motivation and writing: Research and school practice* (pp. 141–162). Dordrecht, The Netherlands: Kluwer.

Palmquist, M., & Young, R. (1992). The notion of giftedness and student expectations about writing. *Written Communication, 9*(1), 137–169. doi:10.1177/0741088392009001004

Phillips, G. M. (1968). Reticence: Pathology of the normal speaker. *Speech Monographs, 35*, 39–49. doi:10.1080/03637756809375564

Phillips, G. M., & Metzger, N. J. (1973). The reticence syndrome: Some theoretical considerations about etiology and treatment. *Speech Monographs, 40*, 220–230. doi:10.1080/03637757309375799

Piazza, C., & Siebert, C. (2008). Development and validation of a writing dispositions scale for elementary and middle school students. *The Journal of Educational Research, 101*, 275–285. doi:10.3200/JOER.101.5.275-286

Piniel, K., & Csizér, K. (2014). Changes in motivation, anxiety and self-efficacy during the course of an academic writing seminar. In Z. Dörnyei, P. MacIntyre, & A. Henry (Eds.), *Motivational dynamics in language learning* (pp. 164–194). Bristol, UK: Multilingual Matters.

Piniel, K., Csizér, K., Khudiyeva, S. R., & Gafiatulina, Y. (2016). A comparison of Hungarian and Kazakh university students' language learning profiles. *WoPaLP, 10*, 39–55.

Pintrich, P. R. (2000). The role of goal orientation in self-regulated learning. In M. Boekaerts, P. R. Pintrich, & M. Zeidner (Eds.), *Handbook of self-regulation* (pp. 451–502). San Diego, CA: Academic Press.

Pintrich, P. R., Smith, D. A., Garcia, T., & McKeachie, W. J. (1991). *A manual for the use of the motivated strategies for learning questionnaire (MSLQ)*. Ann Arbor, MI: The University of Michigan Press.

Richardson, F. C., & Suinn, R. M. (1972). The mathematics anxiety rating scale: Psychometric data. *Journal of Counseling Psychology, 19*(6), 551–554. doi:10.1037/h0033456

Richmond, V., & Dickson-Markman, F. (1985). Validity of the writing apprehension test. *Psychological Reports, 56*, 255–259. doi:10.2466/pr0.1985.56.1.255

Riffe, D., & Stacks, D. (1988). Dimensions of writing apprehension among mass communication students. *Journalism Quarterly, 65*(2), 384–391. doi:10.1177/107769908806500218

Rose, M. (1981). Questionnaire for Identifying Writer's Block (QIWB). ERIC Document, ED 236 652.

Rose, M. (1984). *Writer's block: The cognitive dimension*. Carbondale, IL: Southern Illinois University Press.

Rose, M. (1985). *When a writer can't write: Studies in writer's block and other composing-process problems*. New York, NY: Guilford Press.

Sanders-Reio, J., Alexander, P., Reio, T., & Newman, I. (2014). Do students' beliefs about writing relate to their writing self-efficacy, apprehension, and performance? *Learning and Instruction, 33*, 1–11. doi:10.1016/j.learninstruc.2014.02.001

Sarason, I. G. (1984). Stress, anxiety, and cognitive interference reactions to test. *Journal of Personality and Social Psychology, 46*, 929–938. doi:10.1037//0022-3514.46.4.929

Sasaki, M., & Hirose, K. (1996). Explanatory variables for EFL students' expository writing. *Language Learning, 46*(1), 137–174. doi:10.1111/j.1467-1770.1996.tb00643.x

Shaver, J. (1990). Reliability and validity of measures of attitudes toward writing and toward writing with the computer. *Written Communication, 7*(3), 375–392. doi:10.1177/0741088390007003004

Selfe, C. (1984). The predrafting processes of four high- and four low-apprehensive writers. *Research in the Teaching of English, 18*(1), 45–64.

Shell, D., Colvin, C., & Bruning, R. (1995). Self-efficacy, attributions, and outcome expectancy mechanisms in reading and writing achievement: Grade-level and achievement-level differences. *Journal of Educational Psychology, 87*, 386–398. doi:10.1037/0022-0663.87.3.386

Shell, D., Murphy, C., & Bruning, R. (1989). Self-efficacy and outcome expectancy mechanisms in reading and writing achievement. *Journal of Educational Psychology, 81*, 91–100. doi:10.1037/0022-0663.81.1.91

Skehan, P. (1989). *Individual differences in second language learning*. London: Edward Arnold.

Solomon, L. J., & Rothblum, E. D. (1984). Academic procrastination: Frequency and cognitive-behavioral correlates. *Journal of Counseling Psychology, 31*, 503–509. doi:10.1037/0022-0167.31.4.503

Spielberger, C. D., Gorsuch, R. L., & Lushene, R. (1970). *State-trait anxiety inventory manual*. Palo Alto, CA: Consulting Psychologists Press.

Spielberger, C. D., Gorsuch, R. L., Lushene, R., Vagg, P. R., & Jacobs, G. A. (1983). *State-trait anxiety inventory (form Y)*. Redwood City, CA: Mind Garden.

Thompson, M. O. (1978). *The development and evaluation of a language study approach to a college course in freshman composition*. PhD thesis, The American University, Washington D.C., USA.

Tobias, S. (1978). *Overcoming math anxiety*. Boston, MA: Houghton Mifflin.

Teng, L. S., Sun, P., & Xu, L. (2018). Conceptualizing writing self-efficacy in English as a foreign language contexts: Scale validation through structural equation modeling. *TESOL Quarterly, 52*(4), 911–942. doi:10.1002/tesq.432

Teng, L. S., Yuan, R. E., & Sun, P. P. (2020). A mixed-methods approach to investigating motivational regulation strategies and writing proficiency in English as a foreign language contexts. *System, 88*, 1–12. doi:10.1016/j.system.2019.102182

Teng, L. S., & Zhang, L. J. (2016a). A questionnaire-based validation of multidimensional models of self-regulated learning strategies. *Modern Language Journal, 100*(3), 674–701. doi:10.1111/modl.12339

Teng, L. S., & Zhang, L. J. (2016b). Fostering strategic learning: The development and validation of the writing strategies for motivational regulation questionnaire (WSMRQ). *Asia-Pacific Education Researcher, 25*, 123–134. doi:10.1007/s40299-015-0243-4

Teng, L. S., & Zhang, L. J. (2018). Effects of motivational regulation strategies on writing performance: A mediation model of self-regulated learning of writing in English as a second/foreign language. *Metacognition and Learning, 13*(2), 213–240. doi:10.1007/s11409-017-9171-4

Tremblay, P. F., & Gardner, R. C. (1995). Expanding the motivation construct in language learning. *Modern Language Journal 79*, 505–20. Doi:10.1111/j.1540-4781.1995.tb05451.x

Troia, G. A., Harbaugh, A. G., Shankland, R. K., Wolbers, K. A., & Lawrence, A. M. (2013). Relationships between writing motivation, writing activity, and writing performance: Effects of grade, sex, and ability. *Reading and Writing, 26*, 17–44. doi:10.1007/s11145-012-9379-2

Troia, G. A., Shankland, R. K., & Wolbers, K. A. (2012). Research in writing motivation: Theoretical and empirical considerations. *Reading & Writing Quarterly, 28*(1), 5–28. doi:10.1080/10573569.2012.632729

Tsao, J., Tseng, W., & Wang, W. (2017). The effects of writing anxiety and motivation on EFL college students' self-evaluative judgments of corrective feedback. *Psychological Reports, 120*(2), 219–241. doi:10.1177/0033294116687123

Tsai, H. M. (2008). The development of an English writing anxiety scale for Institute of Technology English majors. *Journal of Education and Psychology, 31*(3), 81–107. doi:10.1177/0033294116687123

Waller, L., & Papi, M. (2017). Motivation and feedback: How implicit theories of intelligence predict L2 writers' motivation and feedback orientation. *Journal of Second Language Writing, 35*, 54–65. doi:10.1016/j.jslw.2017.01.004

Wigfield, A., & Eccles, J. (1992). The development of achievement task values: A theoretical analysis. *Developmental Review, 12*, 265–310. doi:10.1016/0273-2297(92)90011-PGet

Wolters, C. A. (1999). The relation between high school students' motivational regulation and their use of learning strategies, effort, and classroom performance. *Learning & Individual Differences, 11*, 281–299. doi:10.1016/S1041-6080(99)80004-1

Woodrow, L. (2006). Anxiety and speaking English as a second language. *RELC Journal, 37*, 308–328. doi:10.1177/0033688206071315

Woodrow, L. (2011). College English writing affect: Self-efficacy and anxiety. *System, 39*, 510–522. doi:10.1016/j.system.2011.10.017

Wright, K. L., Hodges, T. S., & McTigue, E. M. (2019). A validation program for the self-beliefs, writing-beliefs, and attitude survey: A measure of adolescents' motivation toward writing. *Assessing Writing, 39*, 64–78. doi:10.1016/j.asw.2018.12.004

Wynne, C., Guo, Y., & Wang, S. (2014). Writing anxiety groups: A creative approach for graduate students. *Journal of Creativity in Mental Health, 9*, 366–379. doi:10.1080/15401383.2014.902343

Yao, Q. (2019). Direct and indirect feedback: How do they impact on secondary school learners' writing anxiety and how do learners perceive them? *The Asian Conference on Language Learning 2019, Official Conference Proceedings*, 1–12.

Yilmaz Soylu, M., Zeleny, M. G., Zhao, R., Bruning, R., Dempsey, M., & Kauffman, D. (2017). Secondary students' writing achievement goals: Assessing the mediating effects of mastery and performance goals on writing self-efficacy, affect, and writing achievement. *Frontiers in Psychology, 8*, 1406. doi:10.3389/fpsyg.2017.01406

Yu, S., Jiang, L., & Zhou, N. (2020). Investigating what feedback practices contribute to students' writing motivation and engagement in Chinese EFL context: A large scale study. *Assessing Writing, 44*, 1–15. doi:10.1016/j.asw.2020.100451

Yu, S., Zhou, N., Zheng, Y., Zhang, L., Cao, H., & Li, X. (2019). Evaluating student motivation and engagement in Chinese EFL writing context. *Studies in Educational Evaluation, 62*, 129–141. doi:10.1016/j.stueduc.2019.06.002

Zabihi, R. (2008). The role of cognitive and affective factors in measures of L2 writing. *Written Communication, 35*(1), 32–57. doi:10.1177/0741088317735836

Zimmerman, B. (2000). Self-efficacy: An essential motive to learn. *Contemporary Educational Psychology, 25*, 82–91. doi:10.1006/ceps.1999.1016

Zimmerman, B. J. (2011). Motivational sources and outcomes of self-regulated learning and performance. In J. Zimmerman & D. H. Schunk (Eds.), *Handbook of self-regulation of learning and performance* (pp. 49–64). Mahwah, NJ: Lawrence Erlbaum.

Zimmerman, B., & Bandura, A. (1994). Impact of self-regulatory influences on writing course attainment. *American Educational Research Journal, 31*, 845–862. doi:10.2307/1163397

Zimmerman, B., & Kitsantas, A. (1999). Acquiring writing revision skill: Shifting from process to outcome self-regulatory goals. *Journal of Educational Psychology, 91*, 241–250. doi:10.1037/0022-0663.91.2.241

Zimmerman, B., & Kitsantas, A. (2002). Acquiring writing revision and self-regulatory skill through observation and emulation. *Journal of Educational Psychology, 94*, 660–668. doi:10.1037/0022-0663.94.4.660

Zimmerman, B., & Kitsantas, A. (2007). A writer's discipline: The development of self-regulatory skills. In S. Hidi, & P. Boscolo (Eds.), *Motivation and writing: Research and school practice* (pp. 51–72). Dordrecht, The Netherlands: Kluwer.

2 Measuring writing motivation

2.1 Introduction

A better understanding of the conceptualizations of writing motivation constructs requires looking closely at the ways they have been measured. On the one hand, this will help us understand the construct from a wider and deeper angle and on the other, we will see whether or not a given measure matches the optimal definition of the targeted construct. The insights gained from comparing the ways of defining and assessing a particular construct will definitely assist in developing more robust and accurate conceptualizations and operationalization of it.

Two main approaches have been followed in assessing writers' motivation in previous studies: the quantitative approach and the qualitative one. As may be expected, the quantitative approach has been far more dominant in these studies. This chapter discusses the issues related to measuring writing motivation constructs. The discussion of the measures of all the constructs is organized according to their order in the framework given at the end of the previous chapter. In other words, it starts with the attitudinal/dispositional constructs and ends with the writing/learning goal ones. The author discusses the construct validity issues in the published scales assessing each of the main writing motivation constructs covered in chapter 1, along with the measures of writing motivation sources. In each subsection, sample items from the scales designed for measuring each construct are provided. All the measurement issues highlighted in this chapter will be linked to the conceptualizations of the constructs discussed in chapter 1. The qualitative approach to assessing writing motivation is also highlighted. The chapter ends with providing guidelines for developing writing motivation measures.

2.2 Measures of attitudinal/dispositional constructs

2.2.1 Writing apprehension and attitude

Given the similarity between learners' apprehension and attitude towards writing, we cannot talk about the measures of both constructs in isolation.

Table (2.1) gives a list of the writing apprehension and attitude scales published since the 1970s. As can be noted in the table, the number of writing attitude scales far exceeds that of the apprehension ones. The table generally implies that the attitude towards writing seems to have been researched more than writing apprehension since the 1990s, particularly in L1 writing settings. Noted also are the different terms given to the attitude scales, including: interests in writing (Hogan, 1980), writing passion (Piazza &

Table 2.1 A list of the writing apprehension and attitude scales published since the 1970s

Construct	Scales developed for assessing it
Writing apprehension	Daly and Miller's (1975) 26-item Writing Apprehension Test (WAT)
	Riffe & Stacks' (1988, 1992) 56-item mass communication writing apprehension measure
	Pajares & colleagues' (2000, 2007) modified writing apprehension scales
	Sanders-Reio, Alexander, Reio, and Newman's (2014) 29-item modified WAT
	Abdel Latif's (2015) 12-item English writing apprehension scale
	Limpo's (2018) 12-item Writing Apprehension Scale
Attitude towards writing	Blake (1976) 20-item Writing and Writers' Attitude Scale
	Thompson's (1978) 30-item Writing Attitude Survey
	Emig and King's (1979) 50-item Writing Attitude Scale for Teachers
	Hogan's (1980) 20-item Interests in Writing Activities Survey (for children)
	Rose's (1984) 24-item Attitude towards Writing Questionnaire
	Shaver's (1990) 9-item Attitudes towards Writing with Computer Scale
	Knudson's (1991) 19-item Writing Attitude Survey (for 4–8 grades)
	Knudson's (1992) 19-item Writing Attitude Survey (for 1–3 grades)
	Graham, Schwartz, and MacArthur's (1993) 6item Attitude towards Writing Scale
	Charney, Newman, and Palmquist's (1995) 12-item Attitude towards Writing Scale
	Kear, Coffman, McKenna, and Ambrosio's (2000) 28-item Attitude to Writing Scale (for children)
	Piazza and Siebert's (2008) 31-item Writing Dispositions (Passion) Scale
	Bruning et al.'s (2013) 4-item Liking Writing Scale
	Lee's (2013) 4 four-item Attitudes towards Writing Scale
	Graham, Berninger, and Fan's (2007) 7-item Attitude towards Writing Scale (for 1–3 grades)
	Hall, Toland, and Guo's (2016) 10-item Writing Attitude Scale for Teachers

Siebert, 2008), and liking writing (Bruning, Dempsey, Kauffman, McKim, & Zumbrunn, 2013). Two issues that need to be considered when evaluating the writing apprehension and attitude scales are given in the table. First, construct validity or the extent to which a scale measures what it claims. Second, construct under-representation, which means that a given scale "is too narrow and fails to include important dimensions or facets of the construct" (Messick, 1989, p. 34).

The construct validity problem can particularly be noted in the early writing apprehension and attitude measures, which include a large number of items (e.g., Daly & Miller, 1975; Emig & King, 1979; Riffe & Stacks, 1988, 1992; Rose, 1984; Thompson, 1978). Daly and Miller (1975) made the first systematic attempt to assess writers' motivation when they developed their Writing Apprehension Test (WAT). The WAT is a 26-item measure with a five-point Likert scale (strongly agree, agree, uncertain, disagree, or strongly disagree). Until recently, the WAT has been the most frequently used instrument for measuring writing apprehension. Some early and recent studies relied on the original scale in assessing writing apprehension (e.g., Britt, Pribesh, Hinton-Johnson, & Gupta, 2018; Olivier & Olivier, 2016; Pajares & Johnson, 1996), whereas others used adapted versions of it to match L2 writing environments (e.g., Gungle & Taylor, 1989), or a modified one to assess an additional motivational dimension (e.g., Sanders-Reio et al., 2014). Additionally, the WAT has been a main source for modelling the items in other writing apprehension and attitude scales (e.g., Cheng, 2004; Knudson, 1991, 1992).

Despite this large-scale use of the Daly-Miller WAT, many published works indicate that it is not a pure measure of writing apprehension. In their early evaluation attempt, Burgoon and Hale (1983) conducted a factor analysis of the WAT and found that 16 out of its 26 items loaded on one of three factors: discomfort or ease in writing (five items), enjoyment of writing (eight items), and rewards of writing (three items). As for the other ten items of the scale, Burgoon and Hale found that these did not match the three factors. In another report, Shaver's (1990) principal component analysis of the WAT revealed that it has three components: writing self-concept, affective performance reaction, and reaction to evaluation. Shaver's results emphasize that low self-confidence is a main component of the WAT. Likewise, the content analysis that McKain (1991) conducted on the WAT showed the possibility to classify its 26 items into five categories, measuring: positive feelings about writing (nine items), writing self-efficacy or outcome expectancies (nine items), writing anxiety (five items), value of writing (one item), and miscellaneous behaviours (two items). Additionally, Cheng, Horwitz, and Schallert's (1999) principal component analysis of an L2 version of the WAT revealed that it has three main components: low self-confidence in English writing (12 items), aversiveness of writing in English (seven items), and evaluation of writing apprehension (six items). In their factor analysis of the WAT, Cornwell and McKay (2000) also found that it has four components: enjoyment of writing, fear of evaluation, negative perceptions about writing ability, and showing writing to others. These reports are also supported by other evaluation reports (e.g., Bline, Lowe, Meixner, Nouri, & Pearce, 2001; Poff, 2004) and by the observations made by some researchers such as Richmond and Dickson-Markman (1985) and Gungle and Taylor (1989). Collectively, the conclusion drawn from all these research findings and observations is that the Daly-Miller WAT is not a pure measure of writing apprehension, and that a main component of it can be used for assessing the perceived value of writing and ability beliefs.

As Table (2.1) shows, the attitude towards writing scales developed from the 1970s and 1980s are also characterized by the large number of their items. Thus, they apparently resemble the Daly-Miller WAT in assessing other writing motivational dimensions along with attitude. This issue is clear indeed in the ways these scales are divided or described by their developers. For example, Emig and King's (1979) 50-item writing attitude scale assesses respondents' general preference for writing, their perceptions of self and others as writers, and writing process awareness. Likewise, Rose's (1984) scale measures writers' attitudes along with their perceptions of writing complexity and their writing lateness, editing, and blocking. According to Phinney (1991), Rose's Writing Attitude Questionnaire does not gauge apprehension or attitude, but it assesses the feelings, beliefs, and behaviours leading to the writer's block. On the other hand, Riffe and Stacks' (1988, 1992) 56-item Mass Communication Writing Apprehension Measure covers the following components: general affect or enjoyment and anticipation of writing, blank page paralysis (i.e., the difficulties occurring while starting the task), perceptions of mechanical skills competence, behavioural and cognitive/affective aspects of apprehension, perceptions of writing relevance to career and essential skills, avoidance of performing writing tasks independent of any blank page paralysis, easiness/difficulty to write about facts versus ideas, and interest in informing and persuading audience. Blake's (1976) Writing and Writers Attitude Scale, and Thompson's (1978) Writing Attitude Survey are no exception. The former scale assesses respondents' interest in writing different genres, attitudes towards writing, perceptions of writers, and their views on some writing skills and processes. Thompson's (1978) scale is also concerned with measuring attitudes towards writing and the perceived value of writing.

Compared to these early writing attitude/apprehension measures, the construct validity problem occurs only in a few scales published since the mid-1990s. Knudson's (1991, 1992) writing attitude surveys include some writing value, self-concept, and self-efficacy items. There are also eight items, tapping writing self-concept and learnability beliefs in Charney et al.'s (1995) Attitude towards Writing Scale. Likewise, seven of Hall et al.'s (2016) ten-item scale gauge learners' perceived usefulness of writing and writing self-ability beliefs. Likewise, Limpo (2018) recently validated a 12-item scale adapted from the Daly-Miller WAT, but five items in her scale assess writing self-concept rather than apprehension.

The noted construct validity problems in the early scales of writing apprehension and attitude may have stemmed from the nature of this early or evolving stage in writing motivation research. As indicated in chapter 1, apprehension and attitude were the only writing motivation constructs researched frequently from the mid-1970s to the late 1980s as compared to writing self-efficacy, which was addressed in four studies only during the same period (Graham & Harris, 1989; McCarthy, Meier, & Rinderer, 1985; Meier, McCarthy, & Schmeck, 1984; Shell, Murphy, & Bruning, 1989). In other words, the lack of research on the other writing motivational constructs during this stage may have led researchers to include them as potential correlates of apprehension/attitude in their measures, or perhaps to view apprehension/attitude as an umbrella construct composed of what is related to writing motivation.

In response to the above-mentioned construct validity problems, some studies used more accurate measures of writing apprehension/attitude in the decades following this early writing motivation stage. These measures include: Shaver's (1990) nine-item Attitudes towards Writing with Computer Scale; Graham et al.'s (1993) six-item Attitude towards Writing Scale; Piazza and Siebert's (2008) 31-item Writing Dispositions (Passion) Scale; Bruning et al.'s (2013) four-item Liking Writing Scale; Lee's (2013) four-item Attitudes towards Writing Scale; and the seven-item and four-item scales that Pajares and his colleagues modified from the Daly-Miller WAT (Pajares, Britner, & Valiante, 2000; Pajares & Cheong, 2003; Pajares & Valiante, 1999, 2001; Pajares, Valiante, & Cheong, 2007). However, a construct under-representation problem can be easily noted in the four-item scales used by Pajares and his colleagues, Bruning et al., and Lee. In other words, these scales do not seem to reflect the target construct adequately.

On the other hand, Abdel Latif (2015) synthesized a 12-item L2 writing apprehension measure from three previously published scales (Graham et al., 1993; Gungle & Taylor, 1989; Cheng, 2004). The scale uses a five-point Likert response set (strongly agree, agree, uncertain, disagree, and strongly disagree), and it includes the following statements:

> I usually do my best to avoid writing English essays.
> I am afraid of writing essays in English when I know they will be evaluated.
> Whenever possible, I would use English to write essays.
> I usually seek every possible chance to write English essays outside of class.
> I like writing in English.
> I have no fear of my English writing being evaluated.
> I do not like English writing classes.

I like discussing my English writing with others.
I would rather read than write in English.
I usually do my best to avoid situations in which I have to write in English.
I do not like my English essays to be evaluated.
Unless I have no choice, I would not use English to write essays.

(Abdel Latif, 2015, p. 210)

The characteristics of the children's writing attitude scales are also worth noting. Five of the scales given in Table 2.1 are concerned with assessing young learners' attitudes towards writing (Graham et al., 2007; Hogan, 1980; Kear et al., 2000; Knudson, 1991, 1992). These scales share some common characteristics, namely: including items tapping attitudes towards a variety of activities, wording items differently, and using images in the scale response set. Hogan's (1980) scale asks students about the degree to which they like or dislike a number of writing activities such as spelling words and learning to spell them, writing letters to friends, writing stories, and writing about the things one has done. In the scale Kear et al. (2000) developed, they worded their items in a way matching learners' age. For example: "How would you feel telling in writing why something happened?", "How would you feel if your teacher asked you to go back and change some of your writing?", and "How would you feel about writing a story instead of doing your homework?" (pp. 16–19). Graham et al. (2007) used a similar item — wording in the writing attitude scale they developed for the 1st and 3rd graders. The seven questions in their scale ask about feelings "about writing for fun at home", "when you write in school during free time", "about writing during summer vacation", "about writing instead of playing", "about writing in school", "about spending free time writing", and "when it's time for writing at school." (p. 526). In the two measures developed by Kear et al. (2000) and Graham et al. (2007), they used the four images of Garfield as a four-point Likert scale to represent emotions ranging from "very happy" to "very upset". Kear et al. (2000) rationalize this by referring to the research indicating young learners' inability to simultaneously recognize more than five pieces of information.

It is noted that the above writing apprehension/attitude scales focus only on assessing learners' likes or dislikes of writing, learning, situations, and tasks. They neglect other important dispositional dimensions such as learners' attitudes towards the instructional materials of writing, teaching and testing practices, and the feedback received from the teacher or peers. Teng and Zhang's (2016a) Writing Strategies for Self-Regulated Learning Questionnaire, and Karaca and Inan's (2020) English Writing Demotivation Scale, include items of this type but the two scales were not specifically used for assessing writing apprehension/attitude; they assess multiple motivational and non-motivational dimensions. The sample items representing these neglected dimensions include:

I am open to peer feedback on my writing.
I try to improve my English writing based on teacher feedback.
(Teng & Zhang, 2016a, p. 700)

The way my writing teacher presents the writing course is boring.
I hate excessive amount of assignments in my writing classes.
Writing topics are not interesting for me.
(Karaca & Inan, 2020, p. 12)

Covering these dimensions in future apprehension/attitude scales could be a way for operationalizing and representing the construct more robustly.

2.2.2 Perceived value of writing

Due to the scarce research on the perceived value of writing and the different labels given to the construct (i.e., beliefs about writing, writing interest, and the perceived authenticity of writing), there have been no well-known measures for assessing it. Pajares and his colleagues assessed the construct in a number of studies, using four-item and eight-item scales (Pajares & Cheong, 2003; 2001; Pajares et al., 2007; Pajares & Valiante, 1999). They did not include the complete version of any of the two scales in their published studies; they only included the following two representative items: "Writing is a lot of fun" and "Writing stories is interesting for me" (Pajares & Valiante, 2001, p. 370). Likewise, Troia, Harbaugh, Shankland, Wolbers, and Lawrence (2013) researched the "writing task interest" construct, which they define as learners' writing personal interest and attainment value. They measured the construct using a five-item scale, but no sample items from this scale were reported. Besides, Zhang, Song, Shen, and Huang (2014) published a four-item writing task value scale. The items of this scale are given below:

I think learning writing is important.
I find writing interesting.
What I learn in writing is useful.
Compared to other subjects, writing is useful.
(Zhang et al., 2014, p. 673)

The last decade saw the publication of a few scales operationalizing the perceived value of writing in a way consistent with viewing it as learners' beliefs about the importance, interest, and enjoyment of writing (Pajares & Cheong, 2003; Pajares et al., 2007; Pajares & Valiante, 1999, Pajares & Valiante, 2001). Additionally, some scales claiming to measure other writing motivation variables also include items representing the construct. For example, Hall et al.'s (2016) Writing Attitude Scale for Teachers has the following three items tapping respondents' perceived value of writing: "I write for personal enjoyment", "Writing is important for me to express my feelings", and "Writing is relevant in my life" (p. 219). In Behizadeh and Engelhard's (2014, 2016) original and modified scales of the perceived authenticity in writing, we can also find a number of items gauging the relevance of writing to respondents' academic and personal life. The following two sets of items represent these two dimensions, respectively:

> Writing this paper helped me to understand the topic better.
> Writing this paper helped me to develop my thoughts, opinions, or beliefs.
> Writing this paper was a good learning experience.
> Writing this paper was important to me.
> (Behizadeh & Engelhard, 2014, p. 23)

> English language arts writing assignments relate to topics I care about in the world.
> What I am learning about writing is important to know in my life.
> Writing in my English language arts class connects to my personal interests.
> I am gaining writing skills that I will use later in my life in my English language arts class.
> (Behizadeh & Engelhard, 2016, p. 87)

According to MacArthur, Philippakos, and Graham (2016), when learners view writing as a way of expression and learning, they will be more motivated to perform writing tasks. Some items representing the perceived value of writing construct have also been included in the two beliefs about writing scales developed by MacArthur et al. (2016), and Wright, Hodges, and McTigue (2019). However, these two scales cannot be regarded as pure measures of the perceived value of writing because they include other items irrelevant to the construct, such as beliefs about good writing and writers, and responses to teacher feedback. Below are the items representing the perceived value of writing in the two scales:

> Writing is one of the best ways to explore new ideas.
> I learn new things from writing.
> Writing helps me think about my topic in a new way.
> Writing helps make my ideas clearer.
> (MacArthur et al., 2016, p. 38)

> I believe it is very important to be a good writer.
> I feel most successful if I see that my writing has really improved.
> I think it would be great to become an even better writer than I already am.
> Writing helps me learn.
> (Wright et al., 2019, p. 77)

Future research addressing the perceived value of writing can draw upon the above items or model them to build more valid scales operationalizing the construct robustly. Researchers interested in building scales of this construct can also develop items tapping learners' perceived value of specific writing topics. The construct can be also expanded through reviewing general motivation literature on expectancy-value and learning task value.

2.3 Measures of situational constructs

2.3.1 Writing anxiety

A main problem associated with discussing writing anxiety measurement is the scarcity of the scales previously developed for assessing the construct. This scarcity has mainly resulted from conflating it with writing apprehension in many previous studies relying on measures of the latter construct (e.g., Huerta, Goodson, Beigi, & Chlup, 2017; Zabihi, 2018), and the few available studies addressing the situational nature of writing anxiety (Cheng, 2004; Csizér & Tankó, 2015; Fritzsche, Young, & Hickson, 2003; Han & Hiver, 2018; Meier et al., 1984; Piniel & Csizér, 2014; Piniel, Csizér, Khudiyeva, & Gafiawtulina, 2016; Tsai, 2008; Tsao, Tseng, & Wang, 2017; Woodrow, 2011; Yao, 2019). Table (2.2) shows the scales assessing writing

Table 2.2 A list of the scales assessing the situational writing motivation constructs (writing anxiety and the motivational regulation of writing)

Construct	Scales developed for assessing it
Writing anxiety	Meier et al.'s (1984) 20-item scale (*adapted from Spielberger et al., 1970*)
	Fritzsche et al.'s (2003) 20-item scale (*adapted from Spielberger et al., 1983*)
	Cheng's (2004) 22-item Second Language Writing Anxiety Inventory
	Tsai's (2008) 18-item English Writing Anxiety Scale
	Woodrow's (2011) 20-item Writing Anxiety Scale
	Piniel and Csizér (2014)/ Csizér and Tankó's (2015) 8-item Writing Anxiety Scale
	Piniel et al.'s (2016) 6-item Writing Anxiety Scale
	Han and Hiver's (2018) 7-item Writing Anxiety Scale
	Tsao et al.'s (2017) 21-item English Writing Anxiety Scale (*adapted from Tsai, 2008*)
	Yao's (2019) 28-item English Writing Anxiety Scale (*adapted from Tsai, 2008*)
Motivational regulation of writing	Teng and Zhang's (2016a) Writing Strategies for Self-Regulated Learning Questionnaire (*the 15 items representing the interest enhancement, motivational self-talk, and emotional control dimensions*)
	Teng and Zhang's (2016b) 17-item Second Language Writing Strategies for Motivational Regulation Questionnaire

anxiety along with the motivational regulation of writing, and the two situational constructs of writing motivation.

The previous studies in which writing anxiety scales were not fully described or included are the ones reported by Csizér and Tankó (2015), Fritzsche et al. (2003), Han and Hiver (2018), Meier et al. (1984), Piniel and Csizér (2014), and Piniel et al. (2016). In the two studies conducted by Fritzsche et al. (2003) and Meier et al. (1984), they used a writing anxiety scale adapted from the State-Trait Anxiety Inventory (STAI) (Spielberger, Gorsuch, & Lushene, 1970; Spielberger, Gorsuch, Lushene, Vagg, & Jacobs, 1983). No writing anxiety items were included in Meier et al.'s (1984) study report, but they explained that their 20-item scale requires respondents to describe their feelings about a writing task they are about to complete. Similarly, Fritzsche et al. (2003) did not include any items from their writing anxiety measure either. They indicated that the scale asks respondents to use a four-point format (1 = not at all; 4 = very much so) in rating the feelings they experience while working on their writing assignments. Despite the unavailability of the writing anxiety items in the two research reports, a look at Spielberger et al.'s STAI can inform us about the nature of the situational feelings assessed. The instructions of the STAI require respondents to rate their feelings at a particular moment. The 20 statements of STAI describe how respondents feel; *calm, secure, tense, strained, at ease, upset, satisfied, frightened, comfortable, self-confident, nervous, jittery, indecisive, relaxed, content, worried, steady, confused,* or *pleasant* at the target situation. Given this, we can say that the two writing anxiety scales used by Fritzsche et al. (2003) and Meier et al. (1984) are situational ones.

In the studies reported by Csizér and Tankó (2015), Piniel and Csizér (2014), and Piniel et al. (2016), they reported using eight-item and six-item writing anxiety scales, but only included the following two sample items: "When I hand in a written assignment, I am anxious about my tutor's opinion" (Csizer & Tankó, 2015, p. 7), and "I never seem to be able to clearly write down my ideas in English, in language practice class" (Piniel et al., 2016, p. 45). Piniel et al. (2016) adapted their six-item writing anxiety scale from Cheng et al.'s (1999) measure, in which the construct is not conceptualized as a pure situational one. On the other hand, Han and Hiver (2018) used a seven-item writing anxiety measure that matches their view of the construct as "learners' negative feelings and behavior related to L2 writing" (p. 48). Their measure was adapted from Horwitz, Horwitz, and Cope's (1986) Foreign Language Classroom Anxiety Scale, which assesses anxiety along with self-concept beliefs.

Unlike the above studies, Cheng (2004), Tsai (2008), and Woodrow (2011) fully included the writing anxiety scales they developed in their research reports. Cheng (2004) developed the Second Language Writing Anxiety Inventory to assess the construct from a multidimensional angle. The scale includes 22 items gauging the following three dimensions: a) somatic anxiety: one's perceptions of the physiological effects of the anxiety experience (seven items); b) cognitive anxiety: mental aspects of the anxiety experience (eight items); and c) avoidance behaviours such as procrastination and withdrawal (seven items). As noted, Cheng conflated the terms "writing apprehension" and "writing anxiety", in her measurement attempt. The seven items of her Avoidance Behaviour subscale clearly assess writing apprehension (e.g., "I usually do my best to avoid writing English compositions" and "I usually seek every possible chance to write English compositions outside of class", p. 324). As for the 15 items in the Cognitive Anxiety and Somatic Anxiety subscales, these reflect the situational nature of the construct. Below are sample items from the two subscales (the first four items are from the Cognitive Anxiety subscale, and the last four items are from the Somatic Anxiety one):

> While writing in English, I'm not nervous at all.
> While writing English compositions, I feel worried and uneasy if I know they will be evaluated.
> I'm afraid that the other students would deride my English composition if they read it.
> I don't worry at all about what other people would think of my English compositions.
> I tremble or perspire when I write English compositions under time pressure.
> I feel my heart pounding when I write English compositions under time constraint.
> I often feel panic when I write English compositions under time constraint.
> I usually feel my whole body rigid and tense when I write English compositions.
>
> (Cheng, 2004, p. 324)

Tsai (2008) developed a scale for assessing English writing anxiety in the Taiwanese context. Adapted versions of Tsai's scale were also used in some studies (e.g., Tsao et al., 2017; Yao, 2019). The scale in its final form includes 18 items covering four dimensions of writing anxiety: a) fear of writing — testing situations (six items); b) anxiety about making mistakes in language use while writing (three items); c) fear of receiving negative evaluation from the teacher or classmates (five items); and d) low self-perceptions of one's writing ability while performing the task (four items). The following eight items represent the four dimensions, two for each respectively:

> I feel nervous when reading instructions for the topic in English writing.
> Taking English composition exams makes me feel nervous.
> When writing an English composition, I worry about whether the words and expressions used are correct.

44 *Measuring writing motivation*

> I feel anxious about whether the grammar used is correct when I am writing an English composition.
> I get upset when I find my English composition filled with red marks from the teacher.
> An unfamiliar writing topic makes me anxious.
> I feel panicky when I start writing an English composition.
> Before taking a writing test, I feel jittery about what is going to happen.
>
> (Tsai, 2008, p. 105)

A different writing anxiety measure was developed by Woodrow (2011), who assessed learners' anxious feelings during a number of writing activities. The university student respondents to her measure were asked to use a seven-point Likert scale — with zero indicating "not at all anxious" and seven representing "extremely anxious" — to rate how anxious they felt while performing a variety of micro and macro writing tasks. The micro activities are writing with good handwriting, composing accurate sentences, and using appropriate grammar and vocabulary. The macro ones are concerned with writing at a text level and they include composing well-developed paragraphs and essays, and writing different text types.

The above review of the scales indicates a growing tendency to conceptualize writers' anxiety as a situational construct. The sample items given in this subsection particularly emphasize the situational nature of writing anxiety. Future studies concerned with measuring the construct can rely on these previous scales. They can also expand the construct by covering learners' anxious feelings in writing classes.

2.3.2 Motivational regulation of writing

Since research on the motivational regulation of writing is still in its infancy, only one scale has been developed for assessing it. As indicated in Table (2.2), the scale has been published in two forms in the studies reported by Teng and her colleagues (Teng, Yuan, & Sun, 2020; Teng & Zhang, 2016a; Teng & Zhang, 2016b; Teng & Zhang, 2018). In its first form, the scale was published as a part of the Writing Strategies for Self-Regulated Learning Questionnaire used in Teng and Zhang's (2016a) study. This questionnaire was designed to assess the cognitive, metacognitive, social, and motivational self-regulation dimensions of L2 writing strategies. Along with the cognitive, metacognitive, and social self-regulation dimensions, the questionnaire also includes 15 items gauging three types of motivational regulation writing strategies (interest enhancement, motivational self-talk, and emotional control).

In Teng and Zhang's (2016b) study, a separate scale of motivational regulation of writing is included. Teng and Zhang developed their Second Language Writing Strategies for Motivational Regulation Questionnaire based on Dörnyei's (2001) taxonomy of motivational regulation strategies. In this questionnaire or scale, the interest enhancement and emotional control dimensions remained unchanged, but Teng and Zhang divided motivational self-talk strategies into two types (performance and mastery self-talk) and they also added another dimension related to environment structuring. The same scale was also validated in the two research reports published by Teng et al. (2020), and Teng and Zhang (2018). Teng and Zhang used a seven-point Likert format, ranging from 1 (not at all true of me) to 7 (very true of me), as a response set to the 17 items of their measure. The Second Language Writing Strategies for Motivational Regulation Questionnaire assesses the following five motivational regulation dimensions: interest enhancement, performance self-talk, mastery self-talk, emotional control, and environment structuring (see the definitions of these dimensions in the previous chapter, subsection 1.4.6). Below are sample items representing the five dimensions assessed by the scale, two items for each dimension respectively:

> I look for ways to bring more fun to the learning of writing.
> I connect the writing task with my real life to intrigue me.
> I tell myself that I need to keep studying to improve my writing competence.
> I tell myself that it is important to practice writing.
> I persuade myself to work hard in writing courses to improve my writing skills.
> I persuade myself to keep on learning in writing courses to find out how much I can learn.
> I tell myself not to worry when taking a writing test or answering questions in writing courses.
> I find ways to regulate my mood when I want to give up writing.
> I keep myself away from distraction when writing.
> I change my surrounding so that it is easy to concentrate on writing.
> (Teng & Zhang, 2018, p. 237)

2.4 Measures of writing ability belief constructs

2.4.1 Writing self-efficacy

Since writing self-efficacy has been heavily researched in the last three decades, the number of measures developed for assessing it remarkably exceeds the number of those of any other writing motivation construct. As a result, a wide variance is noted in the published writing self-efficacy scales. This wide variance can be attributed to the changing and different orientations in conceptualizing the construct, and the inconsistencies in the types of the items and tasks given in its measures.

With regard to the different orientations in measuring writers' self-efficacy, these have been mainly concerned with assessing writers' beliefs about their ability to: a) perform particular language-specific and rhetorical skills and tasks (i.e., product-focused or written convention self-efficacy);

b) regulate their composing processes and activities (i.e., process-focused or text composing process self-efficacy); and c) execute some cognitive, linguistic, self-regulatory, or learning actions (i.e., multidimensional self-efficacy). Accordingly, two approaches to assess writing self-efficacy can be characterized: the unidimensional approach represented by the first two types and the multidimensional one. Within each of these three main conceptualization and measurement orientations, there has also been variance in the types of the writing self-efficacy beliefs or the task(s) addressed in the scales. Table (2.3) gives a list of the published writing self-efficacy scales and their types. In addition to these published measures, some studies (e.g., Csizér & Tankó, 2015; Duijnhouwer, Prins, & Stokking, 2010; Han & Hiver, 2018) used writing self-efficacy scales, but their research reports included neither

Table 2.3 A list of the published writing self-efficacy scales and their types

Type of assessment	Scales representing it
Product-focused writing self-efficacy	Meier et al.'s (1984) 19-item writing self-efficacy scale Shell et al.'s (1989) 24-item writing self-efficacy scale Graham and Harris' (1989) 10-item writing self-efficacy scale Shell, Colvin, and Bruning's (1995) modified 9-item Writing Self-Efficacy Scale Pajares and colleagues' (e.g., 1997, 2001, 2007) writing self-efficacy scales Wong, Butler, Ficzere, and Kuperis' (1997) 10-item Writing Self-Efficacy Questionnaire Prat-Sala and Redford's (2010) 12-item self-efficacy in writing scale Woodrow's (2011) 19-item writing self-efficacy scale Abdel Latif's (2015) 18-item English Writing Self-efficacy Scale Kavanoz and Yüksel's (2016) 26-item Scholarly Writing Self-Efficacy Scale Chea and Shumow's (2017) 7-item paragraph-writing self-efficacy scale
Process-focused writing self-efficacy	Graham et al.'s (1993) 8-item Writing Self-Efficacy Scale Zimmerman & Bandura's (1994) 25-item Writing Self-Regulatory Efficacy Scale Schmidt and Alexander's (2012) 20-item Self-Efficacy Scale for Writing Centres Mitchell, Harrigan, Stefansson, and Setlack's (2017) 10-item Self-Efficacy Scale for Academic Writing Chena and Zhang's (2019) 17-item L2 Text Revision Self-Efficacy Scale Golombek, Klingsieck, and Scharlau's (2019) 22-item Self-Efficacy for Self-Regulation of Academic Writing Scale
Multidimensional writing self-efficacy	Jones' (2008) 28-item writing self-efficacy scale Bruning et al.'s (2013) 16-item Self-Efficacy for Writing Scale MacArthur et al.'s (2016) 18-item Self-Efficacy for Writing Scale Teng, Sun, and Xu's (2018) 20-item L2 Writer Self-Efficacy Scale

adequate descriptions of these scales nor representative items from them. Due to the lack of information needed for identifying their types, these scales are not listed in Table (2.3).

Pajares and his colleagues reported using different self-efficacy scales with items ranging in number from 6 to 10. The only writing self-efficacy scale they included fully in their published research is the one used in Pajares, Hartley, and Valiante's (2001) study. This scale consists of 10 items and it is a product-focused one. In their other published studies, Pajares and his colleagues reported using six-item or eight-item writing self-efficacy scales. Though none of the two scales were included in the published reports, the definition provided for the construct measured and the ample representative items given also indicate that these are product-focused or written convention self-efficacy measures. For example, Pajares and Valintine (2001) operationalize writing self-efficacy as "students' judgments of their confidence that they possessed the various composition, grammar, usage, and mechanical skills appropriate to their academic level" (p. 369). The representative items they reported from their scales are: "Correctly punctuate a one page passage", "Organize sentences into a paragraph so as to clearly express a theme" (Pajares & Johnson, 1996, p. 166), "Write a strong paragraph that has a good topic sentence or main idea", and "Structure paragraphs to support ideas in the topic sentences" (Pajares et al., 2007, p. 146). Another unpublished writing self-efficacy scale was used by Spaulding (1995). According to Spaulding (1995), the scale assesses learners' confidence in completing a number of school-based writing tasks requiring some linguistic skills; thus it seems to be a product-focused self-efficacy measure.

Since writing self-efficacy is a task-specific construct, a main problematic issue in its early scales is assessing learners' perceived ability to perform various tasks rather than one task only. In particular, these early scales focus on more than one writing task, for example: assignments and papers (Zimmerman & Bandura, 1994), papers, reports and stories (Graham et al., 1993), letters, instructional manuals, legal documents, resumes, term papers, scholary articles, letter short stories, novels, and class notes (Shell et al., 1989). In their study, In their (1995) study, Shell et al. reduced the number of these tasks to the following five ones: writing game rule descriptions, letters, page reports, book summaries, and stories. Two more recent self-efficacy scales also include a number of writing tasks, specifically: persuasive essays, critique essays, compare-and-contrast essays, summaries (Jones, 2008), cloze passages, essays, letters, and paragraph translation (Woodrow, 2011). Klassen (2002) views that there should be a strong correspondence between the self-efficacy scale used and the criterial writing task to be performed; this is particularly "essential to maximize predictive power of self-efficacy beliefs and to secure confidence that the measure is accurately reflecting the performance task" (p. 184). The scales with items about multiple writing tasks likely lack the strong correspondence between respondents' perceived self-efficacy level and the task they are to perform. According to Pajares

(2003), any self-efficacy scale should always be completed by respondents before getting them to perform the task under investigation, and its items should match this task to reflect the strong relationship between writers' perceived beliefs and their composing output. Accordingly, a well-developed writing self-efficacy scale is supposed to include one task type only.

The list of the published writing self-efficacy scales given in Table (2.3) clearly indicates the varied and changing conceptualizations and operationalizations writing self-efficacy literature is full of. A clearly noted evidence of this variance is the wide differences in the number of the items included in these scales. For instance, some writing self-efficacy measures have fewer than ten items (e.g., Chea & Shumow, 2017; Graham et al., 1993), while others are composed of 15–20 items (Bruning et al., 2013; Teng et al., 2018; Woodrow, 2011) or more than 25 ones (e.g., Jones, 2008; Kavanoz & Yüksel, 2016). Additionally, there have been varied differences in operationalizing a particular dimension of the construct.

As noted in Table (2.3), all the writing self-efficacy scales developed in the 1980s are product-focused, i.e., concerned with written text features or writing conventions only, whereas the process-focused writing efficacy scales occurred in the early 1990s. All the scales developed in the 1980s and 1990s are unidimensional, i.e., just focusing on either writing conventions or process-regulation self-efficacy. Though some writing process-regulation self-efficacy scales (e.g., Graham et al., 1993; Schmidt & Alexander, 2012; Zimmerman & Bandura, 1994) include a few writing convention items, they cannot be regarded as multidimensional ones because their main focus is unidimensional. Jones (2008) is likely the first researcher to conceptualize writing self-efficacy as a multidimensional construct by using three subscales for assessing learners' perceived ability to regulate writing process, perform certain tasks, and execute specific writing conventions skills. Unlike the first decade of the current century, the 2010s saw an active movement in publishing writing self-efficacy scales of all types. The self-efficacy scales listed in Table (2.3) ask respondents to rate their confidence in performing the writing performance aspects assessed by the items. Examples of the Likert response formats used include: not well at all–very well (Prat-Sala & Redford, 2010), no chance–completely certain (Bruning et al., 2013), very unconfident–very confident (Abdel Latif, 2015), totally disagree–totally agree (Chea & Shumow, 2017), and not at all true of me–very true of me (Teng et al., 2018).

The multidimensional writing self-efficacy scales cover varied dimensions of the construct. The items of the scales developed by Bruning et al. (2013), Jones (2008), MacArthur et al. (2016), and Teng et al. (2018) are all organized into three subscales, each addresses a particular writing self-efficacy dimension. Jones' (2008) 28-item scale assesses perceived writing process abilities, regulation of composing challenges, and perceived task and skill competence. Bruning et al.'s (2013) 16-item Self-Efficacy for Writing Scale covers one's perceived capabilities of writing ideation (i.e., perceived ability to generate ideas), text features, and self-regulation. On the other hand,

MacArthur et al.'s (2016) 18-item scale measures writers' perceived ability to demonstrate certain writing skills, use particular strategies, and regulate their composing. Finally, the dimensions assessed in Teng et al.'s (2018) 20-item scale are writers' perceived ability to produce certain textual features and revise the text (i.e., linguistic self-efficacy), regulate composing processes, and perform well in writing courses.

The writing product-focused items in the previously published self-efficacy scales cover a wide range of linguistic and rhetorical skills. These items generally reflect the following sample definitions of writing self-efficacy: learners' evaluation of their writing skills (McCarthy et al., 1985), their confidence in showing particular rhetorical and language skills (Shell et al., 1989), and their perceived ability to demonstrate the writing, grammar usage, and mechanics skills that match the target academic level (Pajares & Valiante, 1999). As noted in the following sample items, they assess learners' perceived ability to use and spell words, write grammatically correct sentences and punctuate them, write well-developed and coherent paragraphs and essays, and demonstrate some features of good scholarly writing:

> Correctly use parts of speech (i.e., nouns, verbs, adjectives, etc.).
> Write a simple sentence with proper punctuation and grammatical structure.
> Write compound and complex sentences with proper punctuation and grammatical structure.
> (Shell et al., 1989, p. 24)

> I can spell my words correctly.
> I can write complete sentences.
> I can punctuate my sentences correctly.
> (Bruning et al., 2013, p. 30)

> Put ideas together in a paragraph in such a way that they are clear to the reader.
> Link sentences together to make a well-organized paragraph.
> Write a good introduction which informs the reader of my intention for a paragraph.
> Make a good conclusion to inform the reader the ending of my paragraph.
> (Chea & Shumow, 2017, p. 190)

> How well can you express your arguments clearly in essays?
> How well can you link the paragraphs to make your essay coherent and make the text flow?
> Before you finish your essay, how well can you make the conclusion relate to the introduction and the essay question?
> (Prat-Sala & Redford, 2010, p. 305)

I can write paragraphs with details to support the main ideas.
I can write a good persuasive essay.
(MacArthur et al., 2016, p. 37)

I can write the topic/problem of the study clearly and intelligibly in English.
I can express the aim of the study clearly and intelligibly in English.
I can clearly express the gap(s) in literature and emphasize the significance of my study.
I can write the method section in manuscripts using clear and intelligible English.
I can use hedges appropriately while writing English texts.
(Kavanoz & Yüksel, 2016, p. 78)

As for the process-focused items in the scales listed in Table (2.3), these assess various aspects of writing process regulation. For example, the items of Zimmerman and Bandura's (1994) Writing Self-Regulatory Efficacy Scale gauge learners' perceived capability to use composing strategies and manage time, stress, and distraction. Meanwhile, Bruning et al. (2013) used items tapping learners' self-regulation beliefs about their ability to avoid distractions while composing texts, but the self-regulation items in Teng et al.'s (2018) scale focus on writers' perceived ability to execute some monitoring strategies and plan their learning-to-write processes. Collectively, the writing process items in the scales and subscales listed cover a number of dimensions, including learners' perceived ability to generate text ideas and organize them, manage and solve composing process problems, avoid distractions while composing, evaluate one's text quality, and make the necessary changes in the written text. Below are sample items representing each of these writing process ability beliefs:

I can think of many words to describe my ideas.
I can think of a lot of original ideas.
I know exactly where to place my ideas in my writing.
(Bruning et al., 2013, p. 30)

I can organize my ideas into a plan that makes sense.
I can find the right words to express my ideas.
(MacArthur et al., 2016, p. 37)

When unexpected problems with writing occur, I do not handle them well.
I do not seem capable of dealing with most problems that come up in completing written work.
(Jones, 2008, p. 235)

I can solve problems which occur during writing.
I can overcome a writer's block and go on writing.
I can avoid repeating an error.
I can judge what I have to do differently next time.
(Golombek et al., 2019, p. 755)

Even when writing feels hard, I know I can complete the task on time.
I will remain calm and in control through the writing process.
(Mitchell et al., 2017, p. 20)

I can find a way to concentrate on my writing even when there are many distractions around me.
I can refocus my concentration on writing when I find myself thinking about other things.
(Zimmerman & Bandura, 1994, p. 850)

I can evaluate whether my paper is well written.
I can evaluate whether I am making progress in learning to write.
(MacArthur et al., 2016, p. 37)

I can evaluate my strength and weakness in writing.
I can evaluate whether a composition is good or bad.
(Teng et al., 2018, p. 32)

I can find and correct my grammatical errors.
I can identify incomplete, or fragment, sentences.
(Schmidt & Alexander, 2012, p. 19)

I can revise a first draft of any paper so that it is shorter and better organized.
When I have written a long or complex paper, I can find and correct all my grammatical errors.
(Zimmerman & Bandura, 1994, p. 850).

I can revise the language in my essay to make it more persuasive to the audience (e.g., to include emotive vocabulary such as "imagine that" or to refer to the reader "you would").
I can revise my essay to ensure it contains all the core argument elements (e.g., position, main points, evidence, re-statement).
(Chena & Zhang, 2019, p. 39)

In addition to these writing conventions and process regulation items, a third type of writing self-efficacy items is concerned with assessing learners' perceived ability to perform well in writing courses and classrooms. Teng et al. (2018) developed a subscale for eliciting respondents' self-efficacy beliefs about understanding and learning the content of writing course learning materials, complete writing assignments, and use the knowledge and skills acquired from writing courses. Below are sample items representing this dimension of writing self-efficacy:

> I can understand the most difficult material presented in writing courses.
> I can do an excellent job on the assignments in writing courses.
> I can master the writing knowledge and strategies being taught in writing courses.
> I can use the writing knowledge and strategies being taught in writing courses.
>
> (Teng et al., 2018, p. 32)

As noted above, there have been varied and changing conceptualizations and operationalizations of writing self-efficacy. In addition to the three main approaches to measuring the construct (i.e., the product-focused, process-focused, and multidimensional ones), the scales belonging to the same approach could be also concerned with different types of writing self-efficacy, for example: paragraph-writing self-efficacy (Chea & Shumow, 2017), essay writing self-efficacy (e.g., Abdel Latif, 2015; Jones, 2008; MacArthur et al., 2016), scholarly writing self-efficacy (Kavanoz & Yüksel, 2016), text revision self-efficacy (Chena & Zhang, 2019), and performance in writing centres self-efficacy (Schmidt & Alexander, 2012). As indicated above, the types of items tapping a particular dimension also vary. These variance issues support the conclusion drawn in the previous chapter (subsction 1.4.2) that writing self-efficacy is optimally viewed as a construct of various types and dimensions. While future research is expected to bring us more different types of writing self-efficacy, these varied conceptualizations and assessment perspectives need to be considered when comparing or generalizing research findings.

It is worth noting that some of the above-mentioned writing self-efficacy scales included some items tapping writers' social or observational comparison and social persuasion (for a review, see Mitchell, Rieger, & McMillan, 2017). Arguably, these items represent aspects of writers' self-concept. The following subsection discusses this issue.

2.4.2 Writing self-concept and similar constructs

The unclear place of self-concept in writing motivation literature has mainly resulted from the scarcity of studies publishing its measures or those of the constructs similar or related to it (i.e., the notion of writing giftedness, the implicit theories of writing, and the entity and incremental theories of writing intelligence), see related definitions in subsection 1.4.3 in the previous chapter and in the glossary. The studies dealing with the

Table 2.4 A list of the scales assessing writing self-concept and related constructs

Construct	Scales assessing it
Writing self-concept	Pajares and colleagues' (1999, 2001, 2003, 2007) 6-item writing concept scale
	Ehm et al.'s (2014) 5-item writing concept scale
Notion of writing giftedness	Palmquist and Young's (1992) 4-tem notion of writing giftedness scale
Implicit theories of writing	Limpo and Alves' (2014) 5-item Implicit Theories of Writing Scale
Entity theory of writing intelligence	Waller and Papi's (2017) 3-item entity theory of writing intelligence scale
Incremental theory of writing intelligence	Waller and Papi's (2017) 2-item incremental theory of writing intelligence scale

similar constructs (Limpo, 2018; Limpo & Alves, 2014; Limpo & Alves, 2017; Palmquist & Young, 1992; Waller & Papi, 2017) depended on scales measuring one aspect of writing self-concept, i.e., these scales seem to under-represent the construct. Meanwhile, some self-concept items were also included in a number of scales assessing other writing motivation variables (e.g., Bottomley, Henk, & Melnick, 1997; Charney et al., 1995; Daly & Miller, 1975; Graham et al., 1993; Limpo, 2018; Neugebauer & Howard, 2015; Wong et al., 1997). Table (2.4) shows the scales previously developed for assessing writing self-concept and the constructs related to it.

As the table shows, two writing self-concept scales were used by Ehm, Lindberg, and Hasselhorn (2014), and Pajares and his colleagues (Pajares & Cheong, 2003; Pajares et al., 2000, 2007; Pajares, Miller, & Johnson, 1999; Pajares & Valiante, 1999, 2001). These scales were adapted from Marsh's (1990) Academic Self-Description Questionnaire. Pajares and his colleagues did not publish their full six-item writing self-concept scale in the several studies they reported. Instead, they only included the following two sample items: "Learning how to be a better writer is easy for me" (Pajares & Valiante, 1999, p. 395) and "I have always done well on writing assignments" (Pajares & Valiante, 2001, p. 370). As for the items of Ehm et al.'s (2014) writing self-concept scale, these are: "In writing, I am the … (worst, best)", "In writing, I make … (a lot of mistakes, no mistakes)", and "In writing, I am … (not gifted, very gifted)" (p. 290). As noted, the items in the two scales reflect respondents' beliefs about their writing self-competence, writing learnability and improvability, and performance social comparison. On the other hand, the items in the scales developed for assessing the four constructs similar to writing self-concept only assess the perceived learnability and improvability of writing.

The four items in Palmquist and Young's (1992) notion of writing giftedness scale assess writing learnability and teachability beliefs. Likewise, the three scales developed by Limpo and Alves (2014) and Waller and Papi

(2017) also gauge writing learnability and performance improvability. Below are the items used in each of these four short scales:

> Good writers are born, not made.
> Some people have said, "Writing can be learned but can't be taught."
> Do you believe it can be learned?
> Do you believe it can be taught?
> Good teachers can help me become a better writer.
>
> (Notion of writing giftedness scale,
> Palmquist & Young, 1992, p. 143)

> My texts will always have the same quality, no matter how much I try to change it.
> No matter how many texts I write, their quality will always be the same.
> If I write well, it's because I was born like that.
> If I do not write as well as I wish, I can't do much to change it.
> I can't change the quality of my texts.
>
> (Implicit Theories of Writing Scale,
> Limpo & Alves, 2014, p. 567)

> You can improve your English writing skills, but you can't really change your writing talent.
> As an English learner, you have a limited amount of talent for developing your English writing skills, and you can't really do much to change it.
> No matter how hard you try, as an English language learner you can never write like a native speaker.
>
> (Entity theory of writing intelligence scale,
> Waller & Papi, 2017, p. 59)

> With enough practice you will be able to write like a native speaker of English.
> No matter who you are, you can always learn to write as well as native speakers of English.
>
> (Incremental theory of writing intelligence scale,
> Waller & Papi, 2017, p. 59)

As can be noted above, all the four constructs (i.e., the notion of writing giftedness, the implicit theories of writing, the entity theory of writing intelligence, and the incremental theory of writing intelligence) are identical. What also supports this view is that the three scales used by Limpo and Alves (2014) and Waller and Papi (2017) were adapted from Dweck's (2000) work on self-theories and motivation. The same applies to the items adapted from the four scales. For example: "The ability to write good academic texts can be learned" (Karlen & Compagnoni, 2017, p. 53).

Apart from the above scales, different types of writing self-concept items were also included in some scales assessing other writing motivation constructs. These items represent the beliefs about general writing ability, social or observational comparison, comparison deficiency, and social feedback. General and educational psychology literature indicates these are important dimensions forming self-concept (e.g., Baumeister, 1999; Bong & Skaalvik, 2003; Marsh & Shavelson, 1985). For example, the following items gauge general writing ability beliefs:

> I'm not good at writing
> I am a good writer.
> I have always been a good writer.
> I believe I was born with the ability to write well.
> (Attitude towards Writing Scale, Charney et al., 1995, p. 307)

Other writers' attitudes and self-efficacy scales also include items tapping their social or observational comparison beliefs (i.e., comparing one's performance with those of peers). These items, for instance, are found in the scales developed by Graham et al. (1993) and Wong et al. (1997). Besides, a comprehensive list of these items is given in Bottomley et al.'s (1997) Writer Self-Perception Scale:

> I write better than other kids in my class.
> When I write, my organization is better than the other kids in my class.
> My writing is more interesting than my classmates' writing.
> The words I use in writing are better than the ones other kids use.
> I put my sentences in a better order than the other kids.
> My sentences and paragraphs fit together as well as my classmates' sentences and paragraphs.
> (Writer Self-Perception Scale, Bottomley et al., 1997, pp. 292–293)

Another related dimension is comparison deficiency, which refers to one's continuous belief that their writing is deficient when compared to what they want it to be (Daly, 1985). Two sample items that represent these comparison deficiency beliefs are included in the Daly-Miller WAT:

> I expect to do poorly in composition classes even before I enter them.
> When I hand in a composition I know I'm going to do poorly.
> (The WAT, Daly & Miller, 1975, p. 246)

Finally, social feedback (i.e., the feedback received from others on one's performance) plays another interactional role in shaping writers' self-concept. Therefore, it is viewed as a dimension of writing self-concept. Below are sample social feedback items:

Other kids think I am a good writer
My teacher thinks my writing is fine.
My teacher thinks I am a good writer.
People in my family think I write pretty well.
 (Writer Self-Perception Scale, Bottomley et al. 1997, pp. 292–293)

It can be easily noted that the scales of writing self-concept and the similar constructs are short ones; they all include a small number of items ranging from two to six. Arguably, the writing self-concept construct is not well represented in these scales. Such construct under-representation can be avoided by including the above-mentioned dimensions when conceptualizing and operationalizing, writing self-concept. In other words, writing self-concept as a construct could encompass one's beliefs about their: perceived general writing ability, writing learnability and teachability and performance improvability, social comparison, comparison deficiency, and social feedback. Taking these dimensions into account in future research will lead to developing a more robust and better represented writing self-concept construct.

2.5 Measures of writing learning goal constructs

As indicated in the previous chapter, there have been three main waves in the writing achievement goal research published since 1989. During the first wave, the construct was named "writing outcome expectancy" or "writing outcome expectations" in the studies published by Shell and Pajares and their colleagues (Pajares & Johnson, 1994; Pajares & Valiante, 1997; Shell et al., 1995, 1989). During this research stage or wave, the only scale used was Shell et al.'s (1989) writing outcome expectancy scale and its adapted versions. The term "writing outcome expectancy" was replaced with "writing achievement goals" in the research published in the last two decades (i.e., the second and third research waves). In the research conducted by Pajares and his colleagues during the second wave, they used one adapted writing achievement goal scale (Pajares & Cheong, 2003; Pajares et al., 2000, 2007; Pajares & Valiante, 2001). The third research wave is characterized by using different writing achievement goal scales (e.g., Chea & Shumow, 2017; Hamilton, Nolen, & Abbott, 2013; He, 2005; Kaplan, Lichtinger, & Gorodetsky, 2009; Limpo, 2018; Limpo & Alves, 2017; MacArthur et al., 2016; Troia et al., 2013; Yilmaz Soylu et al., 2017). The following six writing achievement goal orientation scales were used in the studies representing the three research waves:

Shell et al.'s (1989) 20-item writing outcome expectancy scale.
Pajares and colleagues' (2000, 2001, 2003, 2007) adapted writing achievement goals scale.
Kaplan et al.'s (2009) 14-item writing achievement goal scale.
Hamilton et al.'s (2013) 19-item Motivational Orientation Scale.
MacArthur et al.'s (2016) 12-item writing achievement goal scale.
Yilmaz Soylu et al.'s (2017) 12-item Writing Achievement Goals Scale.

Shell et al. (1989) operationalized writing outcome expectancy using a 20-item scale which asks respondents to rate the importance of writing for achieving different life goals using a seven-point Likert response format ranging from 1 (extremely unimportant) to 7 (extremely important). The scale includes some integrative motivation goals (e.g., making new friends, getting dates, and communicating ideas to others), instrumental/extrinsic motivation goals (e.g., getting a job and progressing in it, obtaining financial security, and getting good school grades), and intrinsic motivation ones (e.g., having self-satisfaction, learning new things, being a creative person, and a good citizen) (Shell et al., 1989, p. 100). In their later study, Shell et al. (1995) used an adapted scale which consists of six goals from the original one: "getting a job when you are an adult", "having a lot of friends", "getting along with your parents", "doing good in school", "going to college", and "telling people things you know" (p. 388). Additionally, they used a five-point response format for this adapted scale: 1 (not important at all), 2 (not very important), 3 (kind of important), 4 (pretty important), and 5 (very important) (Shell et al., 1995, p. 388).

In the two early writing outcome expectancy/achievement goals studies reported by Pajares and his colleagues (Pajares & Johnson, 1994; Pajares & Valiante, 1997), they used an adapted version of Shell et al.'s (1989) scale. In the later studies they published (Pajares & Cheong, 2003; Pajares et al., 2000, 2007; Pajares & Valiante, 2001), Pajares and his colleagues relied on a writing achievement goals scale adapted from Middleton and Midgley's (1997) Patterns of Adaptive Learning Survey. They did not include the full version of this scale in any of their published studies, but their description indicate that the scale is composed of items assessing learners' task goals (e.g., "I like writing assignments that really make me think"), performance approach goals (e.g. "I want to do better than other students in my language arts class"), and their performance avoidance goals (e.g., "I do my writing assignments so others in the class won't think I'm dumb") (Pajares et al., 2007, p. 147).

The three scales developed by Kaplan et al. (2009), MacArthur et al. (2016), and Yilmaz Soylu et al. (2017) include similar number of items gauging the same types of writing achievement goal orientations, i.e., writing mastery, performance approach, and performance avoidance goals. Respondents complete these scales using specific response formats; for example five-point Likert-type scale ranging from 0 (does not describe me at all) to 4 (describes me perfectly) (Yilmaz Soylu et al., 2017), or a seven-point one ranging from 1 (totally disagree) to 7 (totally agree) (Kaplan et al., 2009). Below are the items of three subscales assessing the above-mentioned types of writing achievement goals:

When I do writing assignment, in-class work or homework:

It's important to me that I learn as much as I can.
It's important to me that I improve my skills and knowledge.
One of my goals is to learn as much as I can.

It's important for me to really understand what there is to learn.
One of my goals is to develop deep understanding of what we are learning.
(Writing mastery goals scale, Kaplan et al., 2009, p. 62)

When I'm writing in my English/Language arts class, I'm trying to:

Impress my teacher with my writing.
Be a better writer than my classmates.
Show off my writing skills.
Be the best writer in my class.
(Performance approach subscale, Yilmaz Soylu et al., 2017, p. 4)

When I'm writing in this class, I'm trying to:

Hide that I have a hard time writing.
Avoid making mistakes in front of my classmates.
Hide how nervous I am about writing.
Keep people from thinking I'm a poor writer.
(Performance avoidance subscale, MacArthur et al., 2016, p. 38)

As for Hamilton et al.'s (2013) Motivational Orientation Scale, it consists of items tapping the three types of writing achievement goals and also measures other dimensions, specifically interest in creative self-expression, social communication, and writing work avoidance (i.e., negative attitude towards writing). Therefore, it is not a pure scale of writing achievement goals. The items gauging the three writing achievement goals are listed in the Motivational Orientation Scale under the categories titled: writing mastery, writing ego, and writing ego avoidance. Below are six items representing these goals, two items for each writing achievement goal type, respectively:

I feel most successful:

If I use some really interesting words in my writing.
When I see I'm becoming a better writer.
In writing if I get a higher grade than others kids do.
If I show people I'm one of the best writers in class.
If people don't laugh at my writing.
If people don't make fun of my stories or poems.
(Motivational Orientation Scale, Hamilton et al., 2013, p. 164)

On the other hand, Troia et al. (2013) used a 14-item scale for assessing the three types of writing achievement goal orientations, but no items from this scale were given in their research report. Likewise, no items are published from the short scales assessing "ideal L2 writing self" and "ought-to L2 writing self" – the more recently coined writing learning goal constructs (Han & Hiver, 2018; Lee, Yu, & Liu, 2018).

The relatively increasing attention given recently to researching writing achievement goals and the similar constructs implies that this area could witness further developments in the years to come. These expected future developments may also bring about some changing orientations in conceptualizing and operationalizing writing learning goals.

2.6 Measurers of writing motivation sources

In addition to the above-reviewed measures designed for assessing specific writing motivation constructs, some few scales have been developed to assess the sources of writing motivation. These scales are mainly concerned with the factors causing learners to be motivated or demotivated to write. Two examples of the measures of writing motivation sources are: Pajares, Johnson, and Usher's (2007) Sources of Self-Efficacy Scale, and Karaca and Inan's (2020) English Writing Demotivation Scale.

Pajares et al. (2007) adapted their Sources of Self-Efficacy Scale from the mathematics self-efficacy ones developed by Lent and his colleagues (Lent, Lopez, & Bieschke, 1991; Lent, Lopez, Brown, & Gore, 1996). The scale includes items about the following four potential sources of writing self-efficacy: mastery experience (the interpreted outcome of one's previous writing performance), vicarious experience (observing others' writing performances and comparing theirs to one's performance), social persuasions or feedback received from others about one's writing performance, and physiological indexes or states such as anxiety and stress. Like the case of their other several writing motivation published studies, Pajares and his colleagues did not include their full scale in this research report. Rather, they only provided two items from each subscale of the four potential sources of writing self-efficacy. Below are the eight items representing these four sources (i.e., mastery experience, vicarious experience, social persuasions, and physiological indexes), two for each, respectively:

> I get good grades in writing.
> When I come across a tough writing assignment, I work on it until I complete it.
> Many of the adults I admire are good writers.
> Most of my friends are poor writers.
> People often tell me that I am a good writer.
> My relatives believe that I am a good writer.
> Just thinking about writing makes me nervous.
> Writing makes me feel uneasy and confused.
> (Pajares et al., 2007, p. 110)

As noted, Pajares et al.'s Sources of Self-Efficacy scale measures three of the dimensions viewed as aspects writers' self-concept (i.e., mastery experience, vicarious experience or observational comparison, and social persuasions or feedback received from others), see the issues discussed in subsection 2.4.2. This indicates the strong interaction between writers' self-efficacy and self-concept, and that the two constructs are very close to each other (Zimmerman, 2000).

On the other hand, Karaca and Inan's (2020) English Writing Demotivation Scale was adapted from Kao's (2012) one, which was also used in Wu et al.'s (2020) study. The 34-item instrument adapted by Karaca and Inan assesses the following five possible sources of writing demotivation: a) self-perceived L2 writing competence (11 items), e.g., "I feel I cannot be a good writer"; b) teaching practices (seven items), e.g., "My writing teacher scores my writing assignments fairly"; c) attitudinal aspects (six items), e.g., "Writing in English is unnecessary for my future life"; d) writing instructional materials and methods (five items), e.g., "I think English writing textbooks are boring"; and e) teaching and learning context (five items), e.g., "Writing skill is neglected in English language teaching classes" (Karaca & Inan, 2020, p. 12).

It is worth noting that the scales assessing some of the non-motivational constructs referred to in the previous chapter (subsection 1.4.7), also cover a set of writing motivation sources. These include, for instance, Yu, Jiang, & Zhou (2020) English Writing Motivation and Engagement Scale for University/College Students, and Rose's (1984) Attitude towards Writing Questionnaire, which is a measure of writer's block correlates. Qualitative research addressing the factors influencing writers' motivation can significantly contribute to developing scales gauging various types of writers' motivation sources. Issues related to this point are discussed in the next section.

2.7 The qualitative approach to assessing writers' motivation

The issues covered in the above five sections are all related to the quantitative measures of writing motivation constructs. Apart from these quantitative measures, some studies adopted a qualitative approach to assessing writing motivation. The use of the qualitative data sources does not require the process of verifying the psychometric properties (e.g., validity, reliability, and factor analysis) needed in developing the quantitative measures. In most of the cases, these qualitative data sources have been employed in previous research for exploring more than one writing motivation construct. They have also been used in writing motivation research for a number of purposes; including:

> Generating tentative items for inclusion in a given scale.
> Exploring motivational dimensions, potentially unelicitable by quantitative data sources.
> Assessing changes in learners' writing motivation in action research interventions.
> Supplementing quantitative data.
> Identifying the sources of learners' writing demotivation.

On the other hand, six qualitative data sources have been used in previous writing motivation research: semi-structured interviews, focus group interviews, open-ended questionnaires, think-aloud method, learners' journals, and reflective essays.

To generate the items of their Second Language Writer Self-Efficacy Scale, Teng et al. (2018) depended on interviewing 15 participants from the target student population about their perceived writing ability beliefs. Dörnyei (2003) suggests that researchers can improve the quality of the psychological scale items by involving learners in the item generation process. Teng and her colleagues used the following questions in their semi-structured interviews:

1 Are you confident in your English writing proficiency and competence? Why?
2 Do you feel confident when you are writing a composition in English? Why?
3 Do you have any challenges in the writing process?
4 Do you feel confident in your writing course performance? Why?
5 Do you have any challenges in the learning-to-write process?
6 Do you feel confident in regulating your learning behaviour in the learning-to-write process? Why? (p. 941)

Another qualitative approach to generating items was used by Cheng (2004) in her development of the Second Language Writing Anxiety Inventory. She gave 67 students, in three intact English writing classes in Taiwan, an open-ended questionnaire with four questions written in their first language (i.e., Chinese). These four questions asked the students to describe their anxious feelings, and physiological and psychological reactions while performing writing tasks, and explain the causes of such feelings and reactions. Based on the students' responses to the questionnaire, Cheng generated an initial pool of 33 items which were modelled after the statements found in previous relevant scales.

Some exploratory studies have relied mainly on qualitative data to gain insights obtainable from no quantitative source about specific writing motivation dimensions. For example, Mahfoodh (2017) combined the think-aloud method with the semi-structured interviews to explore L2 students' responses to teacher feedback. In an early phase of the study, each student attended a session, in which they were asked to think-aloud while referring to the teacher comments given on their essay first draft. In a later phase, each student was interviewed about their reactions to the teacher comments on the essay second draft. A third stage of the study also involved interviewing the students about their responses to the comments on the final essay draft. Below are examples of the interview questions Mahfoudh used in his study:

> What is your reaction to teacher written comments? Are you happy with it or you feel angry or disappointed when you read the comments given

by the teacher? Are you satisfied? ... Do you like the teacher to continue giving comments and corrections on your essays? (p. 61)

So you better prefer using comments that praise? (p. 62)

Do you feel frustrated when you see these comments and corrections in your drafts? (p. 64)

In analyzing the students' think-aloud and interview protocols, Mahfoodh particularly focused on their feelings of happiness, dis-/satisfaction, disappointment, and frustration.

Another writing motivation area in which qualitative data can be insightful is exploring writers' anxious feelings and their sources. For example, Barwick (1995) interviewed three students five times, 45 minutes for each interview, about their writing anxiety. His aim was to identify "the deeply rooted, inter-related, developmental factors" influencing learners' anxious feelings during essay writing (p. 560). In their ten-week qualitative study on L2 learners' writing anxiety, Saghafi, Adel, and Zareian (2017) used student journals to gain insights into the factors influencing their L2 writing anxiety. Their four study participants were asked to write a journal following each class to explain any potential causes of their anxiety during classroom tasks. The qualitative data Saghafi et al. collected enabled them to describe the procedural, individual, and contextual causes accounting for foreign language classroom writing anxiety.

In some action research studies, focus group interviews were used to assess the changes in students' writing motivation and in turn, to determine the impact of the instructional intervention used. Lo and Hyland (2007) followed this approach in their study of the role of topics in motivating students to write. During the different stages of their action research study, Lo and Hyland used six semi-structured interview sessions with each focus group of students to explore their feelings about writing in general, and their perceptions of the writing topics and instructional procedures they were exposed to. Specifically, they used the focus group interviews to obtain data about: the students' general writing motivation background (e.g., "Do you enjoy writing in general? Why?...What kinds of topics do you like to write about? What topics did you find the most difficult/easiest? Why?" p. 234); their responses to the traditional writing programme (e.g., "How did you feel about these composition topics?.... Every time I looked at your composition I used a red pen to mark the good points and the problems. Did you find that helpful to develop your writing?" p. 234); and their responses to the new writing programme (e.g., "How did you feel about the pre-writing and post-writing activities (peer discussion, etc.)?... Take a good look at your compositions. Tell me any other thoughts/feelings you had during or after the lessons." p. 234).

Piniel and Csizér (2014) also assessed the changes in students' writing attitude and anxiety during an academic writing seminar course by asking them to write a reflective essay at the end of the semester. They used the students' written reflections to supplement the qualitative data gathered by a group of psychological scales. The instructions of the reflective essay task used read as follows:

> Write a short descriptive essay of 200 words on the topic of how your attitudes and feelings towards academic essays have changed throughout the Academic Skills 2 course. Use specific reasons and examples to illustrate your point. Elaborate on how you felt at the beginning, before the Academic Skills Test, after the Test, and towards the end of the course. (p. 171)

The changes in learners' writing motivation were assessed in Han and Hiver's (2018) study using reflective journals. In their nine-week study of the impact of genre-based L2 writing instruction on changing middle school language learners' motivation, Han and Hiver asked them to submit a weekly reflective journal, in which they report their thoughts on the writing tasks performed in the class. They used the following open-ended prompt to obtain wide and informative responses from their participants: "Think back to everything you did in your writing classes this week. Write some notes about what you experienced, thought about, and felt while in class." (Han & Hiver, 2018, p. 48).

On the other hand, Abdel Latif (2015) used semi-structured interviews to explore the sources of L2 learners' writing apprehension and self-efficacy levels. Below are some of the guiding interview questions used in his study:

> Do you like writing in English? Why or why not?
>
> What do you think about the English writing instruction you have received at the university?
>
> Do you ask others (e.g. your teacher or your peers) to read your English essays and evaluate them? If so, how do they usually comment on your English essays?
>
> Compared to your freshman year, do you think writing essays in English has become easier for you? Why or why not?
>
> Compared to the English essays written by your peers, how do you evaluate your own essays?
>
> Do you think you are a good writer in English? Why or why not?
>
> Which writing skills (e.g. spelling, vocabulary, forming a paragraph, etc.) do you think you are good at? (p. 212)

As noted in the above examples, the use of qualitative data sources can add important dimensions to assessing writing motivation. They are particularly used to elicit participants' detailed accounts of their writing motivation experiences. Qualitative sources can also reveal situational writing motivation data unobtainable from quantitative measures. Most importantly, we can also gain insights from learners' qualitative accounts into the sources of their motivation or demotivation. Despite these benefits, the qualitative assessment approach is not generally dominant in writing motivation research.

2.8 Guidelines for developing and validating writing motivation measures

As implied in the above sections, developing and validating a scale measuring a specific writing motivation construct is a multistage process. Overall, such process includes the following four main stages: defining the construct and its dimensions and naming it, generating items and revising them and identifying the appropriate Likert scale response format, administering the scale to the target sample, and analyzing the data collected.

Before developing a scale for assessing the writing motivation construct to be researched, we have to define it and identify its dimensions. At this stage, researchers need to thoroughly review previous relevant literature in order to come up with the most optimal conceptualization and label of the target construct. As indicated in the previous chapter and the above sections in the present one, many overlapping and underrepresented conceptualizations of particular writing motivation constructs have occurred as a result of not considering more relevant literature (e.g., writing apprehension, anxiety, attitude, and the constructs similar to writing self-concept). As we have seen above and in the previous chapter, some researchers have used different writing motivation constructs synonymously, whereas others named the same construct differently. This has in turn caused a case of terminological and definitional confusion of some writing motivation constructs. To avoid these conceptual and terminological problems, researchers at this stage need to answer the following three important questions: "To what extent does the researched construct differ from the other similar ones? Which dimension(s) of the construct do they investigate? And is the construct labelled properly and in a way consistent with writing motivation literature?" (Abdel Latif, 2019, p. 8).

There are a number of approaches to generating the items of writing motivation scales. As shown in the above section, a common approach to doing this is to involve learners in the item generation process, though using open-ended questionnaires (e.g., Cheng, 2004) or semi-structured interviews (e.g., Teng et al., 2018). It is worth noting also that some writing motivation studies have adopted different approaches to generating scale items. For example, Meier et al. (1984) reported generating the items of their writing self-efficacy scale based on reviewing the objectives of the writing courses studied by the target student population. Recently, Karaca and Inan (2020) developed the tentative items of their English Writing Demotivation Scale through the systematic review of language learning and writing motivation studies. This concurs with the psychological literature (e.g., DeVellis, 2016; Dörnyei, 2003), suggesting this alternative approach to scale item generation. After generating the initial item pool for their scale, Karaca and Inan involved field experts in evaluating the items, and also piloted them and made the necessary revisions to some items.

Researchers need to make sure that the items generated or selected for the scale match their definition of the construct. A writing apprehension scale, for instance, is not supposed to include anxiety or self-efficacy items and vice versa. Likewise, product-based writing self-efficacy items should not be given in a process-focused writing self-efficacy scale or subscale. Therefore, it is important that no item conflation is made in one scale. A significant gain obtained from avoiding any overlap or confusion in construct conceptualization and operationalization is making the comparability of research findings easier.

It is important also to choose an appropriate response set for the items of the scale. As indicated above, the four-point, five-point and seven-point Likert response formats are most commonly used in the scales assessing writing motivation constructs. In some writing motivation scales designed for children, researchers used specific response sets such as images of Garfield (e.g., Graham et al., 2007; Kear et al., 2000). A wide variance can be particularly noted in the response sets of the published writing self-efficacy scales. Pajares, Hartley, and Valiante (2001) compared writing self-efficacy scales with different response formats, and found that the 0–100 format is psychometrically stronger than the traditional Likert one in influencing the predicative value of the scale. This supports Bandura's (1997) conclusion that self-efficacy "scales that use only a few steps should be avoided because they are less sensitive and less reliable" (p. 44). It is worth noting, however, that these conclusions may be only true for writing self-efficacy, and perhaps self-concept scales. As for the other writing motivation constructs, this issue may still be questionable. At any rate, researchers developing a measure of a particular writing motivation construct are advised to review relevant literature before deciding upon the response set for the items generated.

Before administering a given scale to a target sample, researchers need to write it in the language facilitating respondents' understanding of its items. If some language barriers are likely to influence L2 respondents' interpretations of items, translating the scale into their L1 will be the optimal option. When giving the scale to respondents, researchers need to consider the nature of its instructions and title. For example, a scale with a title "writing apprehension" or whose instructional part reads as "This scale assesses your writing apprehension..." may stimulate respondents' social desirability, and get them to choose the responses indicating they are non-apprehensive writers. Therefore, a better alternative title for the scale version given to respondents may be, for instance, "a writing learning questionnaire" and its instructional part may read as "This scale assesses your views on learning writing...". Scale instructions, in general, should be phrased in a way inhibiting learners' biased responses to items. Thus, it is important to explain to respondents in the instructional part of the scale that there are no right or wrong answers to its items or statements, and that they ought to provide as honest and realistic answers as possible. Jargon terms should be also avoided. For example, respondents are unlikely to understand scale instructional sentences such as "This scale assesses your writing self-efficacy/motivational regulation of writing/implicit theories of writing/ought-to writing self...etc.". Few scale respondents may be familiar with these terms. This issue has to be considered also in developing writing motivation interview questions.

Respondents can complete writing motivation scales in two formats: the electronic or online format and the printed one. When designing the scale electronically, researchers need to find a respondent-friendly format for presenting the scale. Thanks to technological developments, there are many available online templates researchers can use for designing learning motivation scales. Since scale validation research usually involves collecting other types of motivational and/or performance data, it is noted that researchers in the very vast majority of previous writing motivation studies depended on giving scales to respondents in their classes. Given that this is the dominant scale administration mode, it is recommended that researchers should be there where respondents are completing the scale to answer any questions raised about the meanings of its items. While a given writing motivation scale is completed by children, researchers had better read its items to them and ask them to mark their chosen response (see for example, Graham et al., 2007).

While administering the scale, researchers ought to verbally remind respondents that they need to provide as realistic answers as possible to its items. A problematic issue that could stimulate respondents' social desirability is to ask them to write their names on the scale copies completed. A far better alternative is to assign each participant a number and ask them to write it down on all the research instruments they complete, including the writing motivation scale(s). This procedure is likely to minimize their social desirability response bias.

In testing the construct validity of writing motivation scales, previous studies relied widely on factor analysis. A robust statistical tool used in testing construct validity is Rasch analysis (see Boone, 2016; Hendriks, Fyfe, Styles, Skinner, & Merriman, 2012; McNamara, Knoch, & Fan, 2019). Combining Rasch analysis with factor analysis or using it solely in future writing motivation studies could help in obtaining more valid and accurate measures.

2.9 Conclusion

The above review of the measures of writing motivation constructs complements the conceptualization perspectives discussed in the previous chapter. Thus, readers have a much clearer picture now of how each writing motivation construct has been conceptualized and assessed, and what types of items reflect it more validly. As noted, there have been problematic issues in assessing some writing motivation constructs, such as writing attitude/apprehension, anxiety and self-concept, and the perceived value of writing. These have resulted either from using inaccurate measures or construct under-representation. Terminological problems can be also noted in many measures of these constructs.

The review indicates the changing developments the writing motivation assessment area has witnessed. As has been seen, the assessment of some constructs (e.g., writing apprehension/attitude and self-efficacy) has undergone major changes. The more recent apprehension/attitude measures, for example, are generally shorter compared to the ones developed in the 1970s and 1980s. Meanwhile, the writing self-efficacy scales published in the late 1980s and the 1990s are unidimensional, whereas the ones developed in the last decade cover more varied types of writing and some of them are multidimensional. The assessment of other writing motivation constructs (i.e., perceived value of writing, motivational regulation of writing, and writing self-concept) is still evolving and could witness further developments in the near future. As for the qualitative assessment of writers' motivation, it has not received adequate attention yet.

To summarize, writing motivation assessment has been progressing. An increasing number of measures have been published, and new constructs and construct dimensions have been operationalized. However, some problematic assessment issues are yet to be resolved in future writing motivation research.

References

Abdel Latif, M. M. M. (2015). Sources of L2 writing apprehension: A study of Egyptian university students. *Journal of Research in Reading*, *38*(2), 194–212. doi: 10.1111/j.1467-9817.2012.01549.x

Abdel Latif, M. M. M. (2019). Unresolved issues in defining and assessing writing motivational constructs: A review of conceptualization and measurement perspectives. *Assessing Writing*, *42*. doi: 10.1016/j.asw.2019.100417

Bandura, A. (1997). *Self-efficacy: The exercise of control*. New York: W. H Freeman.

Barwick, N. (1995). Pandora's box: An investigation of essay anxiety in adolescents. *Psychodynamic Counseling*, *1*(4), 560–575. doi: 10.1080/13533339508404154

Baumeister, R. F. (Ed.) (1999). *The self in social psychology*. Philadelphia, PA: Psychology Press (Taylor & Francis).

Boone, W. (2016). Rasch analysis for instrument development: Why, when, and how? *CBE-Life Sciences Education*, *15*(4), rm4. doi: 10.1187/cbe.16-04-0148

Behizadeh, N., & Engelhard, G., Jr. (2014). Development and validation of a scale to measure perceived authenticity in writing. *Assessing Writing*, *21*, 18–36. doi: 10.1016/j.asw.2014.02.001

Behizadeh, N., & Engelhard, G., Jr. (2016). Examining the psychometric quality of a modified perceived authenticity in writing scale with Rasch measurement theory. In Zhang, Q. (Ed.). Pacific Rim Objective Measurement Symposium (PROMS) 2015. Conference Proceedings, pp. 71–87. Singapore: Springer. doi: 10.1007/978-981-10-1687-5_5

Blake, R. W. (1976). Assessing English and language arts teachers' attitudes toward writers and writing. *The English Record*, *27*, 87–97.

Bline, D., Lowe, D. R., Meixner, W. F., Nouri, H., & Pearce, K. (2001). A research note on the dimensionality of Daly and Miller's writing apprehension scale. *Written Communication, 18*(1), 61–79. doi: 10.1177/0741088301018001003

Bong, M., & Skaalvik, E. M. (2003). Academic self-concept and self-efficacy: How different are they really? *Educational Psychology Review, 15*(1), 1–40. https://doi.org/10.1023/A:1021302408382

Bottomley, D. M., Henk, W. A., & Melnick, S. A. (1997). Assessing children's views about themselves as writers using the writer self-perception scale. *The Reading Teacher, 51*, 286–296.

Britt, M., Pribesh S., Hinton-Johnson, K., & Gupta, A. (2018). Effect of a mindful breathing intervention on community college students' writing apprehension and writing performance. *Community College Journal of Research and Practice, 42*(10), 693–707. doi: 10.1080/10668926.2017.1352545

Bruning, R., Dempsey, M., Kauffman, D., McKim, C., & Zumbrunn, S. (2013). Examining dimensions of self-efficacy for writing. *Journal of Educational Psychology, 105*(1), 25–38. doi: 10.1037/a0029692

Burgoon, J., & Hale, J. (1983). A research note on the dimensions of communication reticence. *Communication Quarterly, 31*, 238–248. doi: 10.1080/01463378309369510

Charney, D., Newman, J. H., & Palmquist, M. (1995). "I'm just no good at writing": Epistemological style and attitudes toward writing. *Written Communication, 12*(3), 298–329. doi: 10.1177/0741088395012003004

Chea, S., & Shumow, L. (2017). The relationships among writing self-efficacy, writing goal orientation, and writing achievement. In K. Kimura and J. Middlecamp (Eds.), *Asian-focused ELT research and practice: Voices from the far edge*, (pp. 169–192). IDP Education (Cambodia) Ltd: Cambodia.

Cheng, Y. S. (2004). A measure of second language writing anxiety: Scale development and preliminary validation. *Journal of Second Language Writing, 13*(4), 313–335. doi: 10.1016/j.jslw.2004.07.001

Cheng, Y. S., Horwitz, E., & Schallert, D. (1999). Language anxiety: Differentiating writing and speaking components. *Language Learning, 49*(3), 417–446. doi: 10.1111/0023-8333.00095

Chena, J., & Zhang, L. J. (2019). Assessing student-writers' self-efficacy beliefs about text revision in EFL writing. *Assessing Writing, 40*, 27–41. doi: 10.1016/j.asw.2019.03.002

Cornwell, S., & McKay, T. (2000). Establishing a valid, reliable measure of writing apprehension for Japanese students. *JALT Journal, 22*(1), 114–139.

Csizér, K., & Tankó, G. (2015). English majors' self-regulatory control strategy use in academic writing and its relation to L2 motivation. *Applied Linguistics, 38*(3), 386–404. doi: 10.1093/applin/amv033

Daly, J. A. (1985). Writing apprehension. In M. Rose (Ed.), *When a writer can't write: Studies in writer's block and other composing process problems*, (pp. 43–82). New York: Guilford Press.

Daly, J., & Miller, M. D. (1975). The empirical development of an instrument to measure writing apprehension. *Research in the Teaching of English, 9*(3), 242–249.

DeVellis, R. F. (2016). *Scale development: Theory and applications* (4th ed.). Thousand Oaks, CA: Sage.

Dweck, C. (2000). *Self-theories: Their role in motivation, personality and development.* Philadelphia, PA: Psychology Press.

Dörnyei, Z. (2003). *Questionnaires in second language research.* New York: Routledge.

Dörnyei, Z. (2001). *Motivation strategies in the language classroom.* Cambridge: Cambridge University Press.

Duijnhouwer, H., Prins, F. J., & Stokking, K. M. (2010). Progress feedback effects on students' writing mastery goal, self-efficacy beliefs, and performance. *Educational Research and Evaluation, 16*(1), 53–74. doi: 10.1080/13803611003711393rm4

Ehm, J., Lindberg, S., & Hasselhorn, M. (2014). Reading, writing, and math self-concept in elementary school children: Influence of dimensional comparison processes. *European Journal of Psychology of Education, 29*(2), 277–294. doi: 10.1007/s10212-013-0198-x

Emig, J., & King, B. (1979). *Emig-King attitude scale for teachers.* ERIC Document, ED 236 629.

Fritzsche, B. A., Young, B. R., & Hickson, K. C. (2003). Individual differences in academic procrastination tendency and writing success. *Personality and Individual Differences, 35*, 1549–1557. doi: 10.1016/S0191-8869(02)00369-0

Golombek, C., Klingsieck, K. B., & Scharlau, I. (2019). Assessing self-efficacy for self-regulation of academic writing: Development and validation of a scale. *European Journal of Psychological Assessment, 35*(5), 751–761. doi: 10.1027/1015-5759/a000452

Graham, S., Berninger, V., & Fan, W. (2007). The structural relationship between writing attitude and writing achievement in first and third grade students. *Contemporary Educational Psychology, 32*, 516–536. doi:10.1016/j.cedpsych.2007.01.002

Graham, S., & Harris, K. R. (1989). Components analysis of cognitive strategy instruction: Effects on learning disabled students' compositions and self-efficacy. *Journal of Educational Psychology, 81*(3), 353–561. doi: 10.1037/0022-0663.81.3.353

Graham, S., Schwartz, S., & MacArthur, C. (1993). Learning disabled and normally achieving students' knowledge of writing and the composing process, attitude toward writing, and self-efficacy. *Journal of Learning Disabilities, 26*, 237–249. doi: 10.1177/002221949302600404

Gungle, B. W., & Taylor, V. (1989). Writing apprehension and second language writers. In D. M. Johnson and D. H. Roen (Eds.), *Richness in writing: Empowering ESL students*, (pp. 235–248). New York: Longman, Inc.

Hall, A. H., Toland, M. D., & Guo, Y. (2016). The writing attitude scale for teachers (WAST). *International Journal of Quantitative Research in Education, 3*(3), 204–221. doi: 10.1504/IJQRE.2016.077801

Han, J., & Hiver, P. (2018). Genre-based L2 writing instruction and writing-specific psychological factors: The dynamics of change. *Journal of Second Language Writing, 40*, 44–59. doi: 10.1016/j.jslw.2018.03.001

Hamilton, E. W., Nolen, S. B., & Abbott, R. D. (2013). Developing measures of motivational orientation to read and write: A longitudinal study. *Learning & Individual Differences 28*, 151–166. doi: 10.1016/j.lindif.2013.04.007

He, T. (2005). Effects of mastery and performance goals on the composition strategy use of adult EFL writers. *The Canadian Modern Language Review, 61*(3), 407–431. doi: 10.1353/cml.2005.0017

Hendriks, J., Fyfe, S., Styles, I., Skinner, S., & Merriman, G. (2012). Scale construction utilizing the Rasch unidimensional measurement model: A measurement of adolescent attitudes towards abortion. *The Australasian Medical Journal, 5*(5), 251–261. doi: 10.4066/AMJ.2012.952

Hogan, T. P. (1980). Students' interests in writing activities. *Research in the Teaching of English, 14*(2), 119–125.

Horwitz, E. K., Horwitz, M. B., & Cope, J. (1986). Foreign language classroom anxiety. *Modern Language Journal, 70*(2), 125–132. doi: 10.1111/j.1540-4781.1986.tb05256.x

Huerta, M., Goodson, P., Beigi, M., & Chlup, D. (2017). Graduate students as academic writers: Writing anxiety, self-efficacy and emotional intelligence. *Higher Education Research & Development, 36*(4), 716–729. doi: 10.1080/07294360.2016.1238881

Jones, E. (2008). Predicting performance in first-semester college basic writers: Revisiting the role of self-beliefs. *Contemporary Educational Psychology, 33*, 209–238. doi: 10.1016/j.cedpsych.2006.11.001

Kaplan, A., Lichtinger, E., & Gorodetsky, M. (2009). Achievement goal orientations and self-regulation in writing: An integrative perspective. *Journal of Educational Psychology, 101*(1), 51–69. doi: 10.1037/a0013200

Karaca, M., & Inan, S. (2020). A measure of possible sources of demotivation in L2 writing: A scale development and validation study. *Assessing Writing, 43*. Doi: 10.1016/j.asw.2019.100438

Kao, T. N. R. (2012). *Factor analysis of English writing demotivation among Central Taiwan University students*. MA thesis, Providence University, Taichung, Taiwan.

Karlen, Y., & Compagnoni, M. (2017). Implicit theory of writing ability: Relationship to metacognitive strategy knowledge and strategy use in academic writing. *Psychology Learning & Teaching,16*, 47–63. doi: 10.1177/1475725716682887

Kavanoz, S., & Yüksel, G. (2016). Developing and validating a self-efficacy scale for scholarly writing in English. *International Online Journal of Educational Sciences, 8*(2), 71–82.

Kear, D., Coffman, G., McKenna, M., & Ambrosio, A. (2000). Measuring attitude toward writing: A new tool for teachers. *The Reading Teacher, 54*(1), 10–23.

Klassen, R. (2002). Writing in early adolescence: A review of the role of self-efficacy beliefs. *Educational Psychology Review, 14*, 173–203.

Knudson, R. E. (1991). Development and use of a writing attitude survey in grades 4 to 8. *Psychological Reports, 68*(3), 807–816. doi: 10.2466/pr0.1991.68.3.807

Knudson, R. E. (1992). Development and application of a writing attitude survey for grades 1 to 3. *Psychological Reports, 70*(3), 711–720. doi: 10.2466/pr0.1992.70.3.711

Lee, I., Yu, S., & Liu, Y. (2018). Hong Kong secondary students' motivation in EFL writing: A survey study. *TESOL Quarterly, 52*(1), 176–187. doi: 10.1002/tesq.364

Lee, J. (2013). Can writing attitudes and learning behavior overcome gender difference in writing? Evidence from NAEP. *Written Communication, 30*(2) 164–193. doi: 10.1177/0741088313480313

Lent, R. W., Lopez, F. G., & Bieschke, K. J. (1991). Mathematics self-efficacy: Sources and relation to science-based career choice. *Journal of Counseling Psychology, 38*, 424–430. doi: 10.1037/0022-0167.38.4.424

Lent, R. W., Lopez, F. G., Brown, S. D., & Gore, P. A. (1996). Latent structure of the sources of mathematics self-efficacy. *Journal of Vocational Behavior, 49*, 292–308. doi: 10.1006/jvbe.1996.0045

Limpo, T. (2018). Development of a short measure of writing apprehension: Validity evidence and association with writing frequency, process, and performance. *Learning and Instruction, 58*, 115–125. doi: 10.1016/j.learninstruc.2018.06.001

Limpo, T., & Alves, R. (2014). Implicit theories of writing and their impact on students' response to a SRSD intervention. *British Journal of Educational Psychology, 84*, 571–590. doi: 10.1111/bjep.12042

Limpo, T., & Alves, R. (2017). Relating beliefs in writing skill malleability to writing performance: The mediating role of achievement goals and self-efficacy. *Journal of Writing Research, 9*(2), 97–125. doi: 10.17239/jowr-2017.09.02.01

Lo, J., & Hyland, F. (2007). Enhancing students' engagement and motivation in writing: The case of primary students in Hong Kong. *Journal of Second Language Writing, 16*, 219–237. doi: 10.1016/j.jslw.2007.06.002

MacArthur, C., Philippakos, Z., & Graham, S. (2016). A multicomponent measure of writing motivation with basic college writers. *Learning Disability Quarterly*, *39*(1), 31–43. doi: 10.1177/0731948715583115

Mahfoodh, O. H. A. (2017). "I feel disappointed": EFL university students' emotional responses towards teacher written feedback. *Assessing Writing*, *31*, 53–72. Doi: 10.1016/j.asw.2016.07.001

Marsh, H. (1990). The structure of academic self-concept: The Marsh–Shavelson model. *Journal of Educational Psychology*, *82*, 623–636. doi: 10.1037//0022-0663.82.4.623

Marsh, H. W., & Shavelson, R. J. (1985). Self-concept: Its multifaceted, hierarchical structure. *Educational Psychologist*, *20*, 107–125. doi: 10.1207/s15326985ep2003_1

McCarthy, P., Meier, S., & Rinderer, R. (1985). Self-efficacy and writing: A different view of self-evaluation. *College Composition and Communication*, *36*, 465–471. doi: 10.2307/357865

McKain, T. L. (1991). Cognitive, affective, and behavioural factors in writing anxiety. *PhD Dissertation, the Catholic University of America*, USA.

McNamara, T., Knoch, U., & Fan, J. (2019). *Fairness, justice and language assessment*. Oxford: Oxford University Press.

Meier, S., McCarthy, P., & Schmeck, R. (1984). Validity of self-efficacy as a predictor of writing performance. *Cognitive Therapy and Research*, *8*, 107–120.

Messick, S. (1989). Validity. In R. L. Linn (Ed.), *Educational measurement* (pp.13–103). New York: Macmillan.

Middleton, M., & Midgley, C. (1997). Avoiding the demonstration of lack of ability: An underexplored aspect of goal theory. *Journal of Educational Psychology*, *89*(4), 710–718. doi: 10.1037/0022-0663.89.4.710

Mitchell, K. M., Harrigan, T., Stefansson, T., & Setlack, H. (2017). Exploring self-efficacy and anxiety in first-year nursing students enrolled in a discipline-specific scholarly writing course. *Quality Advancement in Nursing Education*, *3–4*, 1–20. http://dx.doi.org/10.17483/2368-6669.1084

Mitchell, K. M., Rieger, K. L., & McMillan, D. E. (2017). A template analysis of writing self-efficacy measures. *Journal of Nursing Measurement*, *25*(2), 205–223. doi: 10.1891/1061-3749.25.2.205

Neugebauer, S. R., & Howard, E. R. (2015). Exploring associations among writing self-perceptions, writing abilities, and native language of English-Spanish two-way immersion students. *Bilingual Research Journal*, *38*(3), 313–335. doi: 10.1080/15235882.2015.1093039

Olivier, L., & Olivier, J. (2016). Exploring writing apprehension amongst Afrikaans-speaking first-year students. *Reading & Writing-Journal of the Reading Association of South Africa*, *7*(1), a89. doi: 10.4102/rw.v7i1.89

Pajares, F. (2003). Self-efficacy beliefs, motivation, and achievement in writing: A review of the literature. *Reading and Writing Quarterly*, *19*, 139–158. doi: 10.1080/10573560390143085

Pajares, F., Britner, S., & Valiante, G. (2000). Relation between achievement goals and self-beliefs of middle school students in writing and science. *Contemporary Educational Psychology*, *25*, 406–422. doi: 10.1006/ceps.1999.1027

Pajares, F., & Cheong, Y. (2003). Achievement goal orientations in writing: A developmental perspective. *International Journal of Educational Research*, *39*, 437–455. doi: 10.1016/j.ijer.2004.06.008

Pajares, F., Hartley, J., & Valiante, G. (2001). Response format in writing self-efficacy assessment: Greater discrimination increases prediction. *Measurement and Evaluation in Counseling and Development*, *33*(4), 214–221. doi: 10.1080/07481756.2001.12069012

Pajares, F., & Johnson, M. J. (1994). Confidence and competence in writing: The role of writing self-efficacy, outcome expectancy, and apprehension. *Research in the Teaching of English*, *28*, 313–331.

Pajares, F., & Johnson, M. (1996). Self-efficacy beliefs and the writing performance of entering high school students. *Psychology in the Schools*, *33*, 163–175. doi: 10.1002/(SICI)1520-6807(199604)33:2<163::AID-PITS10>3.0.CO;2-C

Pajares, F., Johnson, J., & Usher, E. (2007). Sources of writing self-efficacy beliefs of elementary, middle, and high school students. *Research in the Teaching of English*, *42*(1), 104–120.

Pajares, F., Miller, M., & Johnson, M. (1999). Gender differences in writing self-beliefs of elementary school students. *Journal of Educational Psychology*, *91*, 50–61. Doi: 10.1006/ceps.1998.0995

Pajares, F., & Valiante, G. (1997). Influence of writing self-efficacy beliefs on the writing performance of upper elementary students. *The Journal of Educational Research*, *90*, 353–360. doi: 10.1080/00220671.1997.10544593

Pajares, F., & Valiante, G. (1999). Grade level and gender differences in the writing self-beliefs of middle school students. *Contemporary Educational Psychology*, *24*(4), 390–405. doi: 10.1006/ceps.1998.0995

Pajares, F., & Valiante, G. (2001). Gender differences in writing motivation and achievement of middle school students: A function of gender orientation? *Contemporary Educational Psychology*, *26*, 366–381. doi: 10.1006/ceps.2000.1069

Pajares, F., Valiante, G., & Cheong, Y. F. (2007). Writing self-efficacy and its relation to gender, writing motivation, and writing competence: A developmental perspective. In S. Hidi, & P. Boscolo (Eds.). *Motivation and writing: Research and school practice* (pp. 141–162). Dordrecht, The Netherlands: Kluwer.

Palmquist, M., & Young, R. (1992). The notion of giftedness and student expectations about writing. *Written Communication*, *9*(1), 137–169. doi: 10.1177/0741088392009001004

Phinney, M. (1991). Word processing and writing apprehension in first and second language writers. *Computers and Composition*, *9*(1), 65–82. doi: 10.1016/8755-4615(91)80039-G

Piazza, C., & Siebert, C. (2008). Development and validation of a writing dispositions scale for elementary and middle school students. *The Journal of Educational Research*, *101*, 275–285. doi: 10.3200/JOER.101.5.275-286

Piniel, K., & Csizér, K. (2014). Changes in motivation, anxiety and self-efficacy during the course of an academic writing seminar. In Z. Dörnyei, P. MacIntyre, & A. Henry (Eds.), *Motivational dynamics in language learning*, (pp. 164–194). Bristol: Multilingual Matters.

Piniel, K., Csizér, K., Khudiyeva, S. R., & Gafiatulina, Y. (2016). A comparison of Hungarian and Kazakh university students' language learning profiles. *WoPaLP*, *10*, 39–55.

Poff, S. (2004). *Regimentation: A predictor of writer's block and writing apprehension*. PhD dissertation, University of Southern California, USA.

Prat-Sala, M., & Redford, P. (2010). The interplay between motivation, self-efficacy, and approaches to studying. *The British Journal of Educational Psychology*, *80*(2), 283–305. doi: 10.1348/000709909x480563

Richmond, V., & Dickson-Markman, F. (1985). Validity of the writing apprehension test. *Psychological Reports*, *56*, 255–259. doi: 10.2466/pr0.1985.56.1.255

Riffe, D., & Stacks, D. (1988). Dimensions of writing apprehension among mass communication students. *Journalism Quarterly*, *65*(2), 384–391. doi: 10.1177/107769908806500218

Riffe, D., & Stacks, D. W. (1992). Student characteristics and writing apprehension. *The Journalism Educator*, *47*(2), 39–49. doi: 10.1177/107769589204700206

Rose, M. (1984). *Writer's block: The cognitive dimension*. Carbondale: Southern Illinois University Press.

Sanders-Reio, J., Alexander, P., Reio, T., & Newman, I. (2014). Do students' beliefs about writing relate to their writing self-efficacy, apprehension, and performance? *Learning and Instruction*, *33*, 1–11. doi: 10.1016/j.learninstruc.2014.02.001

Saghafi, K., Adel, S. M. R., & Zareian, G. (2017). An ecological study of foreign language writing anxiety in English as a foreign language classroom. *Journal of Intercultural Communication Research*, *46*(5), 424–440. doi: 10.1080/17475759.2017.1367954

Shaver, J. (1990). Reliability and validity of measures of attitudes toward writing and toward writing with the computer. *Written Communication*, *7*(3), 37–392. doi: 10.1177/0741088390007003004

Schmidt, K. M., & Alexander, J. E. (2012). The empirical development of an instrument to measure writerly self-efficacy in writing centers. *Journal of Writing Assessment*, *5*(1), 1–19.

Shell, D., Murphy, C., & Bruning, R. (1989). Self-efficacy and outcome expectancy mechanisms in reading and writing achievement. *Journal of Educational Psychology*, *81*, 91–100. doi: 10.1037/0022-0663.81.1.91

Shell, D., Colvin, C., & Bruning, R. (1995). Self-efficacy, attributions, and outcome expectancy mechanisms in reading and writing achievement: Grade-level and achievement-level differences. *Journal of Educational Psychology*, *87*, 386–398. doi: 10.1037/0022-0663.87.3.386

Spaulding, C. L. (1995). Teachers' psychological presence on students' writing-task engagement. *Journal of Educational Research*, *88*(4), 210–219. doi: 10.1080/00220671.1995.9941302

Spielberger, C. D., Gorsuch, R. L., & Lushene, R. (1970). *State-trait anxiety inventory manual*. Palo Alto, CA: Consulting Psychologists Press.

Spielberger, C. D., Gorsuch, R. L., Lushene, R., Vagg, P. R., & Jacobs, G. A. (1983). *State-trait anxiety inventory (form Y)*. Redwood City, CA: Mind Garden.

Thompson, M. O. (1978). *The development and evaluation of a language study approach to a college course in freshman composition*. PhD dissertation, The American University, Washington D.C., USA.

Teng, L. S., Sun, P., & Xu, L. (2018). Conceptualizing writing self-efficacy in English as a foreign language contexts: Scale validation through structural equation modeling. *TESOL Quarterly*, *52*(4), 911–942. doi: 10.1002/tesq.432

Teng, L. S., Yuan, R. E., & Sun, P. P. (2020). A mixed-methods approach to investigating motivational regulation strategies and writing proficiency in English as a foreign language contexts. *System*, *88*, 1–12. doi: 10.1016/j.system.2019.102182

Teng, L. S., & Zhang, L. J. (2016a). A questionnaire-based validation of multidimensional models of self-regulated learning strategies. *Modern Language Journal*, *100*(3), 674–701. doi: 10.1111/modl.12339

Teng, L. S., & Zhang, L. J. (2016b). Fostering strategic learning: The development and validation of the writing strategies for motivational regulation questionnaire (WSMRQ). *Asia-Pacific Education Researcher*, *25*, 123–134. doi: 10.1007/s40299-015-0243-4

Teng, L. S., & Zhang, L. J. (2018). Effects of motivational regulation strategies on writing performance: A mediation model of self-regulated learning of writing in

English as a second/foreign language. *Metacognition and Learning, 13*(2), 213–240. doi: 10.1007/s11409-017-9171-4

Troia, G. A., Harbaugh, A. G., Shankland, R. K., Wolbers, K. A., & Lawrence, A. M. (2013). Relationships between writing motivation, writing activity, and writing performance: Effects of grade, sex, and ability. *Reading and Writing, 26*, 17–44. Doi: 10.1007/s11145-012-9379-2

Tsai, H. M. (2008). The development of an English writing anxiety scale for Institute of Technology English majors. *Journal of Education and Psychology, 31*(3), 81–107. Doi: 10.1177/0033294116687123

Tsao, J., Tseng, W., & Wang, W. (2017). The effects of writing anxiety and motivation on EFL college students' self-evaluative judgments of corrective feedback. *Psychological Reports, 120*(2), 219–241. Doi: 10.1177/0033294116687123

Waller, L., & Papi, M. (2017). Motivation and feedback: How implicit theories of intelligence predict L2 writers' motivation and feedback orientation. *Journal of Second Language Writing, 35*, 54–65. doi: 10.1016/j.jslw.2017.01.004

Wong, B. Y. L., Butler, D. L., Ficzere, S. A., & Kuperis, S. (1997). Teaching adolescents with learning disabilities and low achievers to plan, write, and revise compare-and-contrast essays. *Learning Disabilities Research and Practice, 12*(1), 2–15.

Woodrow, L. (2011). College English writing affect: Self-efficacy and anxiety. *System, 39*, 510–522. doi: 10.1016/j.system.2011.10.017

Wright, K. L., Hodges, T. S., & McTigue, E. M. (2019). A validation program for the self-beliefs, writing-beliefs, and attitude survey: A measure of adolescents' motivation toward writing. *Assessing Writing, 39*, 64–78. doi: 10.1016/j.asw.2018.12.004

Wu, W. V., Yang, J. H., Hsieh, J. H. C., & Yamamoto, T. (2020). Free from demotivation in EFL writing: The use of online flipped writing instruction. *Computer Assisted Language Learning, 33*(4), 353–387. doi: 10.1080/09588221.2019.1567556

Yao, Q. (2019). Direct and indirect feedback: How do they impact on secondary school learners' writing anxiety and how do learners perceive them? *The Asian Conference on Language Learning 2019, Official Conference Proceedings*, 1–12.

Yilmaz Soylu, M., Zeleny, M. G., Zhao, R., Bruning, R., Dempsey, M., & Kauffman, D. (2017). Secondary students' writing achievement goals: Assessing the mediating effects of mastery and performance goals on writing self-efficacy, affect, and writing achievement. *Frontiers in Psychology, 8*, 1406. doi: 10.3389/fpsyg.2017.01406

Yu, S., Jiang, L., & Zhou, N. (2020). Investigating what feedback practices contribute to students' writing motivation and engagement in Chinese EFL context: A large scale study. *Assessing Writing, 44*, 1–15. doi: 10.1016/j.asw.2020.100451

Zabihi, R. (2018). The role of cognitive and affective factors in measures of L2 writing. *Written Communication, 35*(1), 32–57. doi: 10.1177/0741088317735836

Zhang, H., Song, W., Shen, S., & Huang, R. (2014). The effects of blog-mediated peer feedback on learners' motivation, collaboration, and course satisfaction in a second language writing course. *Australasian Journal of Educational Technology, 30*, 670–685. doi: 10.14742/ajet.860

Zimmerman, B. (2000). Self-efficacy: An essential motive to learn. *Contemporary Educational Psychology, 25*, 82–91. doi: 10.1006/ceps.1999.1016

Zimmerman, B., & Bandura, A. (1994). Impact of self-regulatory influences on writing course attainment. *American Educational Research Journal, 31*, 845–862. doi: 10.2307/1163397

3 Profiling motivated and demotivated writers

3.1 Introduction

Having discussed the conceptualizations and operationalizations of writing motivation constructs, there is a need now to identify the correlates and sources of writers' motivation and demotivation. Reviewing research on these correlates and factors will help us in identifying the characteristics of motivated writers and symptoms of writing demotivation. The detailed discussion of these issues is closely related to the two main topics covered in chapters 4 and 5 which deal with the writing motivation instructional research and how to motivate students to write, respectively. Overall, the factors associated with writing motivation can be grouped into three categories: personal variables; language and writing performance and beliefs; and learning and instruction practices. In this chapter, the author discusses these potential predictors and sources of writing motivation. The chapter starts with discussing how three personal variables (i.e., gender, age, and cultural background) may influence writers' motivation. Then, the author reviews the research addressing the performance and belief predictors of writers' motivational levels, and the motivating influence of learning and instruction practices and the issues related to them. In light of discussing all these issues, the author ends the chapter with summarizing the characteristics of motivated and demotivated writers.

3.2 The role of personal variables in writing motivation

The "personal variables" term is used here to refer to learners' gender, age, and cultural background factors. Not many studies have addressed the role of these three variables in writing motivation. Before referring to these few studies, it will be important to shed light on the role of the three variables in language learning motivation, the more general area.

3.2.1 Gender

L2 learning motivation research generally indicates that female students are more motivated to language learning than male ones (Coleman, Galaczi, &

Astruc, 2007; Okuniewski, 2014; Sylvén & Thompson, 2015); though very few studies (e.g., Iwaniec, 2019) found no gender differences in some variables such as students' L2 learning self-efficacy beliefs, self-concept, or intrinsic motivation. Research has also shown that as compared to their female peers, male students' intrinsic language learning motivation decreases more rapidly as age increases (Lee & Kim, 2014; Yeung, Lau, & Nie, 2011), and that they have lower motivational intensity (e.g., Kissau, Quach Kolano, & Wang, 2010; Williams, Burden, & Lanvers, 2002). The noted stronger motivation among females has also been found across a number of cultural settings (Dörnyei, Csizér, & Németh, 2006; Kim & Kim, 2011) and various languages (e.g., Chavez, 2014; Dörnyei et al., 2006; Henry, 2009; Kim & Kim, 2011; Öztürk & Gürbüz, 2013).

On the other hand, a few studies have investigated the relationship between gender and writing motivation. Gender influence in writing motivation research has been addressed as a potential correlate of some constructs rather than others. Most reported research findings are related to writing self-efficacy and apprehension. In the writing self-efficacy studies, females were found to have higher writing self-efficacy beliefs than males (Andrade, Wang, Du, & Akawi, 2009; Hidi, Berndorff, & Ainley, 2002; Pajares, 2003; Pajares, Miller, & Johnson, 1999; Pajares & Valiante, 1997; 2001; 2006; Pajares, Valiante, & Cheong, 2007). Pajares, Britner, and Valiante (2000) and Pajares and Cheong (2003) also found gender-related differences in students' writing goals. The two studies revealed that girls had more task goals, whereas boys had more performance approach and avoidance goals. In their study about the sources of writing self-efficacy, Pajares, Johnson, and Usher (2007) found that girls had greater writing mastery and vicarious experiences and higher social persuasion beliefs. As indicated in the previous chapter, these can be regarded as dimensions forming writers' self-concept. Pajares and colleagues (Pajares, Johnson, & Usher, 2007a; Pajares & Valiante, 2001) attributed females' high self-efficacy scores to viewing writing as gender stereotyped and to the femininity associated with writing self-efficacy. Despite the results revealing that females are likely to have a higher level of writing motivation than males, it is worth to note that the studies reported by Pajares and Johnson (1996) and Pajares et al. (1999) indicate that gender-related differences in writing motivation disappear or go in the reverse direction when students reach the high school. Meanwhile, Lee, Yu, and Liu (2018) found no impact for gender on a number of L2 learners' writing motivation variables.

Other fewer studies reported findings on gender differences in writing apprehension. In some of these studies, males were found to be more apprehensive than female writers (Elias, 1999; Pajares et al., 2007b; Riffe & Stacks, 1992; Simons, Higgins, & Lowe, 1995), others revealed that female writers are more apprehensive (Faris, Golen, & Lynch, 1999; Huerta, Goodson, Beigi, & Chlup, 2017; Martinez, Kock, & Cass, 2011), and a third group of studies showed no relationship between gender and writing apprehension

(Abu Shawish & Atea, 2010; Massé & Popovich, 2005). With regard to writing anxiety, Yu et al. (2019) found that female students feel worry more than males about not doing well on the assigned tasks. Given these scarce and varied research findings, no decisive conclusions can be drawn from these studies with regard to the role of learners' gender in their writing apprehension or anxiety levels.

3.2.2 Age

The age variable has been used interchangeably in motivation research with other terms such as the educational grade or stage. Unlike gender, not much research is available on age-related differences in language learning motivation. For example, Ghenghesh (2010) found that students' L2 learning motivation decreases with age. Research also indicates that students have different motivational orientations in different ages. Tragant's (2006) study, for instance, revealed that young Catalonian learners of English had more intrinsic and instrumental motivation types, while adult ones had more instrumental motives. Age-related differences in L2 learning motivation were also found by Kormos and Csizér (2008), whose study showed a higher level in university students' motivated behaviours than that of high school students. In a recent study examining age-related motivational differences in the Chinese context, Xu and Case (2015) conclude that:

> Students' motivation to learn English shift with each level of schooling… instrumental motivation starts to develop when students enter middle school. Elementary students begin with unbiased motivations toward learning English. They share similar levels of integrative motivation with their middle school peers but a higher level than their high school peers. As for instrumental motivation, they do not differ significantly with middle school or high school students. (p. 77).

Collectively, the previous few studies addressing the role of age in L2 learning motivation generally indicate the construct is dynamic, i.e., it varies from one age to another, particularly with regard to motivational goal orientations. As for motivational ability beliefs, no conclusive evidence seems to have occurred from relevant research.

Very few studies have investigated the relationship between learners' age and their writing motivation. Like the case of gender, these studies have been mainly concerned with writing self-efficacy. In Shell, Colvin, and Bruning's (1995) study, students' writing self-efficacy increased as they progressed from elementary to high school grades. Contrarily, Pajares and Valiante (1999) found a decrease in middle school students' self-efficacy scores as they move to upper grades. Similarly, Pajares et al.'s (2007a) study showed a decline in students' writing efficacy beliefs as they move from elementary to middle school, and a stable level in these beliefs during the high school stage.

The same declining trend was also noted in middle and high school students' reported writing mastery, vicarious, and social persuasion experiences compared to elementary graders' stronger ones (Pajares et al., 2007b). In a more recent study, Lee et al. (2018) also found a decline in students' writing efficacy as they move to upper school grades.

3.2.3 Socio-cultural background

Learners' socio-cultural background means their ethnicity or the environment in which they have grown up or to which they belong. In the language learning motivation area, some works have addressed the association between students' varied L2 learning motivational levels and socio-cultural factors (e.g., Graham & Hudley, 2007; van Laar, 2001). The main assumption underlying this cross-cultural research strand is that particular cultural values mediate language learners' cognition, behaviours, and achievement (Dörnyei & Ushioda, 2011). In the Chinese schooling context, for example, Hong (2001) found that performance outcomes are ascribed to students' efforts, rather than abilities. Some more recent studies (e.g., Amirian & Komesh, 2018; Mostafaei Alaei & Ghamari, 2013) investigated the relationship between L2 learners' ethnic backgrounds and their motivation to learn English.

In writing classes, we may also expect that learners' socio-cultural background exerts some influence on their motivational beliefs. However, there is a clear scarcity of writing motivation studies dealing with this issue. The only available quantitative study is perhaps the one reported by Pajares and Johnson (1996), who found that Hispanic high school students had lower writing self-efficacy and higher apprehensive writing levels than non-Hispanic White ones. Meanwhile, the qualitative study reported by Saghafi, Adel, and Zareian (2017) implies that family pressure and the dominance of language learning extrinsic motivation goals in the Iranian context are associated with increasing students' English writing anxiety. An early reference to the role of contextual factors in writing motivation was made by Bloom (1985) who states that "when contexts not conducive to writing interfere with those that are, the conflict may produce little writing and little desire to do any" (p. 131).

Due to the scarce studies on the above-mentioned three personal variables (i.e., age, gender, and socio-cultural background), we do not have conclusive evidence about the directions in which they influence writers' motivation. It can be noted also that the larger number of these studies concern writing motivation in L1 contexts. Despite the lack of relevant research evidence, motivational writing instruction is supposed to be tailored in a way considering learners' gender, age, and socio-cultural characteristics. Until decisive research evidence occurs, writing teachers may deal with these learner personal variables in their classes depending on intuition and previous experiences.

3.3 Performance, belief, and behaviour correlates of writing motivation

Learners' writing motivation interacts with a set of performance aspects, beliefs, and behaviours. The performance correlates are writers' actual language level and their composing processes and texts. The belief predictors include the perceived beliefs about one's language proficiency, writing mastery experiences, and the way writing motivation constructs interact with each other. As for the behavioural correlates, these are the learning habits or orientations associated with writing demotivation or motivation, such as taking particular types of writing courses, performing writing tasks, and doing extracurricular activities. In what follows, these correlates are discussed in detail.

3.3.1 Language ability level

Writing calls upon using a linguistic knowledge base which is usually operationalized by researchers as language proficiency. Grammar and vocabulary knowledge are the two main linguistic resources that writers use to express ideas in appropriate syntactic structures. Grammar knowledge refers to learners' repertoire of the target language structures and ability to use them. Vocabulary knowledge, labelled by other researchers as lexical proficiency (e.g., Baba, 2009), is one's awareness of the meaning of lexical items and their ability to use these items in written or spoken forms. Due to the limited linguistic resources available in L2 writers' long-term memory, they experience much more complicated text composing processes than their L1 peers. Empirical studies comparing writers' L1 and L2 composing processes found that the latter type of composing involves more difficulties and is less fluent than the former one due to the linguistic constraints and vocabulary and grammar problems encountered (e.g. Albrechtsen, Haastrup, & Henriksen, 2008; Fagan & Hayden, 1988; Pennington & So, 1993; Silva, 1993; Skibniewski, 1988; Uzawa, 1996; Wolfersberger, 2003). Given this empirical evidence, we can expect that in L2 environments, learners' ability levels play a more influential role in shaping their writing motivation, and that many L2 learners who have not developed facility with the textual or communicative aspects of the target language are likely to be less motivated to write.

Not many studies have addressed the correlation between writers' linguistic ability levels and their motivation. The findings of these few studies show significant correlation between writers' motivation and the quality of the texts they produce. Specifically, they emphasize the strong correlation between writers' motivation and the language-related features in their texts. Victori's (1995) study revealed that Spanish English-as-a-foreign-language (EFL) writers with higher self-confidence had more problems in cohesion than in grammar, while writers with lower self-confidence had more problems in grammar than in cohesion. Language deficiency was found to influence writers' motivation in L1 contexts as well. In Sanders-Reio, Alexander, Reio, and Newman's (2014) study, for instance, apprehension about grammar correlated negatively with L1 writers' performance. In the Malaysian context, Daud, Daud, and Abu Kassim (2005) also found that L2 university students' writing apprehension levels are associated significantly with the language-related dimensions (i.e., vocabulary and language use) in their texts, but not with the other aspects of the text related to content, organization, and mechanics. Similar results were also found by Abdel Latif (2015), whose study showed a higher negative correlation of Egyptian EFL learners' writing apprehension with both text vocabulary and language use scores than text content, organization, and mechanics ones.

The comparative association of both linguistic knowledge and writing motivation with learners' writing ability has hardly been researched. In a rare study addressing this issue, Abdel Latif (2009) found that compared to writing apprehension and self-efficacy, vocabulary and grammar knowledge, respectively, had higher correlations with learners' composing processes and texts. The conclusion drawn from this study is that L2 learners' linguistic knowledge levels mediate the relationship of their writing motivation with performance. In other words, the higher linguistic knowledge levels L2 learners have the more motivated and competent writers they are expected to be, and vice versa. Thus, linguistic knowledge is the variable playing the central role in this net of relationships as it is a prerequisite for facilitating the composing process and producing a good quality text and in turn it also influences writers' apprehension and self-efficacy levels. Abdel Latif (2015) also provided further evidence that L2 students' linguistic knowledge levels are associated negatively with their writing apprehension and positively with writing self-efficacy beliefs. In an L1 writing context, Sims' (1995) study showed a negative correlation between students' writing apprehension and their English scores as measured by the American College Testing (ACT).

Some research suggests that the mediating influence of language ability on writing motivation is likely to disappear at a particular developmental stage. The results of some studies (e.g., Concepcion, 1992; Ryu, 1997) support the threshold hypothesis that when L2 learners reach a specific level of language proficiency, their writing would be more influenced by rhetorical dimensions than language ability ones and in this case, only motivation is expected to play a more influential role in writing performance. This case is obvious in L1 writing environments where students do not encounter many language barriers. The threshold hypothesis seems to be consistent with Roca de Larios, Murphy, and Martin's (2002) opinion that the relationship between writing and language proficiency "should not be viewed as an all-or-nothing business but as a continuum" (p. 39).

3.3.2 Perceived language ability beliefs

While learners' language ability – demonstrated in their test scores or task performance – is an indicator of their actual linguistic knowledge or proficiency level, their perceived language ability beliefs – which may or may not be consistent with actual language performance – is another potential correlate of their writing motivation. In a case similar to the linguistic knowledge research reviewed in the above subsection, the studies dealing with the relationship between the two variables (i.e., perceived language ability beliefs and writing motivation) are also very scarce.

Three studies reported qualitative data about how students' perceived language problems cause their writing demotivation. In Abdel Latif's (2015) study, the apprehensive writers reported vocabulary, grammar, and spelling as their main problems. Contrarily, the problems reported by non-apprehensive interviewees were mainly related to text content and organization. Thus, it is concluded that the perceived low language ability beliefs cause Egyptian students to have higher English writing apprehension. In Saghafi et al.'s (2017) study, they found linguistic block a major hindrance to Iranian learners' L2 writing process fluency. This linguistic block – resulted mainly from limited vocabulary repertoires – caused their participants to have some writing anxiety symptoms such as a running-down state of mind, and panic and uneasy feelings. One of their participants did not have these anxious writing feelings because of her higher English proficiency level. In describing this student, Saghafi and her colleagues stated that the "constant use of English during the immigration time helped her speed up with the generation of insightful ideas and extend her linguistic knowledge which assuaged her writing anxiety" (p. 433). In their study about US Hispanic students' perceptions of their Spanish language writing abilities, Torres, Arrastia-Chisholm, and Tackett (2020) found the language difficulties these students experienced caused them to have low writing-self-efficacy and higher writing apprehension levels. Explaining the students' perceived causes of their writing demotivation, Torres et al. listed "limited vocabulary, inadequate understanding of grammatical rules, and inexperience with formal Spanish writing" (p. 89). Some quantitative research findings support the above qualitative data. For instance, the results reported by Cheng, Horwitz, and Schallert (1999), and Hertz-Lazarowitz & Bar-Natan, 2002) indicate that L2 writers worry more about the form or linguistic aspects than the content of their texts.

As noted above, the above-reviewed research about the influence of writers' linguistic knowledge levels and perceived language ability on their motivation has addressed writing self-efficacy, apprehension, and anxiety only. No research seems to be available about the influence of these two factors on other writing motivation constructs such as achievement goals or perceived value of writing.

3.3.3 Writing performance

Writing motivation is associated with certain performance features or aspects at both the composing process and written text level. The studies on the latter correlate are relatively larger in number than those reported on the former one. Additionally the available research on the relationship between writers' motivation and their performance are concerned with some constructs rather than others.

3.3.3.1 Writing process

The few studies examining the relationship between writers' motivation and their text composing processes can be divided into two categories: a) the studies dealing with writing motivation as peripheral variable; and b) in-depth studies focusing on writers' motivation as a main potential correlate of their composing strategy use. The studies reported by Angelova (1999), Gungle and Taylor (1989), Masny and Foxall (1992), Sasaki and Hirose (1996), and Victori (1995) belong to the first category. These studies addressed the target issue by including a few items, ranging from 2 to 5 on average, in a background questionnaire to gauge writers' motivation, and then correlated the respondents' answers to these items with their responses to another set of items in a writing strategy questionnaire.

The writing process studies dealing with writing motivation as peripheral variable reported inconsistent results. Gungle and Taylor (1989) did not find any significant correlation between writers' apprehension levels and their attention to form or content. They attributed these results to the possibility that their revised version of the Daly and Miller (1975) Writing Apprehension Test (WAT) was not an accurate measure of the construct. Pursuing the same issue, Masny and Foxall (1992) found that the low apprehensive students were more concerned with form than the high apprehensive ones. On the other hand, Victori's (1995) study showed that Spanish L2 writers with higher self-confidence did not attend much to the pre-writing planning and the content of their writing, whereas writers with lower self-confidence depended on pre-writing outline and followed it strictly. In contrast, Sasaki and Hirose's (1996) study revealed no significant relationship between writers' self-confidence and their strategy use. Using the Hirose and Sasaki's (1994) writing metacognitive knowledge survey and supplementing it with video-stimulated recall interview, Angelova (1999) also found that writers with positive attitudes and stronger confidence used pre-writing and online planning strategies and attended to content and organization, while writers with negative attitude and lower confidence relied on online planning related to the text written and encountered difficulties in organizing their ideas. As noted, the discrepancies in these results have likely been caused by the different and inaccurate writing motivation measures used in some studies.

The in-depth studies on the composing processes of writers with different motivation levels were reported by Abdel Latif (2009), Bannister (1982), Butler (1980), Hayes (1981), He (2005), Karlen and Compagnoni (2017), Selfe (1984), and Teng, Yuan, and Sun (2020). The larger number of these studies, however, was concerned with writing apprehension only. Butler (1980) investigated the writing strategies used by four secondary school students whose writing apprehension and ability levels were identified based on the WAT and teacher's rating, respectively. Two of the four students were high apprehensive writers, while the other two were low apprehensive writers (one with a high writing ability and one with a low writing ability in each pair). They were observed and videotaped while composing two tasks, then they were interviewed about their writing processes. Differences in some aspects of the composing process (the amount of physical activity, re-reading behaviours, and considering audience) were found between these writers due to writing apprehension rather than writing ability. On the other hand, Hayes' (1981) study engaged an apprehensive writer and another non-apprehensive in composing two texts in two separate sessions, in which they were videotaped and their verbalizations were recorded. In addition, the two writers were stimulated to retrospect their composing behaviours by replaying their videotaped composing sessions. While the apprehensive writer was found to seldom write a part of a text in a single sitting and to have anxious feelings during writing, the non-apprehensive one composed her texts in one sitting mostly and had non-anxious composing habits. In addition, the non-apprehensive writer wrote more than one draft and up to four drafts, of which the final one was completed in the shortest time, but the apprehensive writer wrote only one draft. The composing process of the apprehensive writer, who was concerned more with the linguistic form, was less recursive and more rigid than that of the non-apprehensive writer.

Bannister (1982) examined the composing strategies of four high apprehensive writers and four low apprehensive ones, identified by the WAT, using planning activity forms and interviews. The study found that low apprehensive writers planned more productively through generating ideas and evaluating them, while high apprehensive writers wrote down the ideas generated initially without assessing them and did little while-writing revisions. Selfe (1984) investigated the composing behaviours of four high and four low apprehensive writers using think-aloud protocols, video recording of the writing sessions, retrospective interview, and the WAT. The study revealed that the high apprehensive writers, who had an impulsive and anxious composing style, spent less time pre-writing and engaged in less ideational and organizational planning than the low apprehensive writers. Moreover, the low apprehensive writers spent more time between sentences, on casting individual sentences, and on reviewing and correcting their texts at the post-writing stage than high apprehensive writers. Abdel Latif's (2009) study supports the results reported in the above early in-depth research. He explored the composing strategies used by demotivated and motivated writers (i.e., the writers with high apprehension and lower self-efficacy levels versus the ones with low apprehension and high self-efficacy levels, respectively). In this study, the demotivated writers had more linguistic composing problems than their motivated peers. Specifically, the demotivated writers rehearsed their texts more at the word level, used more word spelling strategies, retrieved ideas or linguistic structures by reading the last written part repeatedly, and made more deletion and intra-sentential text-changes. In addition, the demotivated writers spent less time composing their texts. But as mentioned above, this study indicates that writers' language ability mediates the relationship of their motivation with composing processes. In other words, the composing problems the demotivated writers had were mainly caused by their language ability deficiency.

Apart from the above writing process studies concerned with apprehension and self-efficacy, three other studies examined the composing processes used by writers with varied self-concept, achievement goals, and motivational regulation levels. He (2005) classified 38 Taiwanese EFL students into two groups ($n = 19$ each) based on their scores on a writing achievement goal scale: a) high-mastery-low-performance group (writers who had stronger mastery but weaker performance goals), and b) the low-mastery-high-performance group (writers who had weaker mastery but stronger performance goals). The think-aloud protocols generated by the students while performing an expository task revealed that the high-mastery-low-performance group used more monitoring/evaluating and revising strategies than the low-mastery-high-performance ones. This indicated that the former group tended to ensure the comprehensibility of the ideational and textual features of their writing more than the latter group.

On the other hand, Karlen and Compagnoni (2017) examined the relationship between learners' implicit theories of writing ability and their self-reported strategy use. They found that the students with malleable writing ability beliefs theory used more planning and monitoring strategies and better strategy awareness than their peers with a fixed theory of writing ability. Recently, Teng et al. (2020) also found that learners with high writing-proficiency levels reported using more mastery and performance self-talk, and demonstrated better maturity and flexibility in implementing some motivational regulation strategies than the ones with low writing-proficiency.

The results of the above-reviewed in-depth studies are consistent in emphasizing the differences in the composing processes of writers with different motivation levels. Specifically, these results indicate that compared to demotivated ones, motivated writers – i.e., those with lower apprehension and higher self-efficacy and self-concept beliefs, and mastery goals – spend more time composing, write more drafts, plan more ideas, review their produced texts, and revise them more frequently.

3.3.3.2 Writing product

Research findings indicate that writers' motivation variables are associated with some features in the texts they produce. The textual features examined in the previous related studies are: text quality, text linguistic complexity, and text length. It is unfortunate, however, that these studies were mainly related to writers' attitudinal and self-ability beliefs.

Previous studies indicate that some written text quality features are associated with writers' apprehension/attitude and self-ability beliefs. These studies are congruent in confirming the negative correlation between writers' apprehension and performance (e.g. Bennett & Rhodes, 1988; Erkan & Saban, 2011; Faigley, Daly, & Witte, 1981; Feng, 2001; Lee, 2005; Magno, 2008; Podsen, 1987; Thompson, 1986; Wu, 1992; Yarbrough, 1985). Contrarily, previous research consistently showed a positive correlation between writers' self-ability beliefs and the quality of their texts (e.g., Angelova, 1999; Limpo & Alves, 2017; Pajares et al., 2007a, 2007b; Sanders-Reio, 2010; Sasaki & Hirose, 1996).

Previous research findings also emphasize the strong relationship between writers' apprehension and the linguistic richness in their texts. For example, a negative correlation was found between writers' apprehension and the number of cohesive ties in their texts (Thompson, 1986). In Hadaway's (1987) study, the total number of t-units in written texts (which is used as a measure of writing syntactic complexity) correlated negatively with writers' apprehension levels. Likewise, Wu (1992) found a positive correlation between students' attitude to writing in Chinese and the number of t-units in their Chinese essays, and a negative correlation between their English writing apprehension and the number of t-units and average t-unit length in English essays. Recently, Rahimi and Zhang (2019) also found a negative relationship between writing apprehension and the mean length of t-units. Congruent research findings also confirm the higher correlations of apprehension with the linguistic aspects than with the ideational and organizational ones in writers' texts (Daud et al., 2005; Sanders-Reio, 2010; Sanders-Reio et al., 2014).

As for text length or quantity features, the few reported research findings are inconsistent with regard to their relationship with writing motivation. Some previous studies found that demotivated writers' texts are shorter (Yarbrough, 1985; Wu, 1992), and have a smaller number of sentences (Abdel Latif, 2008) than the texts written by motivated ones. In contrast, Hadaway (1987) did not find any significant correlations between L2 writers' apprehension levels and total number of words in their essays. Similarly, Abdel Latif (2008) found no significant correlation between writers' apprehension and their text quantity. In light of these inconsistent research findings, no clear conclusions can be drawn about the interaction between writers' apprehension and text quantity measures.

3.3.4 Previous writing learning experiences

Previous writing learning experiences represent another correlate of writers' motivation. Students can become motivated or demotivated to write as a result of their interpretation of the outcome of one's previous writing performance and the improvement made in it (i.e., writing mastery experience). Thus, the histories of success and failure in writing may cause differences in students' motivation. Past failure experiences could cause students to avoid writing situations in which the probability of future failure increases and to lose interest in learning to write. In contrast, past successful writing experiences could lead them to become more motivated and continuously try to find ways for improving their performance. In this case, the "Matthew effect" could occur (Merton, 1968). In other words, good writers get better and poor ones get poorer.

Like the case of the above reviewed correlates of writing motivation, previous research seems to have only investigated how writers' success and failure experiences influence their apprehension and self-efficacy beliefs. Some studies (Abdel Latif, 2015; Crumbo, 1999; Washholz & Etheridge, 1995; Wittman, 1991) showed that the history of students' poor writing performance predicts their apprehension. L2 students' writing success and failure histories can be also related to their L1 learning experiences. This conclusion is supported by the research findings indicating a positive relationship between L1 and L2 writing apprehension (e.g., Cheng, 2002; Fayer, 1986; Hadaway, 1987). On the other hand, few studies looked at the influence of previous writing experiences on students' self-efficacy. For example, Pajares et al. (2007b) found that writers' mastery experience is the most influential source of their self-efficacy.

3.3.5 The interaction among writing motivation constructs

Research indicates that writing motivation constructs potentially interact with each other, either positively or negatively. The research reported so far has addressed the relationship among some writing motivation constructs, whereas the correlations among other ones are yet to be examined. Below is a summary of the pertinent research findings.

The results of previous studies seem to be consistent with regard to the negative relationship between writers' apprehension and their self-ability beliefs (e.g., Abdel Latif, 2015; Blasco, 2016; Cheng, 2002; Crumbo, 1999; Erkan & Saban, 2011; Huerta et al., 2017; MacArthur, Philippakos, & Graham, 2016; Mitchell, Harrigan, & McMillan, 2017; Onwuegbuzie, 1999; Onwuegbuzie & Collins, 2001; Pajares et al., 2000, 2007a; Palmquist & Young, 1992; Rankin-Brown, 2006). These studies confirm that writers' apprehension correlates negatively with their self-ability beliefs (i.e., writing self-efficacy and self-concept). In other words, high apprehensive writers (i.e., the ones with negative attitudes towards writing) are likely to have low self-efficacy and self-concept levels, whereas low or non-apprehensive ones are expected to have higher self-efficacy and self-concept levels.

Research also implies that writers' self-efficacy is strongly associated with their writing self-concept beliefs (Pajares et al., 2007a, 2007b; Palmquist & Young, 1992). In Palmquist and Young's (1992) study, for example, writers' notion of writing giftedness and its learnability correlated positively with their confidence in completing certain writing tasks and demonstrating particular skills. Likewise, Pajares et al. (2007a, 2007b) found that writers' vicarious experience and social persuasions beliefs – two dimensions of their self-concept – predicted their product-based (i.e., writing convention) self-efficacy. On the other hand, Limpo and Alves' (2017) recent study showed that both students' writing self-efficacy and malleability beliefs are associated positively with the writing mastery goals they pursue. In fact, such relationship seems to be expected, given that both constructs (i.e., writing self-efficacy and malleability) are related to one's writing ability beliefs, i.e., they belong to the same type of writing motivational constructs. Additionally, the same relational pattern will likely apply to the other writing motivation constructs of the same type (see the conclusion section in chapter 1). For example, writers' attitude/apprehension perceptions are likely to be positively associated with their perceived value of writing (another attitudinal/dispositional construct). In other words, writers with a high apprehension/negative attitude level are expected to have a low perceived value of writing, and those with a low apprehension/positive attitude level will develop a high perceived value of writing.

Writers' achievement goals have also been found to interact with other motivational perceptions. For example, they seem to influence writing anxiety. Saghafi et al.'s (2017) study indicates that writers' anxiety is alleviated when they are extrinsically motivated, i.e., interested in achieving worldly goals such as immigrating to a foreign country. Meanwhile, Pajares et al. (2000) found a negative association between writers' performance avoidance goals and their apprehension. Similarly, the study conducted by Yilmaz Soylu et al. (2017) also showed that learners' positive attitude towards writing is related positively to their writing mastery goals and negatively to performance avoidance ones, but not related to their performance approach goals. They interpret these results as follows:

> (1) students with mastery goals may view the processes and products of writing itself as rewarding and thus enjoy engaging in writing activities; (2) students with performance avoidance goals are more likely to possess feelings of low competence and anticipate failure; and (3) students endorsing performance approach goals may view writing outcomes as more important than the writing process, that is, mainly as a means to an end and thus less relevant to affective experiences. (p. 8)

Previous research also indicates that writers' achievement goals are related in some way or another to their self-ability beliefs (i.e., self-efficacy and self-concept). Pajares et al. (2000), for example, found that writers' self-efficacy and self-concept beliefs related positively to their task mastery goals and negatively to the performance avoidance ones. In Yilmaz Soylu et al.'s (2017) study, writers' performance approach goals correlated positively with three dimensions of their self-efficacy (writing convention self-efficacy, ideation self-efficacy, and self-regulation self-efficacy). A negative correlation pattern was also found between the three self-efficacy types and writers' performance avoidance goals. Besides, writers' mastery goals had a strong positive relationship with self-efficacy for self-regulation, but not with self-efficacy for conventions or ideation. Relatively different results were revealed by Limpo and Alves' (2017) study, in which writers' mastery goals correlated positively with their skill malleability beliefs and self-efficacy for conventions, ideation, and self-regulation. Writers' performance approach goals correlated positively only with self-efficacy for ideation and self-regulation. As for writers' performance avoidance goals, they correlated negatively with writing skill malleability beliefs but not with any self-efficacy type. Limpo and Alves (2017) conclude that as compared to performance goals, writers' mastery goals have a more clear-cut relationship with their perceived ability beliefs. The two researchers interpreted this stronger relationship as follows:

> [M]astery goals contributed to students' confidence to carry out specific writing processes. It is likely that students more oriented towards mastery goals may actively strive to improve their competence, for example, by taking on challenges, working hard, and confronting deficiencies, which may give them a strong sense of efficacy to accomplish specific processes fundamental to successful writing. Specifically, the more students were oriented toward developing their writing ability, the higher their self-perceptions of ability to generate and organize ideas (ideation), translate them into text (conventions), and manage the numerous processes involved in writing (self-regulation). (p. 115)

The relatively different results revealed by Limpo and Alves' study about the interaction of performance goals with writers' self-efficacy could be attributed to the measure used in assessing the latter construct (i.e., the multidimensional self-efficacy scale developed by Bruning, Dempsey, Kauffman, McKim, & Zumbrunn, 2013). Perhaps due to the same cause, MacArthur et al. (2016) found no significant correlations between writers' self-efficacy and their performance or mastery goals. As for the varied interactions of writing goals with skill malleability, these have likely resulted from the fact that the latter construct is an under-represented form of writing self-concept.

A main issue about which there is no decisive research evidence yet is the mediating influence of writing motivation constructs. Referring to this mediating effect, Pajares et al. (2007a) state that the influence of both writing apprehension and the perceived value of writing on students' written texts was nullified when including writing self-efficacy in the statistical model used. The same effect is also noted in the earlier research reported by Pajares and his colleagues (Pajares et al., 1999; Pajares & Valiante, 1997, 1999). Contrarily to these results, Goodman and Cirka (2009) found that writing apprehension partially mediated the influence of self-efficacy on writing performance. Since a few studies have addressed such mediating influence issue, a clearer picture is yet to be drawn about which writing motivation constructs influence writers' performance more or less.

3.3.6 Behaviorual correlates of writing motivation

Apart from the above highlighted performance and belief correlates, research also indicates that writing motivation is associated with some behaviours, which represent the learning habits demonstrated by motivated and demotivated students. The main writing learning behaviours reported by previous studies include: the nature of the writing courses attended, writing procrastination and the regularity of performing writing task, extracurricular activities, and writing learning style. As will be noted in the following paragraphs, the research probing these issues was limited to writing apprehension, anxiety, self-efficacy, and goals.

The studies on whether writers' motivation is associated or not with the type of writing courses attended have been only concerned with apprehension. Previous studies seem to be consistent in indicating that as compared to their low or non-apprehensive peers, high apprehensive students choose majors perceived to be low in requirements for writing and are less interested in taking advanced writing courses (Daly & Shamo, 1978; Faris et al., 1999; Gungle & Taylor, 1989; Masny & Foxall, 1992; Mausehund, 1993; Riffe & Stacks, 1992; Simons et al., 1995; Todd, 2003). The only exception is Lew's (2001) study which showed that high apprehensive L2 students did not avoid advanced writing classes.

On the other hand, some studies suggest that learners' motivation is associated with the frequency of performing writing tasks and their task performance procrastination. Podsen (1987) found a significant inverse relationship between writing apprehension and the number of writing tasks performed. Meanwhile, some studies revealed that apprehensive and demotivated writers tended to procrastinate performing writing tasks (Fritzsche, Young, & Hickson, 2003; Onwuegbuzie & Collins, 2001). With regard to writing goals, Troia, Harbaugh, Shankland, Wolbers, and Lawrence (2013) found that the learners writing more often for different purposes had higher motivational beliefs and more performance approach goals, whereas the learners reporting writing less often had more task avoidance goals. Writing mastery goal orientation, on the other hand, had no association with the frequency of writing activities.

Previous studies also revealed that demotivated writers put in less extracurricular effort, i.e., reading of their own volition, to improve their writing and language skills, do not perform free writing tasks on their own, and resist new ideas and experiences for facilitating writing (Lee, 2005; Lee & Krashen, 1997; Walsh, 1989). This suggests that free, voluntary reading and writing activities are negatively related to writing apprehension. In Martinez et al.'s (2011) study, the students with higher writing self-efficacy levels also reported their interest in leisure writing activities. Research also showed that writing motivation is associated with feedback seeking orientation and handling (Waller & Papi, 2017). In another study conducted by Tsao, Tseng, and Wang (2017), the learners with intrinsic writing motivation (i.e., writing mastery goals) showed interest in receiving written corrective feedback and handling it.

Finally, Onwuegbuzie's (1998) study revealed important information about the learning style of demotivated writers. In this study, graduate students with high writing apprehension levels reported their preference to learn writing in structured, group, and authority-oriented environments. This clearly indicates that they are unlikely to have an autonomous learning style.

3.4 Learning and instructional practices as sources of writing motivation

Learning and instructional practices also play an essential role in motivating or demotivating students to write. Much language and writing learning motivation research has addressed this role. It is worth noting that the larger portion of the demotivating factors listed in the language learning motivation literature is related to instructional practices rather than learning ones. For example, Gorham and Christophel (1992) provided a list of the demotivating factors mentioned by the student participants in their study. Of the first five categories mentioned by the students, four are associated with instructional practices only; these are: students' dissatisfaction with teachers' evaluation and assignments, boring and unorganized teaching, malorganized learning materials, and teachers' unfavourable characteristics. Similarly, out of the eight main language learning demotivating factors, Dörnyei (1998) identified the following four ones related to instruction and schooling: teacher's personality, commitment, competence, and instructional method, inadequate school facilities (e.g., large class size), compulsory nature of language learning, and course books or language learning materials. These factors are also emphasized in Oxford's (1998) work, which focused on analyzing the content of the essays written by US high school and university students about their demotivating learning experiences. The more dominant factors mentioned in the students' essays include: improper teacher-student relationship, teacher's inappropriate delivery of the course and its learning materials, teaching-learning style conflict, and the unfavourable characteristics of the classroom activities. In some L2 learning contexts, teaching- and teacher-related factors could play a more influential role. For example, based on their review of a number of studies addressing demotivation to learn English in the Japanese context, Sakai and Kikuchi (2009) identified six common demotivating factors, four of which are related to the teacher and teaching only. These are: teacher attitude, competence, personality and instructional style, characteristics of classroom instruction (e.g., course monotonous activities and pace), class environment, and unsuitable or uninteresting materials.

With regard to the learning and teaching variables influencing writers' motivation, literature indicates that five main factors can cause students to become demotivated or motivated to write. Collectively, these factors are: the medium of writing, the assigned writing topics, the nature of writing instruction and learning materials, teacher feedback, and peer feedback. In the following subsections, these five sources are discussed.

3.4.1 Medium of writing: Typing versus handwriting tools

Nowadays, student writers have access to an increasing number of the technological tools and applications available for text composing along with the traditional handwriting tools (i.e., paper-and-pen/pencil). Definitely, these different typing and handwriting tools have varied motivational impacts on students. There have been historical stags for viewing the relationship between the writing medium and motivation. Before the 1980s, such relationship was neglected simply because people during this era used to perform writing tasks in the handwritten form. A new stage occurred in the 1980s and the 1990s when people began to increasingly depend on Word processors. During this stage, techno-literacy played an important role in shaping learners' computer-based writing motivation. Not all people worldwide during that time were techno-literate; therefore we can say that techno-literate learners' attitudes towards computer-based writing were positive, whereas techno-illiterate ones had negative attitudes towards it. Perhaps due to these techno-literacy-related differences, writing motivation constructs were addressed very peripherally in the computer-based writing studies reported during the 1980s and the 1990s. For example, the main focus in the computer-based writing studies included in the two reviews reported by Cochran-Smith (1991) and Goldberg, Russell, and Cook (2003) was on learners' writing quality and quantity and keyboarding skills. Likewise, some early studies (Hert, 1988; Johnson, 1987; Phinney, 1991; Sullivan & Pratt, 1996; Zuercher, 1986) found no significant effects for Word processers on reducing writers' apprehension. In her seminal review on using Word processing studies in language classrooms, Cochran-Smith (1991) interpreted the relationship between students' attitudes and computer-based writing as follows:

> In informal interviews as well as written surveys, student writers and/or their teachers at elementary through college levels report they like using word processing and have generally positive attitudes towards writing with word processing...Probably the most salient explanation of positive attitudes toward word processing is the most obvious one: It is less physically demanding of writers, and it takes the recopying/retyping penalty out of the production of the final drafts and the cutting-and-pasting penalty out of revision and refinement of texts. Teachers and researchers also speculate that students like word processing because they feel powerful when they control the technology, are less intimated as writers

because a machine rather than a person is the first audience for their efforts, and are impressed by the professional looking results of their products...The most important reason to consider student attitudes toward writing with word processing is its potentially powerful mediating effect on allocation of time spent on writing, willingness to revise and edit, and the quantity of texts produced. (pp. 143–144)

As indicated in Cochran-Smith's explanation, the ability to use Word processors at that time was viewed as conditional to learners' positive attitudes towards computer-based writing.

The last two decades saw a radical change in viewing the relationship between writing motivation and the use of technological tools and applications. With the increasingly widespread use of the Internet, the technological revolution and the occurrence of mobile-assisted-language-learning (MALL) devices (laptops, tablet computers, and smart mobile phones), technology has become part and parcel of everyday writing practices. Therefore, instead of comparing learners' writing performance and motivation on paper-and-pen/pencil tasks versus computer-based ones (i.e., the tasks performed through Word processors), we now talk about the influence of using different technological tools and applications on writing performance and motivation. In other words, writing research examining the writing medium-related motivational impact is only concerned now with the technological tools with different design, typing, and information access facilities. Since students attending a particular educational stage are now supposed to have familiarity with certain technological devices and applications, the issue of techno-literacy-related differences seems to be no longer tackled in the current writing motivation research.

As a result of the influence of the technological and communication revolution on everyday writing practices, motivation has gained more ground in the studies dealing with technology-mediated writing. For example, the studies reported in the last decade indicate that children become more motivated when they compose their texts using touchscreen tablets (e.g., Bigelow, 2013; Dunn & Sweeney, 2018). Technology has also contributed to the increasing use of particular types of motivating writing tasks such as collaborative digital story creation (Bratitsis, Kotopoulos, & Mandila, 2012) and multimodal composing activities involving learners in not only using words to communicate their thoughts, but also in integrating other visual elements such as photographs, drawings, and videos to enrich their texts (e.g., Jiang & Luk, 2016; McVee & Miller, 2012; Yuan, 2015). For a review of more technological tools and applications recently integrated into writing learning, see Kucirkova, Rowe, Oliver, and Piestrzynski (2019).

To conclude, technology is continuously bringing us novel tools and applications with potentially varied effects on learners' writing motivation, especially young generations. Meanwhile, we may also expect that there are some people or older students whose text-composing habits are incompatible with the use of these novel tools; they resist them and feel more motivated to use the writing media they have been familiar with. Thus, people's use of a particular writing medium is associated with some emotional attitude and feelings, and will in turn influence their text composing processes and outcomes.

3.4.2 Assigned writing topics

The topics students are asked to write about represent another potential source of their writing motivation. Students will be motivated to write about a topic they like and are familiar with. Meanwhile, if they are to write about a topic they are unfamiliar with or uninterested in, this can cause them to be demotivated. As Behizadeh and Engelhard (2014) point out:

> [S]tructured choice of a valued topic means that students want to be able to choose a topic that connects to them and allows them to express their feelings and thoughts, although they may need help making a meaningful choice.... For writing to be authentic, students need to write about a topic they value. Students' valued topics were personal interests, people they love, role models they admire, and community and global issues. (pp. 31–32)

Previous studies emphasize the importance of writing topics in motivating students (e.g., Daly, 1979; Atay & Kurt, 2006). This motivating impact can be seen, for instance, in the increasing quantity of the texts students produce (Hidi & McLaren, 1990, 1991). The results of some studies also indicate the importance of topic attractiveness as the main motivational source of writing (e.g., Albin, Benton, & Khramtsova, 1996; Benton, Corkill, Sharp, Downey, & Khramtsova, 1995; Boscolo, Del Favero, & Borghetto, 2007). Given these results, writing teachers need to carefully consider the topics assigned to their students, due to their important motivating effect.

3.4.3 Teaching methods and learning materials

Writing instruction is also another source of learners' writing motivation/demotivation. As indicated above, research implies the essential role of teaching methods and learning materials in L2 learning motivation (e.g., Dörnyei, 1998; Gorham & Christophel, 1992; Sakai & Kikuchi, 2009). With regard to writing motivation, there is a paucity of the studies dealing with the motivating impact of writing teaching methods and learning materials on students' affect.

The few relevant studies available collected peripheral data about the motivating influence of teaching methods and learning materials. These studies revealed that students' writing demotivation can be developed as a result of inappropriate instruction practices (Atay & Kurt, 2006; Hadaway,

1987) or the lack of interesting teaching materials (Lo & Hyland, 2007). In Abdel Latif's (2015) study, the students were found demotivated due to their teachers' focus on teaching them writing theoretically rather than practically; i.e., the teachers' negligence of process writing instruction. Tsao, Tseng, and Wang (2017) also refer to the role of high-pressure and test-driven writing instruction environments in causing students' anxiety and demotivating them to seek feedback from their teachers. In contrast, Saghafi et al. (2017) found that the teacher's style and supportive interactions helped learners in alleviating their writing anxiety. In light of these research findings, it is assumed that the nature of writing instructional practices and learning materials can influence students' writing motivation either positively or negatively.

3.4.4 Teacher feedback

Much published research shows the very influential role of teacher feedback in shaping learners' writing motivation. Research indicates that overuse of teacher written corrective feedback and criticism can particularly result in writing demotivation (Hyland & Hyland, 2001; Lee, 2019; Lee et al., 2018; Mahfoodh, 2017; Truscott, 1996; Wiltse, 2002). In some cases, overuse of praise can also give learners the impression that there is no further need to improve their writing and thus it has its demotivating effect (Lipnevich & Smith, 2009). Not only could writing demotivation be caused by the large amounts of praise, criticism, and the overuse of error correction in teacher feedback, but it may also result from the lack of adequate feedback (Abdel Latif, 2015).

In their large-scale study, Yu, Jiang, and Zhou (2020) investigated how 1190 students from 35 Chinese universities rate the influence of five feedback types on their writing motivation. The five feedback types they included in their 23-item scale are: scoring or evaluative feedback (i.e., rating written texts according to various descriptors); process-oriented feedback given on the content of text drafts; expressive feedback encompassing praise, criticisms, and suggestions; peer and self-feedback (i.e., students' critical evaluation of their own texts); and written corrective feedback. The participant students' responses indicate that writing motivation and engagement are discouraged by both process-oriented feedback and written corrective feedback, but fostered by scoring, peer and self-feedback, and expressive feedback. Yu and his colleagues conclude that:

> L2 writing teachers…should realize that although all the types of feedback strategies may lead to student text revisions and enhance text quality, some feedback strategies can be motivating whereas others may demotivate student writers. For instance, while WCF [i.e., written corrective feedback] can trigger maladaptive motivation and engagement, other forms of feedback (e.g., peer and self-feedback, expressive

feedback) can be integrated in practice to reduce the maladaptive motivation and engagement of WCF. Students' motivation and engagement should be monitored closely and dynamically so that the use of WCF can be reduced to moderate its negative impact if extremely low levels of motivation and engagement are observed. Thus, it is important for L2 writing teachers to learn how to use feedback to enhance student writing motivation and engagement and to avoid the demotivating effects of some feedback strategies. Moreover, to enhance student writing motivation and engagement, L2 writing teachers may also consider adopting criteria-based scoring feedback instead of only giving holistic scores. They can also make use of expressive feedback to provide support and scaffolding, and engage students. (p. 12)

It is noteworthy that some instructional research findings do not concur with the results revealed by Yu et al.'s (2019) study (see subsection 4.4 in the next chapter).

Research also indicates that students' responsiveness to teacher feedback and handling it depend on some factors. For example, students' motivation to revise their texts in response to teacher feedback could be influenced by the type of the written corrective feedback given. Specifically, these types are: a) direct error correction, where errors are corrected by the teacher and the student is to transcribe the corrections in the text; and b) indirect error correction, which is a guided problem-solving activity in which the teacher highlights errors and the student is to correct them (Ferris, 2002). Some studies suggest that indirect error correction may be more effective than direct error correction (Ferris, 1995; Ferris & Hedgcock, 1998; Lalande, 1982) which may result in appropriating student texts (Ferris, 2002), and causing negative attitudes towards writing (Semke, 1984). Meanwhile, Ferris (2002) views that direct error correction can be more effective when responding to low proficient students. According to Hendrickson (1980), low self-confident student writers need more supportive error correction than their high self-confident peers, and this can be achieved through focusing on the salient errors and tolerating less important ones.

The timing of feedback provision could also influence students' motivation to handle the teacher's comments. While L2 students in Yu et al.'s (2019) above-mentioned study reported that the process-oriented feedback given on text drafts is discouraging their motivation, some early studies suggest that responding to drafts is more effective than responding to the final product (Hillocks, 1982; Leki, 1990, 1991; Zamel, 1985). On the other hand, some studies indicate the need for considering error selectivity when providing feedback on students' writing (e.g., Cardelle & Corno, 1981; Ferris, 2002). This selective approach to feedback and error correction provision should also interact with students' writing needs and language proficiency (Dheram, 1995; Hendrickson, 1980; Lee, 1997). Besides, some researchers (e.g., Dheram, 1995; Krest, 1988; Straub & Lunsford, 1995) suggest that writing teachers should focus on content and organization when responding to early drafts and on surface aspects when responding to later drafts; this combined pattern of content and form seems to be better than the content pattern or the form one only (Ashwell, 2000).

As has been noted above, feedback provision on students' writing is a complicated process, particularly in L2 writing settings. It has also to interact with students' characteristics, including their responsiveness, writing and language development, age, and perhaps gender and cultural background. Overall, the studies reviewed in this subsection imply that the overuse of criticism and error correction – and praise in many cases – is very likely to cause students' writing demotivation. Other issues associated with the motivational influence of teacher feedback seem to differ relatively from one educational setting to another. That is why teachers need to consider students' characteristics and responsiveness in the feedback provision process. Further issues related to the influence of teacher feedback on students' writing motivation are discussed in the next two chapters.

3.4.5 Peer feedback

Peer feedback activities represent another instructional source that could shape learners' writing motivation. In some classroom activities, writing demotivation may occur as a result of peers' over-criticism and negative attitude. Abdel Latif (2015) found that L2 students avoid showing their essays to peers due to their fear of criticism. Peer feedback activities in writing classes can cause motivation problems due to students' individual differences and varied writing attitudes. Some studies indicate that students' attitudes to and handling of the feedback given by peers depend on their perceived usefulness of peers' comments (see for example, Wang, 2014; Yu, 2020; Yu & Hu, 2017).

Other studies imply that students' cultural background could negatively influence and create barriers to interactions in peer feedback activities (e.g., Hu & Lam, 2010; Lee, 2017; Yu & Lee, 2016; Yu, Lee, & Mak, 2016). Thus, motivational problems can potentially occur in the peer feedback activities organized in the writing classes which include students with multicultural backgrounds. To avoid the potential demotivating influence of the above-mentioned obstacles, there is a need for organizing peer feedback activities in the optimal way. Obviously, lack of orchestrating these factors can cause detrimental effects such as increasing students' negative attitudes towards participating in peer assessment activities and having anxious feelings while taking part in them.

3.5 Characteristics of demotivated and motivated writers

In light of the above review of the correlates and sources of writing motivation, it is possible now to build initial profiles of demotivated and motivated writers. The consistent research findings highlighted above indicate that both types of writers have specific affective, behavioural, and performance characteristics.

Demotivated writers normally suffer from some language and writing ability deficiencies, and they are likely to have previous unsuccessful writing learning and performance experiences. Due to this, they are expected to develop some low writing self-ability beliefs and negative dispositional perceptions about writing. This could lead them, for instance, to have negative attitudes towards writing, i.e., they will apprehend the situations in which they may write or in which their written texts may be discussed. They may also try to avoid taking optional writing courses; in other words, they will only attend compulsory writing courses. Thus, demotivated writers generally do not like taking writing courses unless it is necessary and are likely to select the majors or attend educational programmes not requiring much writing. In general, they do not have writing mastery goals. They are usually uninterested in developing their writing competence; that is why they do not usually do extracurricular activities to improve their writing performance. Meanwhile, they do not normally seek feedback on their writing from the teacher or peers. Besides, they procrastinate performing writing tasks.

When performing composition tasks, demotivated writers are expected to demonstrate some certain composing behaviours. They normally have anxious feelings and habits while composing. These anxious feelings may increase in some classroom writing situations they do not like. They do not motivate themselves while composing the text either. Demotivated writers do not generally spend much time composing their texts. They do not attend much to planning their texts or revising them. Overall, their composing processes are characterized by superficiality. Due to their limited language abilities, they are likely to encounter many linguistic difficulties while composing their texts. At the product level, demotivated writers are likely to produce low-quality texts whose word count may be below the expected range.

As for motivated writers, they do not normally suffer from language or writing ability deficiencies at the target developmental language level, and they are likely to have previous successful writing learning history and experienced satisfactory progress in their writing performance. Their satisfactory writing learning and performance experiences have helped them to develop positive writing self-ability beliefs and not to apprehend writing or writing testing situations, i.e., they have positive attitudes towards writing. Due to this positive disposition, motivated writers are expected to have a high perceived value of writing and writing mastery goals. This could lead them, in turn, to be interested in attending optional writing courses or select the majors or attend educational programmes requiring much writing. In their attempts to improve writing performance, motivated writers will be also interested in seeking feedback on their writing from the teacher or/ and perhaps from peers with better writing experiences. Besides, they are unlikely to have symptoms of writing procrastination.

While writing their texts, motivated writers are expected to have no text composing dysfluency symptoms. Since they have adequate linguistic resources in their long-term memory, they will be able to solve the language problems encountered while composing the text. This will not make them preoccupied with linguistic retrieving and planning in most of the writing task time; thus, they will allocate balanced efforts to their composing process components, including planning ideas and text, monitoring text production, retrieving, reviewing, and revising. Therefore, motivated writers spend adequate time composing their texts and do not show anxious feelings or anxiety symptoms while performing the target task. Additionally, they will likely use motivational self-talk strategies to encourage themselves to complete the writing task successfully. Due to these fluent, non-anxious, and motivational writing processes and the adequate time and efforts allocated to text composing components, motivated writers will be able to produce texts meeting the expected quality and quantity criteria.

The above initial profiles of demotivated and motivated writers are yet to be completed. They can be expanded in future literature depending on the results of relevant studies and the accumulated research evidence.

3.6 Conclusion

In the above sections, the variables potentially influencing writing motivation have been reviewed. As indicated, the relationship of writers' gender and age with their motivation is still unclear. Findings, however, seem to indicate that females may be more motivated to write than males and that at some educational level, age-related differences in writing motivation may disappear. Though research generally implies that learners' socio-cultural background shapes their writing motivation in a particular direction, no conclusive findings have been reported yet about the relative influence of the different cultures and social backgrounds on writing motivation. Thus, the interaction of writers' motivation with their gender, age, and socio-cultural background remains to be explicated in future research.

The research findings reported so far show a clearer picture about the relationship of writers' motivation with their language and writing performance than with their beliefs. As noted above, research is almost consistent in confirming the direction of the relationship of some writing motivation constructs (e.g., writing apprehension and self-efficacy) with language ability and writing performance variables. As for the relationship between writers' motivation and their language and writing beliefs, the consistency of research findings varies one from variable to another. That is why we need future research covering all writing motivation constructs. Though the direction of the relationship between student writers' motivation and their learning habits and behaviours is relatively clear, stronger research evidence is yet to be provided.

Regarding the learning and instructional practices research, findings vary from one issue to another. Research findings show clear directions about how teacher feedback could motivate or demotivate student writers. Many of the teacher feedback research findings reviewed above are also confirmed by the instructional research highlighted in the next chapter. Findings also indicate the complexity of interactions in peer assessment activities. With regard to research on the other three learning and instructional issues (i.e., medium of writing, assigned writing topics, and teaching methods and learning materials), it generally implies their influential role in motivating students, but we still lack specific details about their interactional patterns with writing motivation constructs. The main cause of the lack of these specific details is the paucity of research dealing with these issues. Addressing all these voids in future research will help us develop clearer and more complete profiles of the characteristics of demotivated and motivated writers.

References

Abdel Latif, M. M. M. (2008). The relationship of linguistic knowledge, affective traits and writing quality with EFL writers' text length aspects. *Essex Graduate Student Papers in Language & Linguistics, 10*, 101–121.

Abdel Latif, M. M. M. (2009). *Egyptian EFL student teachers' writing processes and products: the role of linguistic knowledge and writing affect*. PhD thesis, University of Essex, UK.

Abdel Latif, M. M. M. (2015). Sources of L2 writing apprehension: A study of Egyptian university students. *Journal of Research in Reading, 38*(2), 194–212. doi: 10.1111/j.1467-9817.2012.01549.x

Abu Shawish, J., & Atea, M. (2010). *An Investigation of Palestinian EFL majors' writing apprehension: Causes and remedies*. Paper presented at the First National Conference on 'Improving TEFL Methods & Practices at Palestinian Universities', Al-Quds Open University, Palestine.

Albin, M. L., Benton, S. L., & Khramtsova, I. (1996). Individual differences in interest and narrative writing. *Contemporary Educational Psychology, 21*, 305–324. doi: 10.1006/ceps.1996.0024

Albrechtsen, D., Haastrup, K., & Henriksen, B. (2008). *Vocabulary and writing in a first and second language: Processes and development*. New York: Palgrave Macmillan.

Amirian, S. M. R., & Komesh, N. (2018). A study on the relationship between EFL learners' nationality and language learning motivation. *International Journal of Applied Linguistics & English Literature, 7*(2), 26–32. doi: 10.7575/aiac.ijalel.v.7n.2p.26

Andrade, H., Wang, X., Du, Y., & Akawi, R. (2009). Rubric-referenced self-assessment and self-efficacy for writing. *The Journal of Educational Research, 102*(4), 287–302. doi: 10.3200/JOER.102.4.287-302

Angelova, M. (1999). *An exploratory study of factors affecting the process and product of writing in English as a foreign language*. PhD thesis, State University of New York at Buffalo, USA.

Ashwell, T. (2000). Patterns of teacher response to student writing in a multiple-draft composition classroom: Is content feedback followed by form feedback the best method? *Journal of Second Language Writing, 9*, 22–58. doi: 10.1016/S1060-3743(00)00027-8

Atay, D., & Kurt, G. (2006). Prospective teachers and L2 writing anxiety. *Asian EFL Journal*, *8*(4), 100–118.

Baba, K. (2009). Aspects of lexical proficiency in writing summaries in a foreign language. *Journal of Second Language Writing*, *18*, 191–208. doi:10.1016/j.jslw.2009.05.003

Bannister, L. A. (1982). *Writing apprehension and anti-writing: A naturalistic study of composing strategies used by college freshmen*. University of Southern California, USA.

Behizadeh, N., & Engelhard, G., Jr. (2014). Development and validation of a scale to measure perceived authenticity in writing. *Assessing Writing*, *21*, 18–36. doi: 10.1016/j.asw.2014.02.001

Bennett, K., & Rhodes, S. (1988). Writing apprehension and writing intensity in business and industry. *Journal of Business Communication*, *25*(1), 25–39. doi: 10.1177/002194368802500102

Benton, S. L., Corkill, A. J., Sharp, J. M., Downey, R. G., & Khramtsova, I. (1995). Knowledge, interest, and narrative writing. *Journal of Educational Psychology*, *87*(1), 66–79. doi: 10.1037/0022-0663.87.1.66

Bigelow, E. C. (2013). *Iwrite: digital message making practices of young children*. Doctoral Thesis, Vanderbilt University, USA.

Blasco, J. (2016). The relationship between writing anxiety, writing self-efficacy, and Spanish EFL students' use of metacognitive writing strategies: A case study. *Journal of English Studies*, *14*, 7–45. doi: 10.18172/jes.3069

Bloom, L. (1985). Anxious writers in context: Graduate school and beyond. In M. Ross (Ed.), *When a writer can't write*, (pp. 119–133). New York, NY: Guilford Press.

Boscolo, P., Del Favero, L., & Borghetto, M. (2007). Writing on an interesting topic: Does writing foster interest? In S. Hidi, & P. Boscolo (Eds.), *Motivation and writing: Research and school practice*, (pp. 73–92). Dordrecht, The Netherlands: Kluwer.

Bratitsis, T., Kotopoulos, T., & Mandila, K. (2012). Kindergarten children's motivation and collaboration being triggered via computers while creating digital stories: A case study. *International Journal of Knowledge and Learning*, *8*(3–4), 239–258. doi: 10.1504/IJKL.2012.051677

Bruning, R., Dempsey, M., Kauffman, D., McKim, C., & Zumbrunn, S. (2013). Examining dimensions of self-efficacy for writing. *Journal of Educational Psychology*, *105*(1), 25–38. doi: 10.1037/a0029692

Butler, D. A. (1980). *A descriptive analysis of the relationships between writing apprehension and the composing processes of selected secondary students*. PhD thesis, University of Virginia, USA.

Cardelle, M., & Corno, L. (1981). Effects on second language learning of variations in written feedback on homework assignments. *TESOL Quarterly*, *15*, 251–261. doi: 10.2307/3586751

Chavez, M. (2014). Variable beliefs about the need for accuracy in the oral production of German: An exploratory study. *International Journal of Applied Linguistics*, *24*(1), 97–127. doi: 10.1111/ijal.12029

Cheng, Y. S. (2002). Factors associated with foreign language writing anxiety. *Foreign Language Annals*, *35*, 647–656. doi: 10.1111/j.1944-9720.2002.tb01903.x

Cheng, Y. S., Horwitz, E. K., & Schallert, D. (1999). Language anxiety: Differentiating writing and speaking components. *Language Learning*, *49*(3), 417–446. doi: 10.1111/0023-8333.00095

Cochran-Smith, M. (1991). Word processing and writing in elementary classrooms: A critical review of related literature. *Review of Educational Research*, *61*(1), 107–155. doi: 10.2307/1170669

Coleman, J., Galaczi, Á., & Astruc, L. (2007). Motivation of UK school pupils towards foreign languages: A large-scale survey at key stage 3. *Language Learning Journal*, *35*(2), 245–281. doi: 10.1080/09571730701599252

Concepcion, B. E. (1992). *The Effects of grammar knowledge on the writing skills of business English students in Puerto Rico*. PhD thesis, New York University, USA.

Crumbo, G. B. (1999). *Writing apprehension and the effects of "I think I can, I think I can"*. PhD thesis, Spalding University, USA.

Daly, J. A. (1979). Writing apprehension in the classroom: Teacher role expectancies of the apprehensive writer. *Research in the Teaching of English*, *13*, 37–44.

Daly, J., & Miller, M. D. (1975). The empirical development of an instrument to measure writing apprehension. *Research in the Teaching of English*, *9*(3), 242–249.

Daly, J. A., & Shamo, W. G. (1978). Academic decisions as a function of writing apprehension. *Research in the Teaching of English*, *12*, 119–126.

Daud, N. S. M., Daud, N. M., & Abu Kassim, N. L. (2005). Second language writing anxiety: Cause or effect. *Malaysian Journal of ELT Research (MELTA)*, *1*(1), 1–19.

Dheram, P. (1995). Feedback as a two-bullock cart: A case study of teaching writing. *ELT Journal*, *79*, 100–108. doi: 10.1093/elt/49.2.160

Dörnyei, Z. (March, 1998). Demotivation in foreign language learning. *Paper presented at the TESOL '98 Congress*, Seattle, WA.

Dörnyei, Z., Csizér, K., & Németh, N. (2006). *Motivation, language attitudes and globalisation: A Hungarian perspective*. Clevedon: Multilingual Matters.

Dörnyei, Z., & Ushioda, E. (2011). *Teaching and researching motivation*. Edinburgh: Pearson Education Limited.

Dunn, J., & Sweeney, T. (2018). Writing and iPads in the early years: Perspectives from within the classroom. *British Journal of Educational Technology*, *49*, 859–869. doi 10.1111/bjet.12621

Elias, R. Z. (1999). An examination of nontraditional accounting students' communication apprehension and ambiguity tolerance. *Journal of Education for Business*, *75*(1), 38–41. doi: 10.1080/08832329909598988

Erkan, D. Y., & Saban, A. I. (2011). Writing performance relative to writing apprehension, self-efficacy in writing, and attitudes towards writing: A correlational study in the Turkish tertiary-level EFL context. *Asian EFL Journal*, *13*(1), 164–192.

Fagan, W. T., & Hayden, M. (1988). Writing processes in French and English of fifth grade French immersion students. *The Canadian Modern Language Review*, *44*(4), 653–70. doi: 10.3138/cmlr.44.4.653

Faigley, L., Daly, J., & Witte, S. (1981). The role of writing apprehension in writing performance and competence. *Journal of Educational Research*, *75*, 16–21. doi: 10.1080/00220671.1981.10885348

Faris, K., Golen, S., & Lynch, D. (1999). Writing apprehension in beginning accounting majors. *Business Communication Quarterly*, *62*(2), 9–22. doi: 10.1177/108056999906200203

Fayer, J. M. (1986). *Writing apprehension among Puerto Rican university students*. ERIC Document, ED 280283.

Feng, H. (2001). *Writing an academic paper in English: An exploratory study of six Taiwanese graduate students*. PhD thesis, Teachers College, Columbia University, USA.

Ferris, R. D. (1995). Student reactions to teacher response in multi-draft composition. *TESOL Quarterly, 29*, 33–53. doi: 10.2307/3587804

Ferris, R. D. (2002). *Treatment of error in second language writing*. Ann Arbor: University of Michigan Press.

Ferris, R. D., & Hedgcock, J. S. (1998). *Teaching ESL composition: Purpose, process, and practice*. Mahwah: Lawrence Erlbaum.

Fritzsche, B. A., Young, B. R., & Hickson, K. C. (2003). Individual differences in academic procrastination tendency and writing success. *Personality and Individual Differences, 35*, 1549–1557. doi: 10.1016/S0191-8869(02)00369-0

Ghenghesh, P. (2010). The motivation of L2 learners: Does it decrease with age? *English Language Teaching, 3*(1), 128–141. doi: 10.5539/elt.v3n1p128

Goldberg, A., Russell, M., & Cook, A. (2003). The effect of computers on student writing: A metaanalysis of studies from 1992 to 2002. *Journal of Technology, Learning, and Assessment, 2*(1).

Goodman, S. B., & Cirka, C. C. (2009). Efficacy and anxiety: An examination of writing attitudes in a first-year seminar. *Journal on Excellence in College Teaching, 20*, 5–28.

Gorham, J., & Christophel, D. M. (1992). Students' perceptions of teacher behaviors as motivating and demotivating factors in college classes. *Communication Quarterly, 40*, 239–252. doi: 10.1080/01463379209369839

Graham, S., & Hudley, C. (2007). Race and ethnicity in the study of motivation and competence. In Elliot, A. J., & Dweck, C. S. (Eds.), *Handbook of competence and motivation*, (pp. 392–413). New York: Guilford Press.

Gungle, B. W., & Taylor, V. (1989). Writing apprehension and second language writers. In D. M. Johnson, & D. H. Roen (Eds.), *Richness in writing: Empowering ESL students*, (pp. 235–248). New York: Longman, Inc.

Hadaway, N. L. (1987). *Writing apprehension among second language learners*. PhD thesis, Texas A & M University, USA.

Hayes, C. G. (1981). *Exploring apprehension: Composing processes of apprehensive and non-apprehensive intermediate freshman writers*. ERIC Document, ED210678.

He, T. (2005). Effects of mastery and performance goals on the composition strategy use of adult EFL writers. *The Canadian Modern Language Review, 61*(3), 407–431. doi: 10.1353/cml.2005.0017

Hendrickson, J. M. (1980). The treatment of error in written work. *Modern Language Journal, 64*, 210–221. doi: 10.1111/j.1540-4781.1980.tb05188.x

Henry, A. (2009). Gender differences in compulsory school pupils' L2 self-concepts: A longitudinal study. *System, 37*(2), 177–193. doi: 10.1016/j.system.2008.11.003

Hert, R. S. (1988). *A study of one computer-driven text analysis package for collegiate student writers*. PhD thesis, University of North Texas, USA.

Hertz-Lazarowitz, R., & Bar-Natan, I. (2002). Writing development of Arab and Jewish students using cooperative learning (CL) and computer-mediated communication (CMC). *Computers & Education, 39*, 19–36. doi: 10.1016/S0360-1315(02)00019-2

Hidi, S., Berndorff, D., & Ainley, M. (2002). Children's argument writing, interest, and self-efficacy: An intervention study. *Learning and Instruction, 12*, 429–446. doi: 10.1016/S0959-4752(01)00009-3

Hidi, S., & McLaren, J. (1990). The effect of topic and theme interestingness on the production of school expositions. In: H. Mandl, E. De Corte, N. Bennett, & H. Freidrich (Eds.), *Learning and instruction: European research in an international context*, (Vol. 2.2, pp. 295–308). Oxford: Pergamon Press.

Hidi, S., & McLaren, J. (1991). Motivational factors and writing: The role of topic interestingness. *European Journal of Psychology of Education*, *6*, 187–197. doi: 10.1007/BF03191937

Hillocks, F., Jr. (1982). The interaction of instruction, teacher comment and revision in teaching the composition process. *Research in the Teaching of English*, *16*, 261–278.

Hirose, K., & Sasaki, M. (1994). Explanatory variables for Japanese students' expository writing in English: An exploratory study. *Journal of Second Language Writing*, *3*(3), 203–229. doi: 10.1016/1060-3743(94)90017-5

Hong, Y. Y. (2001). Chinese students' and teachers' inferences of effort and ability. In Salili, F., Chiu, C-Y., & Hong, Y-Y. (Eds.), *Student motivation: The culture and context of learning*, (pp.105–20). New York: Kluwer Academic/Plenum Publishers.

Hu, G., & Lam, S. T. E. (2010). Issues of cultural appropriateness and pedagogical efficacy: Exploring peer review in a second language writing class. *Instructional Science*, *38*(4), 371–394. doi: 10.1007/s11251-008-9086-1

Huerta, M., Goodson, P., Beigi, M., & Chlup, D. (2017). Graduate students as academic writers: Writing anxiety, self-efficacy and emotional intelligence. *Higher Education Research & Development*, *36*(4), 716–729. doi: 10.1080/07294360.2016.1238881

Hyland, F., & Hyland, K. (2001). Sugaring the pill: Praise and criticism in written feedback. *Journal of Second Language Writing*, *10*, 185–212. doi: 10.1016/S1060-3743(01)00038-8

Iwaniec, J. (2019). Language learning motivation and gender: The case of Poland. *International Journal of Applied Linguistics*, *29*, 130–143. doi: 10.1111/ijal.12251

Jiang, L., & Luk, J. (2016). Multimodal composing as a learning activity in English classrooms: Inquiring into the sources of its motivational capacity. *System*, *59*, 1–11. doi: 10.1016/j.system.2016.04.001

Johnson, N. D. (1987). *Effects of inservice training on writing apprehension and computer anxiety in elementary school teachers*. PhD thesis, The University of Wisconsin-Madison, USA.

Karlen, Y., & Compagnoni, M. (2017). Implicit theory of writing ability: Relationship to metacognitive strategy knowledge and strategy use in academic writing. *Psychology Learning & Teaching*, *16*, 47–63. doi: 10.1177/1475725716682887

Kim, Y.-K., & Kim, T.-Y. (2011). Gender differences in Korean secondary school students' learning styles and L2 motivation. *Foreign Languages Education*, *18*(2), 51–71.

Kissau, S. P., Quach Kolano, L., & Wang, C. (2010). Perceptions of gender differences in high school students' motivation to learn Spanish. *Foreign Language Annals*, *43*(3), 703–721. doi: 10.1111/j.1944-9720.2010.01110.x

Kormos, J., & Csizér, K. (2008). Age-related differences in the motivation of learning English as a foreign language: Attitudes, selves and motivated learning behavior. *Language Learning*, *58*, 327–355. doi: 10.1111/j.1467-9922.2008.00443.x

Krest, M. (1988). Student writing: How not to avoid the draft. *Journal of Teaching Writing*, *7*, 27–39.

Kucirkova, N., Rowe, D. W., Oliver, L., & Piestrzynski, L. E. (2019). Systematic review of young children's writing on screen: What do we know and what we do need to know. *Literacy*, *53*(4), 216–225. doi: 10.1111/lit.12173

Lalande, J. F. (1982). Reducing composition errors: An experiment. *Modern Language Journal*, *66*, 140–149. doi: 10.1111/j.1540-4781.1982.tb06973.x

Lee, H., & Kim, Y. (2014). Korean adolescents' longitudinal change of intrinsic motivation in learning English and mathematics during secondary school years:

Focusing on gender difference and school characteristics. *Learning and Individual Differences*, *36*, 131–139. doi: 10.1016/j.lindif.2014.07.018

Lee, I. (1997). ESL learners' performance in error correction in writing: Some implications for college-level teaching. *System*, *25*(4), 465–477. doi: 10.1016/S0346-251X(97)00045-6

Lee, I. (2017). *Classroom assessment and feedback in L2 school contexts*. Singapore: Springer.

Lee, I. (2019). Teacher written corrective feedback: Less is more. *Language Teaching*, *52*(4), 1–13. doi: 10.1017/S0261444819000247

Lee, I., Yu, S., & Liu, Y. (2018). Hong Kong secondary students' motivation in EFL writing: A survey study. *TESOL Quarterly*, *51*, 176–187. doi: 10.1002/tesq.364

Lee, S. Y. (2005). Facilitating and inhibiting factors in English as a foreign language writing performance: A model testing with structural equation modeling. *Language Learning*, *55*(2), 335–374. doi: 10.1111/j.0023-8333.2005.00306.x

Lee, S. Y., & Krashen, S. D. (1997). Writing apprehension in Chinese as a first language. *ITL- International Journal of Applied Linguistics*, 115–*116*, 27–37. doi: 10.1075/itl.115-116.02lee

Leki, I. (1990). Coaching from the margins issues in written response. In B. Kroll (Ed.), *Second language writing: Insights from the classroom*, (pp. 57–68). Cambridge: Cambridge University Press.

Leki, I. (1991). The preferences of ESL students for error correction in college level writing classes. *Foreign Language Annals*, *24*, 203–218. doi: 10.1111/j.1944-9720.1991.tb00464.x

Limpo, T., & Alves, R. (2017). Relating beliefs in writing skill malleability to writing performance: The mediating role of achievement goals and self-efficacy. *Journal of Writing Research*, *9*(2), 97–125. doi: 10.17239/jowr-2017.09.02.01

Lipnevich, A. A., & Smith, J. K. (2009). I really need feedback to learn: Students' perspectives on the effectiveness of the differential feedback messages. *Educational Assessment, Evaluation and Accountability*, *21*, 347–367. doi: 10.1007/s11092-009-9082-2

Lo, J., & Hyland, F. (2007). Enhancing students' engagement and motivation in writing: The case of primary students in Hong Kong. *Journal of Second Language Writing*, *16*, 219–237. doi: 10.1016/j.jslw.2007.06.002

MacArthur, C., Philippakos, Z., & Graham, S. (2016). A multicomponent measure of writing motivation with basic college writers. *Learning Disability Quarterly*, *39*(1), 31–43. doi: 10.1177/0731948715583115

Magno, C. (2008). Reading strategy, amount of writing, metacognition, metamemory, and apprehension as predictors of English written proficiency. *The Asian EFL Journal*, *29*(2), 16–48.

Mahfoodh, O. H. A. (2017). "I feel disappointed": EFL university students' emotional responses towards teacher written feedback. *Assessing Writing*, *31*, 53–72. doi: 10.1016/j.asw.2016.07.001

Martinez, C. T., Kock, N., & Cass, J. (2011). Pain and pleasure in short essay writing: Factors predicting university students' writing anxiety and self-efficacy. *Journal of Adolescent and Adult Literacy*, *54*, 351–360. doi:10.1598/JA AL.54.5.9

Massé, M., & Popovich, M. N. (2005). Individual assessment of media writing student attitudes: Recasting the Riff and Stacks writing apprehension measure. *Journalism & Mass Communication Quarterly*, *82*(2), 339–355. doi: 10.1177/107769900508200207

Masny, D., & Foxall, J. (1992). *Writing apprehension in L2*. ERIC Document, ED020 882.

Mausehund, J. (1993). *An analysis of the relationship of writing ability, writing apprehension, and the interrelationship of peer-review activities in business communication classes*. PhD thesis, Northern Illinois University, USA.

McVee, M. B., & Miller, S. M. (2012). *Multimodal composing in classrooms: Learning and teaching for the digital world*. New York: Routledge.

Merton, R. K. (1968). The Matthew effect in science. *Science, 159* (3810), 56–63.

Mitchell, K. M., Harrigan, T., & McMillan, D. E. (2017). Writing self-efficacy in nursing students: The influence of a discipline-specific writing environment. *Nursing Open, 4*(4), 240–250. doi: 10.1002/nop2.90

Mostafaei Alaei, M., & Ghamari, M. R. (2013). EFL learning, EFL motivation types, and national identity: In conflict or in coalition. *Issues in Language Teaching (ILT), 2*(2), 85–111.

Okuniewski, J. E. (2014). Age and gender effects on motivation and attitudes in German learning: The Polish context. *Psychology of Language and Communication, 18*(3), 251–262. doi: 10.2478/plc-2014-0017

Oxford, R. L. (March, 1998). The unravelling tapestry: Teacher and course characteristics associated with demotivation in the language classroom. *Demotivation in foreign language learning*. Paper presented at the TESOL '98 Congress, Seattle, WA.

Onwuegbuzie, A. J. (1998). The relationship between writing anxiety and learning styles among graduate students. *Journal of College Student Development, 39*, 589–598.

Onwuegbuzie, A. J. (1999). Writing apprehension among graduate students: Its relationship to self-perception. *Psychological Reports, 84*, 1034–1039. doi: 10.2466/pr0.1999.84.3.1034

Onwuegbuzie, A. J., & Collins, K. MT (2001). Writing apprehension and academic procrastination among graduate students. *Perceptual and Motor Skills, 92*, 560–562. doi: 10.2466/PMS.92.2.560-562

Öztürk, G., & Gürbüz, N. (2013). The impact of gender on foreign language speaking anxiety and motivation. *Procedia - Social and Behavioral Sciences, 70*, 654–665. doi: 10.1016/j.sbspro.2013.01.106

Pajares, F. (2003). Self-efficacy beliefs, motivation, and achievement in writing: A review of the literature. *Reading &Writing Quarterly, 19*(2), 139–158. doi: 10.1080/10573560308222

Pajares, F., Britner, S., & Valiante, G. (2000). Relation between achievement goals and self-beliefs of middle school students in writing and science. *Contemporary Educational Psychology, 25*, 406–422. doi: 10.1006/ceps.1999.1027

Pajares, F., & Cheong, Y. (2003). Achievement goal orientations in writing: A developmental perspective. *International Journal of Educational Research, 39*, 437–455. doi: 10.1016/j.ijer.2004.06.008

Pajares, F., Hartley, J., & Valiante, G. (2001). Response format in writing self-efficacy assessment: Greater discrimination increases prediction. *Measurement and Evaluation in Counseling and Development, 33*(4), 214–221. doi: 10.1080/07481756.2001.12069012

Pajares, F., & Johnson, M. (1996). Self-efficacy beliefs and the writing performance of entering high school students. *Psychology in the Schools, 33*, 163–175. doi: 10.1002/(SICI)1520-6807(199604)33:2<163::AID-PITS10>3.0.CO;2-C

Pajares, F., Johnson, J., & Usher, E. (2007a). Sources of writing self-efficacy beliefs of elementary, middle, and high school students. *Research in the Teaching of English, 42*(1), 104–120.

Pajares, F., Miller, M., & Johnson, M. (1999). Gender differences in writing self-beliefs of elementary school students. *Journal of Educational Psychology, 91*, 50–61. doi: 10.1006/ceps.1998.0995

Pajares, F., & Valiante, G. (1997). Influence of writing self-efficacy beliefs on the writing performance of upper elementary students. *The Journal of Educational Research, 90*, 353–360. doi: 10.1080/00220671.1997.10544593

Pajares, F., & Valiante, G. (1999). Grade level and gender differences in the writing self-beliefs of middle school students. *Contemporary Educational Psychology, 24*(4), 390–405. doi: 10.1006/ceps.1998.0995

Pajares, F., & Valiante, G. (2001). Gender differences in writing motivation and achievement of middle school students: A function of gender orientation? *Contemporary Educational Psychology, 26*, 366–381. doi: 10.1006/ceps.2000.1069

Pajares, F., & Valiante, G. (2006). Self-efficacy beliefs and motivation in writing development. In C. A. MacArthur, S. Graham, & J. Fitzgerald (Eds.), *Handbook of writing research*, (pp. 158–170). New York, NY, US: Guilford Press.

Pajares, F., Valiante, G., & Cheong, Y. F. (2007a). Writing self-efficacy and its relation to gender, writing motivation, and writing competence: A developmental perspective. In S. Hidi, & P. Boscolo (Eds.). *Motivation and writing: Research and school practice*, (pp. 141–162). Dordrecht, the Netherlands: Kluwer.

Palmquist, M., & Young, R. (1992). The notion of giftedness and student expectations about writing. *Written Communication, 9*(1), 137–169. doi: 10.1177/0741088392009001004

Pennington, M. C., & So, S. (1993). Comparing writing process and product across two languages: A study of 6 Singaporean university student writers. *Journal of Second Language Writing, 2*(1), 41–63. doi: 10.1016/1060-3743(93)90005-N

Phinney, M. (1991). Word processing and writing apprehension in first and second language writers. *Computers & Composition, 11*(1), 65–82. doi: 10.1016/8755-4615(91)80039-G

Podsen, I. (1987). *School administrators: the role of writing apprehension on job related writing tasks and writing proficiency*. PhD thesis, Georgia State University, USA.

Rahimi, M., & Zhang, L. J. (2019). Writing task complexity, students' motivational beliefs, anxiety and their writing production in English as a second language. *Reading and Writing, 32*, 761–786. doi: 10.1007/s11145-018-9887-9

Rankin-Brown, M. S. (2006). *Addressing writing apprehension in adult English language learners*. Proceedings of CATESOL State Conference.

Riffe, D., & Stacks, D. (1992). Student characteristics and writing apprehension. *Journalism Educator, 47*(2), 39–49. doi: 10.1177/107769589204700206

Roca de Larios, R. J., Murphy, L., & Marin, J. (2002). A critical examination of L2 writing process research. In S. Ransdell, & M. L. Barbier (Eds.), *New directions for research in L2 writing*, (pp. 11–47). Netherlands: Kluwer Academic Publishers.

Ryu, H. (1997). *Threshold level of English language proficiency for EFL writing: Effect on the interaction between English language proficiency and writing skills on Korean college students' EFL writing*. PhD thesis, University of Florida, USA.

Saghafi, K., Adel, S. M. R., & Zareian, G. (2017). An ecological study of foreign language writing anxiety in English as a foreign language classroom. *Journal of Intercultural Communication Research, 46*(5), 424–440, doi: 10.1080/17475759.2017.1367954

Sakai, H., & Kikuchi, K. (2009). An analysis of demotivators in the EFL classroom. *System, 37*, 57–69. doi: 10.1016/j.system.2008.09.005

Sanders-Reio, J. (2010). *Investigation of the relations between domain-specific beliefs about writing, writing self-efficacy, writing apprehension, and writing performance in undergraduates.* PhD diissertation, University of Maryland, USA.

Sanders-Reio, J., Alexander, P., Reio, T., Jr., & Newman, I. (2014). Do students' beliefs about writing relate to their writing self-efficacy, apprehension, and performance? *Learning and Instruction, 33*(1), 1–11. doi: 10.1016/j.learninstruc.2014.02.001

Sasaki, M., & Hirose, K. (1996). Explanatory variables for EFL students' expository writing. *Language Learning, 46*(1), 137–174.

Selfe, C. L. (1984). The predrafting processes of four high- and four low-apprehensive writers. *Research in the Teaching of English, 18*(1), 45–64.

Semke, H. (1984). The effects of the red pen. *Foreign Language Annals, 17*(3), 195–202. doi: 10.1111/j.1944-9720.1984.tb01727.x

Shell, D., Colvin, C., & Bruning, R. (1995). Self-efficacy, attributions, and outcome expectancy mechanisms in reading and writing achievement: Grade-level and achievement-level differences. *Journal of Educational Psychology, 87*, 386–398. doi: 10.1037/0022-0663.87.3.386

Silva, T. (1993). Toward an understanding of the distinct nature of L2 writing: The ESL research and its implications. *TESOL Quarterly, 27*(4), 657–675. doi: 10.2307/3587400

Simons, K., Higgins, M., & Lowe, D. (1995). A profile of communication apprehension in accounting majors: Implications for teaching and curriculum revision. *Journal of Accounting Education, 13*(2), 159–176. doi: 10.1016/0748-5751(95)00001-3

Sims, M. C. (1995). *The effects of a portfolio method of evaluation on the writing apprehension, locus of control, and teacher encouragement rating of community college composition students.* PhD thesis, Delta State University, USA.

Skibniewski, L. (1988). The writing processes of advanced foreign language learners in their native and foreign languages: Evidence from thinking-aloud and behaviour protocol. *Staudi Anglica Posnaniensia, 21*, 177–186.

Straub, R. B., & Lunsford, R. F. (1995). *Twelve readers reading: Responding to student writing.* Cresskill, NJ: Hampton Press.

Sullivan, N., & Pratt, E. (1996). A comparative study of two ESL writing environments: A computer-assisted classroom and a traditional oral classroom. *System, 24*(4), 491–501. doi: 10.1016/S0346-251X(96)00044-9

Sylvén, L. K., & Thompson, A. S. (2015). Language learning motivation and CLIL: Is there a connection? *Journal of Immersion and Content-Based Language Education, 3*(1), 28–50. doi: 10.1075/jicb.3.1.02syl

Teng, L. S., Yuan, R. E., & Sun, P. P. (2020). A mixed-methods approach to investigating motivational regulation strategies and writing proficiency in English as a foreign language contexts. *System, 88*, 1–12. doi: 10.1016/j.system.2019.102182

Thompson, L. G. (1986). *An examination of relationships: writing apprehension levels, semantic encoding performance, and holistic assessments of writing of tenth grade students (writing anxiety, analysis of cohesion, writer's block).* PhD thesis, Georgia State University, USA.

Todd, V. (2003). *Writing and computer apprehension among mass communications majors.* PhD thesis, Texas Tech University, USA.

Torres, K. M., Arrastia-Chisholm, M. C., & Tackett, S. (2020). Perceptions of writing anxiety and self-efficacy among Spanish heritage language learners. *Journal of Hispanic Higher Education, 19*(1) 84–98. doi: 10.1177/1538192718775175

Troia, G. A., Harbaugh, A. G., Shankland, R. K., Wolbers, K. A., & Lawrence, A. M. (2013). Relationships between writing motivation, writing activity, and writing performance: Effects of grade, sex, and ability. *Reading and Writing*, *26*, 17–44. doi: 10.1007/s11145-012-9379-2

Tragant, E. (2006). Language learning motivation and age. In C. Muñoz (Ed.), *Age and the rate of foreign language learning*, (pp. 237–276). Clevedon: Multilingual Matters.

Truscott, J. (1996). The case against grammar correction in L2 writing classes. *Language Learning*, *46*(2), 327–369. doi: 10.1111/j.1467-1770.1996.tb01238.x

Tsao, J., Tseng, W., & Wang, W. (2017). The effects of writing anxiety and motivation on EFL college students' self-evaluative judgments of corrective feedback. *Psychological Reports*, *120*(2), 219–241. doi: 10.1177/0033294116687123

Uzawa, K. (1996). Second language learners' processes of L1 writing, L2 writing, and translation from L1 to L2. *Journal of Second Language Writing*, *5*(3), 271–294. doi: 10.1016/S1060-3743(96)90005-3

Victori, M. (1995). *EFL writing knowledge and strategies: An integrative study (language proficiency and metacognition)*. PhD thesis, Universitat Autonoma de Barcelona, Spain.

Van Laar, C. (2001). Declining optimism in ethnic minority students: The role of attributions and self-esteem. In F. Salili, C-Y. Chiu, and C-Y. Hong (Eds.), *Student motivation: The culture and context of learning*, (pp. 79–104). New York: Kluwer Academic/Plenum Publishers.

Waller, L., & Papi, M. (2017). Motivation and feedback: How implicit theories of intelligence predict L2 writers' motivation and feedback orientation. *Journal of Second Language Writing*, *35*, 54–65. doi: 10.1016/j.jslw.2017.01.004

Walsh, S. M. (1989). *The relationship among three factors–writing apprehension, composition quality and inclination to write voluntarily*. PhD thesis, University of California, USA.

Wang, W. (2014). Students' perceptions of rubric-referenced peer feedback on EFL writing: A longitudinal inquiry. *Assessing Writing*, *19*, 80–96. doi: 10.1016/j.asw.2013.11.008

Washholz, P. B., & Etheridge C. P. (1995). Speaking for themselves: Writing self-efficacy beliefs of high and low apprehensive writers. ERIC Document, ED403563.

Williams, M., Burden, R. L., & Lanvers, U. (2002). "French is the language of love and stuff": Student perceptions of issues related to motivation in learning a foreign language. *British Educational Research Journal*, *28*(4), 503–528. doi: 10.1080/0141192022200000580

Wiltse, E. (2002). Correlates of college students' use of instructors' comments. *Journalism and Mass Communication Educator*, *57*(2), 126–138. doi: 10.1177/107769580205700203

Wittman, E. M. (1991). *Situational factors influencing writing apprehension in the community college composition classroom*. PhD thesis, North Carolina State University, USA.

Wolfersberger, M. (2003). L1 to L2 writing process and strategy transfer: A look at lower proficiency writers. *TESL-EJ*, *7*(2).

Wu, Y. (1992). *First and second language writing relationship: Chinese and English*. PhD dissertation, Texas A & M University, USA.

Xu, W., & Case, R.E. (2015). Age-related differences in motivation in learning English among mainland Chinese students. *International Journal of Applied Linguistic*, *25*(1), 67–82. doi: 10.1111/ijal.12050

Yarbrough, N. (1985). *The effects of cognitive strategy and writing apprehension on quantitative component measures and holistic ratings of creativity in writing (process, expository, narrative)*. PhD thesis, University of Georgia, USA.

Yeung, A. S., Lau, S., & Nie, Y. (2011). Primary and secondary students' motivation in learning English: Grade and gender differences. *Contemporary Educational Psychology*, *36*(3), 246–256. doi: 10.1016/j.cedpsych.2011.03.001

Yilmaz Soylu, M., Zeleny, M. G., Zhao, R., Bruning, R., Dempsey, M., & Kauffman, D. (2017). Secondary students' writing achievement goals: Assessing the mediating effects of mastery and performance goals on writing self-efficacy, affect, and writing achievement. *Frontiers in Psychology*, *8*, 1406. doi: 10.3389/fpsyg.2017.01406

Yu, S. (2020). Giving genre-based peer feedback in academic writing: Sources of knowledge and skills, difficulties and challenges. *Assessment & Evaluation in Higher Education*. doi: 10.1080/02602938.2020.1742872

Yu, S. & Hu, G. (2017). Can higher-proficiency L2 learners benefit from working with lower-proficiency partners in peer feedback? *Teaching in Higher Education*, *22*(2), 178–192. doi: 10.1080/13562517.2016.1221806

Yu, S., Jiang, L., & Zhou, N. (2020). Investigating what feedback practices contribute to students' writing motivation and engagement in Chinese EFL context: A large scale study. *Assessing Writing*, *44*, 1–15. doi: 10.1016/j.asw.2020.100451

Yu, S., & Lee, I. (2016). Peer feedback in second language writing (2005–2014). *Language Teaching*, *49*(4), 461–493. doi:10.1017/S0261444816000161

Yu, S., Lee, I., & Mak, P.(2016). Revisiting Chinese cultural issues in peer feedback in EFL writing: Insights from a multiple case study. *The Asia-Pacific Education Researcher*, *25*(2), 295–304. doi: 10.1007/s40299-015-0262-1

Yu, S., Zhou, N., Zheng, Y., Zhang, L., Cao, H., & Li, X. (2019). Evaluating student motivation and engagement in Chinese EFL writing context. *Studies in Educational Evaluation*, *62*, 129–141. doi: 10.1016/j.stueduc.2019.06.002

Yuan, T. (2015). *Children as multimodal composers: a case study of early elementary students' digital literacy practices*. PhD thesis, Columbia University, USA.

Zamel, V. (1985). Responding to student writing. *TESOL Quarterly*, *19*(1), 79–97. doi: 10.2307/3586773

Zuercher, N. T. (1986). *Word processing and writing apprehension in freshman composition*. PhD thesis, University of South Dakota, USA.

4 Instructional research of writing motivation

4.1 Introduction

After discussing the correlates and sources of writers' varied motivational levels in the previous chapter, the author, in this chapter, highlights the instructional research of writing motivation. Instructional or effectiveness research of writing motivation can generally be classified into two main types. The first type is the interventional research, aiming at helping struggling writers become more motivated. This interventional research normally depends on pre-/post-testing experimental designs or treatments and quantitative data to examine the impact of the instruction used on students' writing motivation. The second type is the observational research aiming at experimenting particular instructional procedures and exploring their influence on writing motivation by depending mainly on qualitative data sources or mix-method designs. This research type normally tries to identify factors influencing the success of a particular instructional scenario.

In the previous writing motivation instructional studies, the following six types of teaching treatments have been experimented: technology-supported instruction, strategy instruction, feedback treatments, genre-based instruction, task interest-based instruction, and therapeutic training. The main aim of the chapter is to not only explain whether or not these instructional treatments improved writers' motivation, but also to show how they were implemented and the factors influencing their effectiveness. As will be noted in the following sections, the place of writing motivation and its constructs in these studies varied. In some studies, writing motivation was addressed as a main dependent variable or perhaps the only one. In the other studies, whose main focus was on writers' processes or texts, writing motivation was dealt with peripherally. Despite these differences, both types of studies provide us with important information about how particular instructional treatments can contribute to motivating writers and when their use can be more or less effective.

4.2 Technology-supported instruction

Technology-supported instructional designs have long been used to motivate students to write. As implied in chapter 3, Word processors represented the only technological tool used in the writing motivation studies conducted in 1980s and 1990s, and these studies were mainly related to writing apprehension/attitude and perceived ability beliefs (e.g., Hert, 1988; Johnson, 1987; Graham & MacArthur, 1988; Phinney, 1991; Schleifer, 1992; Sullivan & Pratt, 1996; Zuercher, 1986). Only a few of these studies found significant positive effects for computer-based instruction on writing motivation (e.g., Graham & MacArthur, 1988; Schleifer, 1992).

Since the turn of the century and with the occurrence of Web 2.0 and Web 3.0 tools, instructional writing motivation studies started to use different technological tools. For example, Skinner and Austin (1999) used computer-based conferencing, i.e., real-time synchronous discussions, and found it had noticeable effects on alleviating students' writing apprehension. In Mabrito's (2000) study, Internet communication newsgroups were used as a tool for helping high apprehensive students overcome their motivation. Besides, Chuo (2007) made use of WebQuest in writing instruction to reduce students' writing apprehension, but found no significant difference between the experimental and control groups in alleviated apprehension. Recently, Wu, Yang, Hsieh, and Yamamoto's (2020) study revealed that college students' demotivation was significantly reduced as a result of using online flipped writing instruction (i.e., understanding writing learning content at home through technology-mediated materials and practicing writing in the classroom).

In the last two decades, three technological tools have been used widely in writing motivation studies. These are: blogs, wikis, and multimodal composing tasks. The writing motivation research implementing these three tools is reviewed in the next subsections.

4.2.1 Blog-mediated writing instruction

Blog-based writing instruction involves students in creating their personal pages, sharing blog posts with their peers, and exchanging feedback on writing performance with them. According to Warschauer (2010), the main advantage of blogs is combining students' published writings and their discussion or feedback in one medium and helping them develop a sense of voice through their contribution to online content. Kramer and Kusurkar (2017) state that the affective impact of using blogs as a writing tool is grounded in the Self Determination Theory positing that self-perceived autonomy, competence, and relevance are requirements for the motivational performance of tasks.

In the blog-mediated instruction studies that dealt peripherally with motivation, a positive impact of blogs on students' writing motivation was noted. For example, Lee (2010) found that blogs fostered students' writing engagement and motivation due to their perceived broad audience.

Likewise, Arslan and Şahin-Kızıl (2010) conclude that the appealing features of blogs enhanced student writers' motive to take up writing outside classrooms. Vurdien's (2013) study also revealed that blogs are conducive to student writers' reflective and collaborative learning, and in turn, to enhancing their motivation. It is worth noting that the reported results of these studies are based on observing students' affective performance rather than assessing it using reliable scales.

Some mixed-method studies showed a motivating impact for blogs on student writers. For example, Zhang, Song, Shen, and Huang (2014) examined the impact of collaborative blog-mediated peer feedback on learners' writing motivation. Thirty-six university L2 students were divided into 3–4-member groups to complete two blog-mediated essay tasks. They were instructed to provide feedback on their peers' writing using specific guidelines related to the text aspects to be evaluated. The multiple groups of students taking part in this study were required to exchange feedback on each other's writing, and each group was supposed to submit revised essays based on feedback provided from another group. Meanwhile, the course teacher made comments on the high-quality essays and feedback produced by the students to guide them on how to effectively evaluate written texts and give efficient feedback. Zhang and his colleagues found that blog-mediated peer feedback contributed significantly to the students' writing self-efficacy and task value perceptions and that it was conducive to their self-reflection. Despite this, they state that the following three pedagogical challenges need to be considered when using blog-mediated peer feedback in writing instruction: the choice of reliable technical blog, teacher's role in fostering the effectiveness of peer feedback, and the teacher's expected workload due to the nature of this online task. In what may be regarded as a writing across the curriculum research project, Kramer and Kusurkar (2017) engaged first-year university biology students in a collaborative science-writing blog project. In their study, Kramer and Kusurkar were mainly concerned with learning motivation experience, for which blog writing represented the main tool. Their instrument was an intrinsic motivation survey that included some writing motivation items. Their study revealed that the students who participated in the science-writing blog project found it an intrinsically motivating and rewarding experience and that it contributed to their mastery goal orientation. The two researchers concluded that the students valued "the freedom of choosing a subject and constructing a blog in their own fashion, i.e. working in autonomy. They ... [expressed] a sense of usefulness (perceived competence) because their efforts are embedded in a broad social context, the web. They ... [expressed] their appreciation in terms of the pleasure of sharing understanding and constructing a blog together (sense of relatedness)" (p. 61).

Contrarily to the above positive effects, the pre-/post-testing experimental studies revealed incongruent results for blog-mediated writing instruction on students' writing motivation. Mixed results were revealed by three studies comparing the writing motivating outcome of experimental versus control group students. Fathi, Ahmadnejad, and Yousofi (2019) found significant differences in writing motivation and self-efficacy in favour of the experimental group students receiving blog-mediated instruction, but contrary results were found in the studies conducted by Lin (2014) and Chen (2016). Lin's (2014) study revealed a positive effect for using blogs on the experimental group students' writing self-efficacy and motivation, but no significant differences were found between them and the control group students in the attitudes towards learning writing. Surprisingly, the control group students had higher writing motivation level as compared to the experimental group ones. Similarly, Chen's (2016) found that the control group students surpassed the experimental group ones in writing self-efficacy.

4.2.2 Wiki-mediated writing instruction

Wikis represent another technological tool that has been experimented in writing research as a means for motivating students. Wikis are more suitable for engaging student writers in collaborative activities and developing collective written content (Warschauer, 2010). Unlike blogs, the use of wikis in writing classes requires engaging students in collaboratively developing successive drafts about certain topics, thus their use involves a number of group editing and revising activities. Normally, the students in one class are grouped into teams including a few members with varied writing abilities and each team has a leader selected by its members, see the early relevant studies reported by Bubas, Kovacic, and Zlatovic (2007); Mak and Coniam (2008); and Li, Chu, Ki, and Woo (2010).

Previous studies integrating wikis in writing instruction showed consistent results with regard to their positive impact on students' writing motivation. In three mixed-method studies, Li and her colleagues (Li et al., 2010, Li, Chu, Ki, & Woo, 2012; Li, Chu, & Ki, 2014) examined the influence of engaging primary school students in a wiki-based collaborative process writing pedagogy on their writing ability and attitudes. Their three studies showed consistent and significant increases in students' attitudes towards writing and writing motivation as a result of working with wikis. Other studies also showed the effectiveness of wiki-mediated instruction in helping students overcome their negative attitudes towards writing (Ducate, Anderson, & Moreno, 2011), motivating them to write (Chao & Lo, 2011; Davidson, 2012; Kassem, 2017), and increasing their writing self-confidence (Wang, 2014). Interpreting this positive impact, Wang (2014) concludes that "students enjoyed performing group tasks in the wiki-mediated environment because they found it to be engaging, challenging and interesting" (p. 383).

It is important to note that the main focus in all the above wiki-mediated instruction studies was on writers' performance rather their motivation. Additionally, writers' motivation was explored using qualitative data sources, with the exception of the three studies conducted by Li and her colleagues, who depended on a quantitative measure.

4.2.3 Multimodal composing tasks

Multimodal composing represents a great shift in text composing practices. As Smith (2014) states, text composing practices "have undergone numerous shifts – from the page to the screen and from text to multimodal" (p. 1). Edwards-Groves (2011) defines multimodal text composing as "the utility of multimedia and technology for the writing process, design and creativity" (p. 53). The motivating features in multimodality lies in involving students in the participatory and collaborative nature of the text composing process (Knobel & Lankshear, 2014), considering their writing interests, experiences and increased engagement (Nash, 2018), and engaging them in using various expressive digital resources.

Research examining the impact of multimodal composing on students' motivation is so scarce indeed. The qualitative and observational data of some studies (Edwards-Groves, 2011; Hafner & Miller, 2011; Knobel & Lankshear, 2014; Yuan, 2015) generally indicate that students become more motivated when they compose multimodal texts, but these studies were not mainly concerned with examining the motivational capacity of multimodality. In other words, motivation was observed as a by-product of the multimodal composing activities used in these studies. In a scarce study focusing only on the potential motivational gains of multimodal composing, Jiang and Luk (2016) collaborated with four teachers in a Chinese university in engaging their students in four multimodal composing projects that were implemented over one academic year. Their interview data showed that the multimodal composing experiences the students were engaged in enhanced their motivation. Many students reported that multimodal text composing is a much more intriguing experience than traditional writing tasks. In discussing the results of their study, Jiang and Luk (2016) point out that the motivational capacity of the multimodal composing tasks was associated with specific factors, including: learners' enjoyment of writing activities characterized by an optimal challenging level, the sensory and cognitive curiosity they experienced, the empowering learning atmosphere in which they had control over meaningful learning outcomes, and the sense of achievement they got when their multimodal composed products were recognized and appreciated by others.

4.3 Strategy instruction

Strategy instruction has commonly been used as a means for fostering students' writing motivation. The use of strategy instruction in writing motivation studies dates back to the 1980s. Two main types of writing strategy instruction have been employed in previous writing motivation studies: writing self-regulation versus general writing strategy instruction. The former type (i.e., writing self-regulation strategy instruction, known also as writing self-regulated strategy development) has been more widely used than the latter one. The writing motivation studies that made use of strategy instruction share three common characteristics. First, they were all conducted in L1 contexts. Second, writers' self-ability beliefs (i.e., their self-efficacy and self-concept) were the only motivational constructs addressed in the majority of these strategy instruction studies. Finally, all these studies were interventional ones that depended on the pre-/post-testing of the variables investigated.

Writing self-regulation strategy instruction (or writing self-regulated strategy development) was introduced in writing motivation research in the late 1980s by Karen Harris and Steve Graham. In the last three decades, the two researchers along with their colleagues published a number of writing self-regulation strategy instruction studies and theoretical relevant works (e.g., Graham & Harris, 2014). Zimmerman and Reisemberg (1997) define writing self-regulation as writers' use of their self-initiated thoughts, perceptions, and processes to accomplish text composing goals. According to Harris, Graham, Mason, McKeown, and Olinghouse (2018), writing self-regulation strategy instruction encompasses the following components:

> (a) interactive, discourse-based, scaffolded, explicit learning of genre knowledge and strategies for writing across and within genres, (b) development of declarative, procedural, and conditional knowledge (the what, when, where, and why) needed to use these strategies, and (c) explicit development of self-regulation strategies for monitoring and managing the writing process, writing strategies, and writing behavior. (p. 326)

Zimmerman and Reisemberg (1997) group writing self-regulation processes into three categories: environmental processes (self-regulating the environment or the physical setting in which the writing task is to be performed); behavioural processes (regulating the cognitive writing activities); and personal processes (self-regulating one's writing beliefs and motivation while composing). They view that these three types of processes interact with each other via what they have labelled as "feedback loops", which monitor the self-regulatory actions performed and inform writers of their effectiveness. Describing the relationship between the feedback loops and writing self-efficacy, Zimmerman and Reisemberg (1997) state that:

> Strategic feedback loops do more than enable writers to be sensitive and adaptive to their output during the course of writing; the resultant feedback alters writers' conceptions of their self-efficacy. In general, when strategic feedback indicates improved or superior textual output, writers' self-efficacy is enhanced, and when such feedback is unfavorable, their self-efficacy is diminished. It is also hypothesized that writers will continue to self-regulate when a self-regulative strategy increases their perceptions of self-efficacy. Thus, writers' sense of

self-efficacy is predictive of not only their self-regulatory processes but also their intrinsic motivation to write and their eventual literary outcomes. (p. 78)

The previous studies examining the impact of self-regulated writing strategy instruction on writing self-efficacy yielded mixed results. Some studies found positive significant effects for self-regulated strategy instruction on fostering learners' writing self-efficacy (e.g., Graham & Harris, 1989a, 1989b). Other studies found no significant effects for such instruction on increasing writing self-efficacy levels (e.g., Garcia-Sanchez & Fidalgo-Redondo, 2006; Graham, Harris, & Mason, 2005; Sawyer, Graham, & Harris, 1992). On the other hand, Limpo and Alves (2014) used self-regulatory strategy instruction to develop L1 students' implicit theories of writing (a construct similar to writing self-concept). As a way of evaluating their intervention, they got their participants, who were 5th and 6th graders, to complete a five-item implicit theories of writing scale before and after the instruction. The self-regulatory strategy instruction used in this study was implemented as follows:

> Students were taught a strategy to plan opinion essays, along with the necessary skills and knowledge to properly use it. This strategy helped students to generate and organize ideas following the opinion essay structure. ... In line with the Self-Regulated Strategy Development (SRSD) model, this strategy was coupled with self-regulation procedures. Goal setting helped students to guide their behaviour in a writing task. Students' goal was to write a complete opinion essay. Self-monitoring helped students to obtain concrete and visible evidence of their progress. Students were given a 'self-monitoring sheet' where they (1) set their goal, (2) registered and counted the number of essay parts, and (3) wrote a self-reinforcement statement. Self-instructions helped students to manage the planning strategy and the other self-regulation procedures. Using a 'writing flow chart', they develop self-instructions to set goals, use the planning strategy, and check goals attainment. The following SRSD practices were used for teaching the writing and self-regulation strategies: development of knowledge for writing and self-regulation; explicit instruction, discussion, and modelling of the planning strategy and self-regulation procedures; promotion of strategies of memorization; collaborative practice supported by teachers and guidance materials gradually faded; and independent practice with minimal teacher support. (p. 578)

Limpo and Alves found that the self-regulatory strategy instruction used helped the students to conceive their writing ability as malleable and learnable, but the improved change in the writing malleability beliefs was associated with an improvement in their planning skills and text quality.

On the other hand, the fewer studies using general writing strategy instruction (i.e., planning, writing, and revising) showed consistent results on its effectiveness in enhancing learners' self-efficacy (De Smedt, Graham, & Van Keer, 2019; Schunk & Swartz, 1991; Wong, Butler, Ficzere, & Kuperis, 1997). For example, De Smedt et al. (2019) examined the impact of explicit strategy instruction with and without peer-assisted writing on primary graders' writing motivation (operationalized by a writing interest measure) and self-efficacy. The five-week instruction they used focused on teaching the students writing knowledge and text planning, writing, and revising strategies. In one experimental condition, this instruction was accompanied by peer-assisted writing and in another one no peer-assisted writing activities were implemented. The three researchers summarize the strategy instruction they provided to their students as follows:

> Teachers explicitly taught students how to plan, write, and revise descriptive texts by applying the following instructional procedure: (1) pointing out the importance and value of a specific strategy, (2) discussing students' strategy use, (3) modelling the writing strategy by demonstrating and thinking aloud how, what, and why the teacher applied the writing strategy, so students gain insights into the teacher's thinking and writing process, and (4) introducing different strategy cards summarizing the steps in applying a strategy (i.e., planning, writing, and revision card). (p. 157)

This study revealed that the students who received explicit strategy instruction with peer-assisted writing were more motivated in the post-instruction testing than the students who received the same instruction type without peer-assisted writing. Gender-related writing motivation differences were also found in the post-testing in favour of girls.

Two issues need to be addressed in the strategy instruction studies concerned with writing motivation. The first one is using observational qualitative data designs instead of solely relying on quantitative pre-/post-testing designs. Such observational designs could reveal new dimensions about students' motivational responses to writing strategy instruction. The second issue is exploring the impact of strategy instruction on the dispositional, situational, and achievement goal constructs of writing motivation. As noted, these constructs have been neglected in the above strategy instruction studies.

4.4 Feedback instructional treatments

Subsections 3.4.4 and 3.4.5 in the previous chapter discuss the issue of how writers' motivation or demotivation can be related to teacher and peer feedback, respectively. The vast majority of the research findings given in these two subsections came from descriptive and correlational studies, i.e., these studies depended mainly on learners' general motivational perceptions of teacher and peer feedback but without using or assessing their responses to particular instructional treatments. On the other hand, some studies had a closer look at teacher or peer feedback by examining the effectiveness of particular feedback provision techniques on learners' writing motivation. In some instructional research of teacher feedback, the main focus was on writing performance, whereas motivation was addressed as a secondary variable. The studies reported by Duijnhouwer, Prins, and Stokking (2010, 2012) and Tang and Liu (2017) are examples of this feedback research. In contrast to these studies, writing motivation was addressed as a main variable in other instructional teacher feedback research reported by Hyland and Hyland (2001), Mahfoodh (2017), and Yao (2019).

The two studies conducted by Tang and Liu (2017) and Yao (2019) investigated the motivating effects of different written corrective feedback techniques. Tang and Liu's (2017) study compared the influence of indirect coded corrective feedback combined with short affective comments and the indirect coded corrective feedback alone on student writers' motivation. In their study, 56 Chinese L2 7th graders were given the two types of feedback on three writing tasks they performed at successive times. The students in the comparison and treatment groups (n = 28 each) had to complete a six-item questionnaire, which also included two open-ended questions. The affective feedback comments the treatment group received:

> [C]onsisted of either a short English sentence or phrase expressing the teachers' affective comments or feelings about the students' writings, such as "A lovely opening!"; "I like your story, and you didn't make many mistakes."; "I am really happy that you used a new word you learned not too long ago."; and "I enjoy reading your story!" (p. 29)

Though Tang and Liu found no significant differences in the writing performance of the two groups, their study revealed a positive impact for the affective comments on the students' motives to improve their writing. That is why they conclude that the two feedback techniques are complementary.

Recently, Yao (2019) explored the impact of the indirect feedback and direct written corrective feedback on Chinese high school L2 writing anxiety. For four weeks, the students in one group received indirect written corrective feedback on their texts, whereas those in the other group received direct written corrective feedback. Their writing anxiety was measured before and after the treatment using Tsai's (2008) scale, and interviews were also held with them in the two occasions. Both quantitative and qualitative data revealed that direct written corrective feedback is more effective in alleviating the students' writing anxiety, and is also preferred by students than the indirect type.

The two studies reported by Hyland and Hyland (2001) and Mahfoodh (2017) looked at student writers' affective responses to the types of teacher written comments. In their oft-cited work, Hyland and Hyland (2001) examined the motivational strategies and impact of teacher written feedback. Their data came from the teachers' written comments on students' drafts, interviews with six L2 students, and their two teachers' thought verbalizations while providing feedback on students' texts and classroom observations. The students in this study reported that the lack of positive comments caused them to become demotivated and to receive teacher feedback negatively. As for the two teachers, they reported attempting to avoid demotivating the students with much criticism by mitigating their negative comments. Such mitigation was accomplished by using some strategies, including paired act patterns (combining critical comments with either praise, suggestions, or both), hedges, personal attribution (criticisms reflecting a personal opinion and teachers' responses as ordinary readers), and interrogative syntax (constructing the criticism in an interrogative form).

Mahfoodh (2017) also examined Yemeni students' emotional responses to their teachers' feedback. The students in his study produced three text drafts. After writing the first draft, they were provided with feedback on it, and then they were asked to verbalize their thoughts while reading the comments given on their texts. This was followed by conducting interviews with them to explore their emotional responses to these comments. Following their writing of the second and final drafts, the students were interviewed about their affective responses to and handling of teacher feedback. The feedback provided on the students' drafts included the following types: direct coded, giving factual information, giving praise, grammar/editing, making a request, negative evaluation, and reflective statements. Mahfoodh's (2017) study showed the association between students' emotional responses to teacher feedback and their use of it in making the required changes to the texts. The study also indicates the strong demotivating influence of teachers' overuse of corrective feedback. Specifically, it revealed that the students "felt frustrated when they read or saw too many written comments in red colour on their drafts. ... [and felt] disappointed when they found their drafts full of comments, corrections, circles, and marks in red colour". (p. 64)

On the other hand, the two studies reported by Duijnhouwer et al. (2010, 2012) tested the effectiveness of providing feedback using one systematic way on students' writing motivation. Specifically, these two studies used progress feedback and providing suggestions for improving performance, respectively. Duijnhouwer et al. (2010) studied the effect of providing university students in the Netherlands with progress feedback on their writing mastery goal and self-efficacy. They define progress feedback as "the information that performance improved, compared to the previous performance on a similar task" (p. 54). The participant students in the progress feedback group performed three assignments over six weeks and received progress feedback via a form in which the teachers ticked the writing performance aspects in which they showed improvement compared to the previous task, and also provided them with explanation for such improvement. The students' writing mastery goal and self-efficacy beliefs were measured using a motivation questionnaire before and after the treatment. Duijnhouwer and her colleagues found that the progress feedback technique improved the students' self-efficacy beliefs but not their writing mastery goals. They ascribed the lack of improvement in the students' writing mastery goals to the short time of their treatment. According to them, "students' mastery goal requires more progress messages than provided in this experiment. To provide students with more and nevertheless realistic progress messages would have required extension of the experiment over a longer time span" (p. 68).

In a later study, Duijnhouwer et al. (2012) examined the influence of providing students with feedback suggestions for improving performance on their motivation. This feedback type is an instructional scaffolding technique through which the teacher tries to help students close the gap between their real performance and the target one. Their treatment is based on the hypothesis that if learners' performance improvement is under their control, their ability beliefs will be fostered. Duijnhouwer and her colleagues describe the feedback treatment they used as follows:

> In the feedback on the first draft, the teachers provided students in the experimental feedback condition with improvement strategies. Teachers were provided with a list of several possible strategies per criterion. Strategies concerned the writing process and aimed at particular text aspects. Examples of strategies are: "You may summarize each paragraph in a few words. These words may help you to order the paragraphs so that the order supports your line of reasoning. You may try to explain to yourself the logic of why a specific paragraph follows another"; and "You may read the text out loud to hear where sentences do not flow smoothly". Part of the strategies suggested the involvement of others. For example: "You may ask someone else to read your paper and ask whether he or she understands the content, or where more clarification is needed". (p. 175)

The study looked at how this experimental treatment relates to learners' writing self-efficacy and their writing mastery and performance goals. Contrarily to their expectations, they found that performance improvement suggestion feedback did not result in improving the students' self-efficacy beliefs, but it positively promoted their writing mastery goals. They also found positive effects for the process-oriented improvement feedback on writing motivation. Overall, the results of this study emphasize the need for using the feedback strategies fitting closely with L2 learners' writing abilities.

Compared to teacher feedback studies, the studies examining the impact of peer feedback on students' writing motivation are much fewer in number. The studies reported by Wang (2014), Yu and Hu (2017), Han and Xu (2019), and Yu, Zhang, Zheng, Yuan, and Zhang (2019) are examples of these few ones. In all these studies, the feedback was provided through oral peer response sessions, i.e., it only included students' oral comments on their peers' writing.

In Wang's (2014) study, the students wrote multiple text drafts and exchanged feedback with their peers through rubric-referenced oral response sessions, each lasted for 40 minutes, over four weeks. Prior to conducting these oral peer response sessions, the students were provided with instructions on how to provide feedback and how to use the rubric. They also received teacher feedback on the second and third drafts written after holding the oral peer response sessions. Wang collected the data using interviews, students' reflective essays, and a peer feedback usefulness questionnaire. The study revealed a gradual decrease in the students' perceptions of the usefulness of peer feedback activities, and found that such perceived usefulness was negatively influenced by the students' unfamiliarity with the assigned essay topics, their limited English proficiency levels and concerns with interpersonal relationship, and the short time allocated to these activities. Similar results were found by Yu and Hu (2017), who engaged two Chinese university L2 students in drafting five essays based on oral peer feedback activities with two other classmates. The students received feedback provision training from their teacher. Yu and Hu collected their data through interviewing the students, video-recording their peer feedback activities, and stimulated recalls. Their study revealed that the students' attitudes towards peer feedback depend mainly on their perceived benefits and their motives and goals for peer feedback.

Drawing on semi-structured interviews, stimulated recalls, audio-recorded oral peer feedback conferences, and text draft analysis, Yu, Zhang, Zheng, Yuan, and Zhang (2019) looked at MA students' motivational, behavioural, and cognitive engagement with their peers' feedback on thesis drafts. To examine the affective or motivational dimensions in their interviews with the students, they used questions like these: "How did you feel upon receiving peers' feedback on your first draft? Are you happy after talking to peers? Are you anxious?" (p. 54). Yu and his colleagues found that while the students valued peer feedback experiences, they neglected handling much of the comments given by their peers and engaged superficially with them from the cognitive dimension. In Yu's (2020) study, the students' difficulties in peer feedback also resulted from their doubts about the usefulness and correctness of their peers' comments, and from their concerns about criticism. With regard to this little cognitive and behavioural engagement with peer feedback, Han and Xu's (2019) study confirms that teacher scaffolding is conditional to fostering their positive attitudes towards peer feedback on writing.

Overall, the reviewed research indicates that peer feedback activities are not always conducive to motivating students' engagement in writing. Compared to teacher feedback, peer feedback activities are more complicated in their implementation and interaction with writers' motivation.

That is why the implementation of these activities requires many planning procedures and much caution. As for teacher feedback, the studies reviewed in this section indicate that student writers get demotivated by much criticism and corrective feedback, and that their engagement in writing is stimulated by teacher suggestions. Though the teacher feedback research findings given here are generally consistent with those of correlational research (see subsection 3.4.4 in the previous chapter), they provide a more realistic picture about students' affective responses due to their dependence on tested instructional treatments.

4.5 Genre-based instruction

Genre-based writing instruction is an explicit, needs-based, and consciousness-raising type of teaching, and it focuses on familiarizing students with the communicative purposes the linguistic structures, and aspects of specific genres (Hyland, 2016). It emphasizes meeting learners' linguistic and communicative needs (Leki, Cumming, & Silva, 2008; Paltridge, 2013). That is why this type of instruction is particularly important in L2 writing settings. According to Van de Poel and Gasiorek (2012), the importance of genre-based instruction lies in enabling learners to be successful members in their academic discipline community by familiarizing them with its norms, and language and genre features constituting its academic discourse. From the motivational angle, Han and Hiver (2018) view that the scaffolding and target genre consciousness-raising elements in genre-based instruction could assist in building learners' writing self-efficacy and alleviating their writing apprehension. Though much has been written on genre-based writing instruction (e.g., Badger & White, 2000; Devitt, 2004; Hyland, 2003, 2004, 2016; Myskow & Gordon, 2010; Tardy, 2009), very few studies investigated its impact on writers' motivation. In a study whose main focus was using genre-based tasks for enhancing L2 students' linguistic knowledge and writing performance and awareness, Yasuda (2011) found through the interview data that some of her participants developed better confidence in their writing ability due to their improved language knowledge.

Van de Poel and Gasiorek (2012) and Han and Hiver (2018) reported two unique studies about the impact of genre-based writing instruction on writers' motivation. Van de Poel and Gasiorek (2012) integrated genre-based instruction in two writing courses taught at a Flemish university. The genre-based instruction was implemented into two writing courses taught to English majors over two academic years. At the beginning and end of each of the two writing courses, the students completed a seven-item scale assessing their writing self-ability beliefs and feelings when discussing their writing with teachers and peers. Van de Poel and Gasiorek stated that the genre-based instruction they used aimed at socializing students with their academic discipline genres. They describe the genre-based instruction provided to their study participants as follows:

> [I]nstruction includes…discussion of what constitutes academic style and register (explicitly discussing the constructs of register and audience, and providing students with banks of words and phrases) as well as an introduction to relevant terminology and metalanguage. Thus, each course includes both socialization and skills components, and both courses aim to raise students' awareness of features of academic writing as well as give them practical experience with analyzing, evaluating, and producing academic writing. For each topic each course covers, students are first presented with short text excerpts (drawn from a corpus of actual work of past years' students) and are guided through a critical analysis of the text as it relates to the topic (e.g., what in the example is or is not correct or appropriate). Then, students write a similar text component themselves on the basis of an excerpt. … Before written assignments are handed in, students learn to work with a rubric listing the key qualities and components their text should have…[and] submit their texts for peer review. … Students then have the opportunity to revise their text, incorporating their peer's comments, before the assignment is handed in for correction by the instructor, who uses the same rubric students were given to evaluate the text. In summary, the pedagogical approach in the academic writing courses borrows from several traditions. … [T]he language learning is tailored to the students' academic purposes, genres and disciplines. … Students are first exposed to "writing-through-reading", are gradually introduced to the different components and aspects of academic writing, first receptively (via questions) and then productively (though still guided by a text excerpt). (pp. 29–298)

The data collected by Van de Poel and Gasiorek indicates that upon the completion of each writing course, the students significantly viewed themselves as more competent writers, and felt more comfortable discussing their written texts with peers and teachers and editing them.

Han and Hiver (2018) also examined the motivating impact of integrating genre-based English writing instruction in three large public middle schools in South Korea. To trace the changes in their middle 7th grader participants' writing self-efficacy and apprehension, they used a questionnaire assessing these constructs prior to the instruction and after it. They also relied on students' reflective journal and interviews. The genre-based instruction was employed in a writing course in nine weeks over one semester. Below is a description of the activities implemented in this course:

> The early weeks involved building context by examining the features and goals of the target genre; several classes were then spent on explicitly modeling and analyzing sample texts with a focus on the genre structure and language conventions; following this, students participated in collaborative writing and were familiarized with evaluative rubrics for

the target genre; individual students completed an independent composition in the final weeks through steps such as planning, writing, revising, and editing their own text. (p. 47)

Han and Hiver found that the genre-based instruction influenced their middle school participants' writing self-efficacy level positively. They attributed this increase to the vicarious and writing mastery experiences the students had throughout the instruction received. Their quantitative data, however, showed elevated levels in the students' writing apprehension. This was ascribed to the students' previous poor writing experiences and their unfamiliarity with the writing of the target genre. Contrarily to the quantitative results, the qualitative data revealed a decrease in the students' writing apprehension, but Han and Hiver acknowledged that they did not give adequate consideration to tracing the qualitative changes in their participants' writing motivation.

The results of the above three studies (i.e., Han & Hiver, 2018; Van de Poel & Gasiorek, 2012; Yasuda, 2011) congruently emphasize the positive impact of genre-based writing instruction on fostering student writers' self-ability beliefs. It is very likely that students' acquisition of the target genre linguistic features is what specifically enhances their writing self-ability perceptions. This conclusion concurs with the descriptive and correlational research findings given in subsections 3.3.1 and 3.3.2 in chapter 3.

4.6 Task interest-based instruction

Task interest-based instruction studies focus on motivating students to write by engaging them in writing about topics of their own interest. The task interest-based instruction used in previous studies depended on pedagogical guidelines such as familiarizing students with the target genre characteristics and text schema, and getting them to write collaboratively and in a supportive environment. Compared to the other motivational instructional types of writing, task interest-based instruction has received little attention.

Two early task interest-based interventional studies were reported by Hidi and McLaren (1991) and Hidi and Anderson (1992). The results of these two studies indicate that topic interest can only be conducive to students' writing motivation if they have adequate background knowledge about the writing topic. For example, Hidi and McLaren (1991) engaged 6th graders in writing about four topics of different interest and knowledge levels (i.e., high-interest/moderate background knowledge versus low-interest/high background knowledge). Their study results imply that prior topic knowledge mediates the motivational influence of writing topic interest.

In a later study, Hidi, Berndorff, and Ainley (2002) tried to develop 8th graders' argumentative writing self-efficacy and attitude using a pre-/post-test intervention focusing on creating a positive writing learning environment through topic interest and knowledge. For over eight weeks, their participant students were engaged in writing about argumentative topics of their choice in collaborative activities, and they were provided with instruction about the characteristics of argumentative texts and the procedural knowledge of argumentative writing. The results of this study showed a positive change in the students' attitude to argumentative writing and increase in their writing self-efficacy. Hidi and her colleagues conclude that:

> [G]eneral interest in writing, enjoying writing in several genres and feeling efficacious about such writing are closely related. This relation seems stable over time (pre- to post-test) and suggests that being interested in writing, enjoying writing in various genres, and having a sense of being able to do so develop in concert and may have reciprocal developmental influences on each other. (p. 442)

In another study, De Bernardi and Antolini (2007) used task interest as a motivational element to develop 8th graders' attitude towards argumentative writing and their writing self-efficacy. They tried to foster students' emotional involvement by: making use of the writing topics of interest to them, raising their awareness of argumentative text schema, providing them with collaborative writing learning environment, and enabling them to use enabling information and resources available on the Internet. Based on their research findings, De Bernardi and Antolini conclude that when students write about the topics important to them, their writing performance is enhanced and this in turn develops their writing self-efficacy and positive attitude towards writing.

All the above studies were conducted in L1 settings. In an L2 context, Lo and Hyland (2007) conducted a three-month action research study to examine the impact of including writing tasks associated with students' life experiences and real audiences on their writing motivation. They collected their data using focus group interviews, research-journal, a short questionnaire, and students' written reflections. Lo and Hyland's study showed that the students became motivated to perform the newly integrated writing tasks due to their relevance, authenticity, and real audience inclusion.

The results of the above studies generally indicate the importance of topic interest and familiarity in enhancing students' writing motivation. These also support the other relevant insights from researchers' observation and correlational research findings (e.g. Atay & Kurt, 2006; Behizadeh & Engelhard, 2014; Boscolo & Cisotto, 1999; Walker, 2003).

4.7 Therapeutic training

Unlike the previously reviewed types of instructional research, therapeutic training studies do not depend on fostering students' writing motivation by meeting their knowledge or composing process needs or changing their writing learning environment. Instead, these therapeutic studies deal directly with students' emotional and affective perceptions about writing and try to optimize them through particular motivational training. That is why they draw mainly upon psychotherapy or counselling principles. The therapeutic training studies of writing motivation are very scarce. The earliest attempt was perhaps made by Fox (1980), who treated writing anxiety by helping students learn in a non-threatening environment involving the use of free writing activities and teacher-student conferencing. In later research, four therapeutic training techniques have been proposed: writing anxiety workshop (Bloom, 1982, 1985), visualization (Ayres & Hopf, 1991), mindful breathing (Britt, Pribesh, Hinton-Johnson, & Gupta, 2018), and writing anxiety groups (Wynne, Guo, & Wang, 2014).

Ayres and Hopf (1991) tried to reduce students' writing apprehension using visualization, a procedure that potentially stimulates students' positive thinking and helps them avoid negative thoughts. Their previous successful experience with experimenting visualization in reducing speech anxiety (e.g., Ayres, 1988; Ayres & Hopf, 1985) encouraged them to use it in reducing writers' apprehension. Through this procedure, they used a visualization script to engage their students in imagining themselves writing two assignments. In each visualization session, the students were asked to sit comfortably, close their eyes, take deep breaths, and to imagine performing a news story writing task. The students were specifically told to imagine themselves feeling "thoroughly prepared for the task at hand" and confident in their ability to complete the whole task and its process stages (text planning, writing, and revising) very successfully, and to end the task with positive beliefs about the quality of the text they have written (p. 190). The students were also told to follow the same visualization procedure whenever performing any writing task in the course they were studying. Based on the results of their pre-/post-testing data and their participants' responses to the multidimensional Daly-Miller (1975) WAT, Ayres and Hopf conclude that the visualization procedure is potentially effective in fostering students' feelings about writing (i.e., their attitudes and enjoyment of writing), but not their ability beliefs.

Britt et al. (2018) used the mindful breathing technique to reduce students' writing apprehension. In using mindful-breathing, Britt and her colleagues depended on psychiatry literature (e.g., Kabat-Zinn, 2003; Kabat-Zinn et al., 1992). According to Britt and her colleagues:

> During mindful breathing, the individual redirects the mind's attention from discursive thoughts to the inhaling and exhaling of breath. Returning one's focus, time and again, to the breath heightens awareness of two critical concepts: (1) the mind has a propensity to wander and (2) the mind's wanderings correspond with emotional responses.... Mindfulness-based anxiety reduction programs typically feature weekly sessions of training and participation in mindfulness practices,

including silent and guided sitting meditations, body-scan, eating and walking meditations. Also common are yoga practice and education regarding the seven principles of mindfulness: acceptance, non-judging, non-striving, beginner's mind, letting-go, patience, and trust, as well as the mindfulness principles of de-centering and non-attachment. (pp. 695–696)

In their four-week intervention, Britt and her colleagues engaged a group of community college students who were studying a writing course in eight short sessions (of about 3–5 minutes), in which they acquainted them with mindful breathing and got them to practice it. The pre-/post-testing procedures in this study showed alleviation in the students' writing apprehension levels.

Bloom (1982, 1985) and Wynne et al. (2014) propose treating graduate students' writing apprehension by using what they have labelled as the "writing anxiety workshop" and the "writing anxiety group", respectively. In her qualitative reports, Bloom (1982, 1985) used a multisession writing anxiety workshop to help graduate students overcome their writing anxiety. In these sessions, each student individually conversed with Bloom about the problems resulting from their writing anxiety. She tried to help them meet the writing requirements in their study programme and guide them for how to monitor their writing progress. Bloom's suggested remedy for students' writing apprehension was based on tracing the contextual sources causing it. She concludes that:

> Teachers, dissertation advisors, researchers, counselors, friends, or others working with anxious writers need to understand the writing problems as fully as possible in the appropriate contexts in order to provide specific, workable solutions adapted to the writer's temperament and to the performance of multiple roles in multiple contexts. An anxious writer, fully understood in context, can be more readily helped to be less anxious, more productive-to be simply, a writer. (p. 133).

On the other hand, Wynne et al. (2014) propose using the writing anxiety group procedure to help graduate students alleviate their stress and anxious writing feelings, but they have not experimented their proposed training. Wynne and his colleagues' proposed treatment draws much upon the insights gained from therapeutic writing (Hagedorn, 2011; Riordan, 1996; Tubman, Montgomery, & Wagner, 2001) and group counseling literature (Gladding, 2012; Corey, 2012; Pauley, 2004). According to them, the writing anxiety group is a self-help one that aims at assisting demotivated students in overcoming their writing motivation and performance problem. The group is supposed to include 8–10 graduate students, who will be meeting several times during a given writing course. The teacher (the leader of the group) will work with a counseling specialist (the co-leader). The leader will implement the writing activities and tasks, whereas the co-leader will facilitate the emotional relief during group interactions by stimulating them to disclose their thoughts and feelings. At the beginning of the intervention, the group members are supposed to complete a writing motivation scale so as to have sense of their motivational levels. The members of the group will express their writing feelings and problems through free writing and keeping a weekly journal, in which they record their writing-related thoughts and feelings. During these weekly meeting sessions, the student members of the groups will share their journals and read them to each other. Combining free writing and group interactions in such way is expected to result in positive therapeutic effects. According to Wynne and his colleagues, getting students to read about the affective dimensions of writing will help them become aware of their writing processes and habits, recognize the sources of their writing motivation, and know how to overcome their writing problems and demotivation. Finally, a follow-up meeting will be held one month after the end of all sessions. In this follow-up meeting, the student members will discuss the writing process and motivation changes they have experienced since completing the group meetings.

As noted, all the above therapeutic training procedures have been used or proposed in L1 writing contexts. Though these studies were all limited to treating students' writing apprehension, their use of the multidimensional Daly-Miller (1975) WAT indicates the embedded inclusion of writers' self-ability beliefs in such treatments. As indicated in the above descriptions of the treatments, they are also concerned with fostering students' writing confidence beliefs.

4.8 Conclusion

In this chapter, different types of writing motivation instructional studies have been reviewed and discussed. As noted in the above sections, some types of instructional studies have been only concerned with L1 writing contexts (i.e., writing strategy and therapeutic training studies), while other types have been more commonly used in L2 ones (i.e., feedback instructional treatment and genre-based writing instruction studies). Table (4.1) provides a summary of the main types of writing motivation instructional studies.

The instructional types have received varied research attention. For example, a much fewer writing motivation studies have dealt with genre-based and task interest-based instruction and therapeutic training as compared to the other three types (i.e., technology-supported, strategy instruction, and feedback instructional treatments). The place of writing motivation constructs in these studies is also worth noting. In many of the studies, writing motivation variables have been dealt with peripherally when compared to writing performance aspects. Meanwhile, the motivational constructs, addressed in the instructional studies, were limited to

Table 4.1 A summary of the main types of writing motivation instructional studies

Type of instructional studies	Types of treatments	Writing motivation constructs addressed
Technology-supported writing instruction studies	• Word processer use (Sullivan & Pratt, 1996) • Computer-based conferencing (Skinner & Austin, 1999) • WebQuest use (Chuo, 2007) • Blog-mediated instruction (e.g., Zhang et al., 2014) • Wiki-mediated instruction (e.g., Li et al., 2012) • Multimodal composing tasks (e.g., Knobel & Lankshear, 2014)	Writing apprehension Attitude towards writing Writing self-efficacy
Writing strategy instruction studies	• Self-regulatory strategy instruction (e.g., Limpo & Alves, 2014) • General writing strategy instruction (e.g., De Smedt et al., 2019)	Writing self-ability beliefs Perceived value of writing
Feedback instructional treatment studies	• Teacher corrective feedback techniques (Tang & Liu, 2017; Yao, 2019) • Teacher feedback comments (Hyland & Hyland, 2001; Mahfoodh, 2017) • Progress feedback (Duijnhouwer et al., 2010) • Feedback suggestions for improving performance (Duijnhouwer et al., 2012) • Peer feedback (e.g., Wang, 2014)	Attitudes towards writing and towards teacher and peer feedback Writing anxiety Writing self-efficacy beliefs Writing mastery goals
Genre-based writing instruction	• Genre-based instruction combined with peer assessment (Van de Poel & Gasiorek, 2012) • Genre-based instruction combined with collaborative writing (Han & Hiver, 2018)	Writing self-ability beliefs and apprehension
Task interest-based writing instruction	• Task interest interventions (e.g., Hidi & McLaren, 1991) • Task interest interventions with collaborative activities (e.g., Hidi et al., 2002) • Using authentic writing topics relevant to students' life experiences (Lo & Hyland, 2007)	Attitude towards writing & writing self-efficacy
Therapeutic training	• Writing anxiety workshop (Bloom, 1985) • Visualization (Ayres & Hopf, 1991) • Writing anxiety group (Wynne et al., 2014) • Mindful breathing (Britt et al., 2018)	Writing apprehension & ability beliefs

writing dispositional perceptions and/or self-ability beliefs in the majority of the cases. Exceptional cases, for example, include researching writing anxiety and mastery goals in the two feedback studies reported by Yao (2019) and Duijnhouwer et al. (2010), respectively. In many studies, the measurement of writing motivation constructs seems to be problematic. This is obvious, particularly in the technology-supported instruction and feedback treatment studies where many researchers depended on short scales which include items synthesized from different sources. In some other cases, the motivation constructs addressed were labelled inappropriately by using broad terms such as writing motivation. These problematic issues may have resulted from the researchers' inadequate background knowledge about the writing motivation research area.

The effectiveness of the used instructional treatments in developing student writers' motivation varied from one type of studies to another. As noted, the lowest degree of the reported effectiveness is perhaps in the peer feedback and self-regulatory strategy instruction studies, while the highest degree is in the genre-based instruction and therapeutic training studies. The studies dealing with other instructional types yielded mixed results. Noted also is the variance found between the findings of the qualitative and quantitative studies addressing the same type of instruction. This is clear, for instance, in the studies dealing with blog-integrated writing instruction. Overall, there are many issues that need to be addressed in future instructional writing motivation research. These issues will be highlighted in the final chapter of the book.

References

Arslan, R. Ş., & Şahin-Kızıl, A. (2010). How can the use of blog software facilitate the writing process of English language learners? *Computer-Assisted Language Learning, 23*(3), 183–197. doi: 10.1080/09588221.2010.486575

Atay, D., & Kurt, G. (2006). Prospective teachers and L2 writing anxiety. *Asian EFL Journal, 8*(4), 100–118.

Ayres, J. (1988). Coping with speech anxiety: The power of positive thinking. *Communication Education, 37*(4), 289–296. doi: 10.1080/03634528809378730

Ayres, J., & Hopf, T. (1985). Visualization: A means of reducing speech anxiety. *Communication Education, 34*(4), 318–323. doi: 10.1080/03634528509378623

Ayres, J., & Hopf, T. (1991) Coping with writing apprehension. *Journal of Applied Communication Research, 19*(3), 186–196. doi: 10.1080/00909889109365302

Badger, R., & White, G. (2000). A process genre approach to teaching writing. *ELT Journal, 54*(2), 153–160. doi: 10.1093/elt/54.2.153

Behizadeh, N., & Engelhard, G., Jr. (2014). Development and validation of a scale to measure perceived authenticity in writing. *Assessing Writing, 21*, 18–36. doi:10.1016/j.asw.2014.02.001

Bloom, L. (1982). Why graduate students can't write: Implications of research on writing anxiety for graduate education. *Journal of Advanced Composition, 2*(1/2), 103–117.

Bloom, L. (1985). Anxious writers in context: Graduate school and beyond. In M. Ross (Ed.), *When a writer can't write*, (pp. 119–133). New York, NY: Guilford Press.

Boscolo, P., & Cisotto, L. (1999). *Making writing an interesting activity in elementary school*. Unpublished manuscript.

Britt, M., Pribesh, S., Hinton-Johnson, K., & Gupta, A. (2018). Effect of a mindful breathing intervention on community college students' writing apprehension and writing performance. *Community College Journal of Research and Practice, 42*(10), 693–707. doi: 10.1080/10668926.2017.1352545

Bubas, G., Kovacic, A., & Zlatovic, M. (2007). *Evaluation of activity with a wiki system in teaching English as a second language*. Proceedings of the International Conference ICT for Language Learning, (pp. 201–21). Florence, Italy.

Chen, P. J. (2016). Learners' metalinguistic and affective performance in blogging to write. *Computer-Assisted Language Learning, 29*(4), 790–814. doi: 10.1080/09588221.2015.1068813

Chao, Y.-C. J., & Lo, H.-C. (2011). Students' perceptions of Wikibased collaborative writing for learners of English as a foreign language. *Interactive Learning Environments, 19*(4), 395–411. doi: 10.1080/10494820903298662

Chuo, T. I. (2007). The effects of the WebQuest writing instruction program on EFL learners' writing performance, writing apprehension, and perception. *TESL-EJ, 11*(3), 1–27.

Corey, G. (2012). *Theory & practice of group counseling* (8th ed.). Belmont, CA: Thomson Higher Education.

Daly, J., & Miller, M. D. (1975). The empirical development of an instrument to measure writing apprehension. *Research in the Teaching of English, 9*(3), 242–249.

Davidson, R. (2012). Wiki use that increases communication and collaboration motivation. *Journal of Learning Design, 5*(2), 28–39. doi: 10.5204/jld.v5i2.110

De Bernardi, B., & Antolini, E. (2007). Fostering students' willingness and interest in argumentative writing: An intervention study. In S. Hidi, & P. Boscolo (Eds.), *Motivation and writing: Research and school practice*, (pp. 183–202). Dordrecht, The Netherlands: Kluwer.

De Smedt, F., Graham, S., & Van Keer, H. (2019). The bright and dark side of writing motivation: Effects of explicit instruction and peer assistance. *The Journal of Educational Research, 112*(2), 152–167. doi: 10.1080/00220671.2018.1461598

Ducate, L. C., Anderson, L. L., & Moreno, N. (2011). Wading through the world of wikis: An analysis of three wiki projects. *Foreign Language Annals, 44*(3), 495–524. doi: 10.1111/j.1944-9720.2011.01144.x

Devitt, A. (2004). *Writing genres*. Carbondale, IL: Southern Illinois University Press.

Duijnhouwer, H., Prins, F., & Stokking, J. K. M. (2010). Progress feedback effects on students' writing mastery goal, self-efficacy beliefs, and performance. *Educational Research and Evaluation, 16*(1), 53–74. doi: 10.1080/13803611003711393

Duijnhouwer, H., Prins, F., & Stokking, K. M. (2012). Feedback providing improvement strategies and reflection on feedback use: Effects on students' writing motivation, process, and performance. *Learning and Instruction, 22*, 171–184. doi:10.1016/j.learninstruc.2011.10.003.

Edwards-Groves, J. (2011). The multimodal writing process: Changing practices in contemporary classrooms. *Language and Education, 25*(1), 49–64. doi: 10.1080/09500782.2010.523468

Fathi, J., Ahmadnejad, M., & Yousofi, N. (2019). Effects of blog-mediated writing instruction on L2 writing motivation, self-efficacy, and self-regulation: A mixed methods study. *Journal of Research in Applied Linguistics, 10*(2), 159–181. doi: 10.22055/RALS.2019.14722

Fox, R. F. (1980). Treatment of writing apprehension and its effects on composition. *Research in the Teaching of English, 14,* 39–49.

Gladding, S. T. (2012). *Groups: Counseling specialty* (6th ed.). Upper Saddle River, NJ: Merrill.

Garcia-Sanchez, J., & Fidalgo-Redondo, R. (2006). Effects of two types of self-regulatory instruction programs on students with learning disabilities in writing products, processes, and self-efficacy. *Learning Disability Quarterly, 29,* 181–211. doi:10.2307/30035506

Graham, S., & Harris, K. (2014). Conducting high quality writing intervention research: Twelve recommendations. *Journal of Writing Research, 62*(2), 89–123. doi: 0.17239/jowr-2014.06.02.1

Graham, S., & Harris, K. R. (1989a). Components analysis of cognitive strategy instruction: Effects on learning disabled students' compositions and self-efficacy. *Journal of Educational Psychology, 81,* 353–361. doi:10.1037/0022-0663.81.3.353

Graham, S., & Harris, K. R. (1989b). Improving learning disabled students' skills at composing essays: Self-instructional strategy training. *Exceptional Children, 56,* 201–214. doi:10.1177/001440298905600305

Graham, S., Harris, K. R., & Mason, L. (2005). Improving the writing performance, knowledge, and self-efficacy of struggling young writers: The effects of self-regulated strategy development. *Contemporary Educational Psychology, 30,* 207–241. doi:10.1016/j.cedpsych.2004.08.001.

Graham, S., & MacArthur, C. (1988). Improving learning disabled students' skills at revising essays produced on a word processor: Self-instructional strategy training. *Journal of Special Education, 22*(2), 133–152. doi: 10.1177/002246698802200202

Hafner, C. A., & Miller, L. (2011). Fostering learner autonomy in English for science: A collaborative digital video project in a technological learning environment. *Language Learning & Technology, 15*(1), 68–86.

Hagedorn, W. B. (2011). Using therapeutic letters to navigate resistance and ambivalence: Experiential implications for group counseling. *Journal of Addictions & Offender Counseling, 31,* 108–126. doi:10.1002/j.2161-1874.2011.tb00071.x

Han, J., & Hiver, P. (2018). Genre-based L2 writing instruction and writing-specific psychological factors: The dynamics of change. *Journal of Second Language Writing, 40,* 44–59. doi:10.1016/j.jslw.2018.03.001

Han, Y., & Xu, Y. (2019). The development of student feedback literacy: The influences of teacher feedback on peer feedback. *Assessment & Evaluation in Higher Education.* doi: 10.1080/02602938.2019.1689545

Harris, K. R., Graham, S., Mason, L. H., McKeown, D., & Olinghouse, N. (2018). Self-regulated strategy development in writing: A classroom example of developing executive function processes and future directions. In L. Meltzer (Ed.), *Executive function in education: From theory to practice,* (pp. 326–356). New York: Guilford Press.

Hert, R. S. (1988). *A study of one computer-driven text analysis package for collegiate student writers.* PhD dissertation, University of North Texas, USA.

Hidi, S., & Anderson, V. (1992). Situational interest and its impact on reading and expository writing. In K. A. Renninger, S. Hidi, & A. Krapp (Eds.), *The role of interest in learning and development,* (pp. 215–238). Hillsdale, NJ: Erlbaum.

Hidi, S., Berndorff, D., & Ainley, M. (2002). Children's argument writing, interest, and self-efficacy: An intervention study. *Learning and Instruction, 12,* 429–446. doi:10.1016/S0959-4752(01)00009-3

Hidi, S., & McLaren, J. A. (1991). Motivational factors and writing: The role of topic interestingness. *European Journal of Psychology of Education, 6,* 187–197. doi:10.1007/BF03191937

Hyland, K. (2003). Genre-based pedagogies: A social response to process. *Journal of Second Language Writing, 12,* 17–29. doi:10.1016/S1060-3743(02)00124-8

Hyland, K. (2004). *Genre and second language writing.* Ann Arbor, MI: University of Michigan Press.

Hyland, K. (2016). *Teaching and researching writing* (3rd ed.). New York: Routledge.

Hyland, F., & Hyland, K. (2001). Sugaring the pill: Praise and criticism in written feedback. *Journal of Second Language Writing, 10,* 185–212. doi:10.1016/S1060-3743(01)00038-8

Jiang, L., & Luk, J. (2016). Multimodal composing as a learning activity in English classrooms: Inquiring into the sources of its motivational capacity. *System, 59,* 1–11. doi:10.1016/j.system.2016.04.001

Johnson, N. D. (1987). *Effects of inservice training on writing apprehension and computer anxiety in elementary school teachers.* PhD dissertation, The University of Wisconsin- Madison, USA.

Kabat-Zinn, J. (2003). Mindfulness-based interventions in context: Past, present, and future. *Clinical Psychology: Science and Practice, 10,* 144–156. doi:10.1093/clipsy.bpg016

Kabat-Zinn, J., Massion, A. O., Kristeller, J., Peterson, L. G., Fletcher, K. E., Pbert, L., & Santorelli, S. F. (1992). Effectiveness of a meditation-based stress reduction program in the treatment of anxiety disorders. *American Journal of Psychiatry, 149,* 936–943. doi:10.1176/ajp.149.7.936

Kassem, M. A. M. (2017). Developing business writing skills and reducing writing anxiety of EFL learners through wikis. *English Language Teaching, 10*(3), 151–163. doi:10.5539/elt.v10n3p151

Knobel, M., & Lankshear, C. (2014). Studying new literacies. *Journal of Adolescent and Adult Literacy, 58*(2), 97–101. doi: 10.1002/jaal.314

Kramer, I. M., & Kusurkar, R. A. (2017). Science-writing in the blogosphere as a tool to promote autonomous motivation in education. *The Internet and Higher Education, 35,* 48–62. doi:10.1016/j.iheduc.2017.08.001

Lee, L. (2010). Fostering reflective writing and interactive exchange through blogging in an advanced language course. *ReCALL, 22*(2), 212–227. doi: 10.1017/S095834401000008X

Leki, I., Cumming, A., & Silva, T. (2008). *A synthesis of research on second language writing in English.* New York: Routledge.

Li, X.-S., Chu, S. K. W., & Ki, W. W. (2014). The effects of a wiki-based collaborative process writing pedagogy on writing ability and attitudes among upper primary school students in mainland China. *Computers & Education, 77,* 151–169. doi:10.1016/j.compedu.2014.04.019.

Li, X., Chu, S. K. W., Ki, W. W., & Woo, M. M. (2010). *Students and teacher's attitudes and perceptions toward collaborative writing with Wiki in a primary four Chinese classroom.* Paper presented at The 3rd International Conference "ICT for Language Learning", Florence, Italy.

Li, X., Chu, S. K. W., Ki, W. W., & Woo, M. M. (2012). Using a wiki-based collaborative process writing pedagogy to facilitate collaborative writing among Chinese primary school students. *Australasian Journal of Educational Technology, 28*(1), 159–181. doi: 10.14742/ajet.889

Limpo, T., & Alves, R. (2014). Implicit theories of writing and their impact on students' response to a SRSD intervention. *British Journal of Educational Psychology, 84*, 571–590. doi:10.1111/bjep.12042

Lin, M. H. (2014). Effects of classroom blogging on ESL student writers: An empirical reassessment. *The Asia-Pacific Education Researcher, 23*(3), 577–590. doi: 10.1007/s40299-013-0131-8

Lo, J., & Hyland, F. (2007). Enhancing students' engagement and motivation in writing: The case of primary students in Hong Kong. *Journal of Second Language Writing, 16*, 219–237. doi:10.1016/j.jslw.2007.06.002

Mabrito, M. (2000). Computer conversations and writing apprehension. *Business Communication Quarterly, 63*(1), 39–49. doi: 10.1177/108056990006300104

Mahfoodh, O. H. (2017). "I feel disappointed": EFL university students' emotional responses towards teacher written feedback. *Assessing Writing, 31*, 53–72. doi:10.1016/j.asw.2016.07.001

Mak, B., & Coniam, D. (2008). Using wikis to enhance and develop writing skills among secondary school students in Honk Kong. *System, 36*(3), 437–455. doi: 10.1016/j.system.2008.02.004

Myskow, G., & Gordon, K. (2010). A focus on purpose: Using a genre approach in an EFL writing class. *ELT Journal, 64*, 283–292. doi:10.1093/elt/ccp057

Nash, B. (2018). Exploring multimodal writing in secondary English classrooms: A literature review. *English Teaching: Practice & Critique, 17*(4), 342–356. doi: 10.1108/ETPC-01-2018-0012

Paltridge, B. (2013). Genre and English for specific purposes. In B. Paltridge, & S. Starfield (Eds.), *Handbook of English for specific purposes*, (pp. 347–366). Malden, MA: Wiley.

Pauley, D. (2004). Group therapy for dissertation-writers: The right modality for a struggling population. *Journal of College Student Psychotherapy, 18*(4), 25–43. doi: 10.1300/J035v18n04_04

Phinney, M. (1991). Word processing and writing apprehension in first and second language writers. *Computers & Composition, 11*(1), 65–82. doi: 10.1016/8755-4615(91)80039-G

Riordan, R. (1996). Scriptotherapy: Therapeutic writing as a counseling adjunct. *Journal of Counseling & Development, 74*, 263–269. doi:10.1002/j.1556-6676.1996.tb01863.x

Schleifer, S. N. (1992). *The effects of using computers in writing instruction on writing apprehension and attitude toward using computers.* PhD dissertation, Nova Southeastern University.

Skinner, B., & Austin, R. (1999). Computer conferencing: Does it motivate EFL students? *ELT Journal, 53*(4), 270–279. doi: 10.1093/eltj/53.4.270

Sawyer, R. J., Graham, S., & Harris, K. R. (1992). Direct teaching, strategy instruction, and strategy instruction with explicit self-regulation: Effects on the composition skills and self-efficacy of students with learning disabilities. *Journal of Educational Psychology, 84*(3), 340–352. doi: 10.1037/0022-0663.84.3.340

Schunk, D. H., & Swartz, C. W. (1991). Writing strategy instruction with gifted students: Effects of goals and feedback on self efficacy and skills. *Roeper Review*, *15*(4), 225–230. doi: 10.1080/02783199309553512

Smith, B. E. (2014). Beyond words: A review of research on adolescents and multimodal composition. In R. R. Ferdig, & K. E. Pytash (Eds.), *Exploring multimodal composition and digital writing*, (pp. 1–19). USA: Information Science Reference.

Sullivan, N., & Pratt, E. (1996). A comparative study of two ESL writing environments: A computer-assisted classroom and a traditional oral classroom. *System*, *24*(4), 491–501. doi: 10.1016/S0346-251X(96)00044-9

Tang, C., & Liu, Y.-T. (2017). Effects of indirect coded corrective feedback with and without short affective teacher comments on L2 writing performance, learner uptake and motivation. *Assessing Writing*, *35*, 26–40. doi:10.1016/j.asw.2017.12.002

Tardy, C. M. (2009). Building genre knowledge. *West Lafayette*. IN: Parlor Press.

Tsai, H. M. (2008). The development of an English writing anxiety scale for Institute of Technology English majors. *Journal of Education and Psychology*, *31*(3), 81–107. doi: 10.1177/0033294116687123

Tubman, J., Montgomery, M., & Wagner, E. (2001). Letter writing as a tool to increase client motivation to change: Application to an inpatient crisis unit. *Journal of Mental Health Counseling*, *23*, 295–311.

Van de Poel, K., & Gasiorek, J. (2012). Effects of an efficacy-focused approach to academic writing on students' perceptions of themselves as writers. *Journal of English for Academic Purposes*, *11*, 294–303. doi:10.1016/j.jeap.2012.07.003

Vurdien, R. (2013). Enhancing writing skills through blogging in an advanced English as a foreign language class in Spain. *Computer-Assisted Language Learning*, *26*(2), 126–143. doi: 10.1080/09588221.2011.639784

Walker, B. (2003). The cultivation of student self-efficacy in reading and writing. *Reading & Writing Quarterly*, *19*(2), 287–302. doi: 10.1080/10573560308217

Wang, W. (2014). Students' perceptions of rubric-referenced peer feedback on EFL writing: A longitudinal inquiry. *Assessing Writing*, *19*, 80–96. doi:10.1016/j.asw.2013.11.008

Wang, Y.-C. (2014). Using wikis to facilitate interaction and collaboration among EFL learners: A social constructivist approach to language teaching. *System*, *42*, 383–390. doi:10.1016/j.system.2014.01.007

Warschauer, M. (2010). Invited commentary: New tools for teaching writing. *Language Learning & Technology*, *14*(1), 3–8.

Wong, B. Y. L., Butler, D. L., Ficzere, S. A., & Kuperis, S. (1997). Teaching adolescents with learning disabilities and low achievers to plan, write, and revise compare-and-contrast essays. *Learning Disabilities Research and Practice*, *12*(1), 2–15.

Wu, W. V., Yang, J. H., Hsieh, J. H. C., & Yamamoto, T. (2020). Free from demotivation in EFL writing: The use of online flipped writing instruction. *Computer Assisted Language Learning*, *33*(4), 353–387. doi: 10.1080/09588221.2019.1567556

Wynne, G., Guo, Y.-J., & Wang, S.-C. (2014). Writing anxiety groups: A creative approach for graduate students. *Journal of Creativity in Mental Health*, *9*(3), 366–379. doi: 10.1080/15401383.2014.902343

Yao, Q. (2019). *Direct and Indirect Feedback: How do they impact on secondary school learners' writing anxiety and how do learners perceive them?* Proceedings of the 2019 Asian Conference on Language Learning, 1–2.

Yasuda, S. (2011). Genre-based tasks in foreign language writing: Developing writers' genre awareness, linguistic knowledge, and writing competence. *Journal of Second Language Writing, 20*, 111–133. doi:10.1016/j.jslw.2011.03.001

Yu., S. (2020). Giving genre-based peer feedback in academic writing: Sources of knowledge and skills, difficulties and challenges. *Assessment & Evaluation in Higher Education.* doi:10.1080/02602938.2020.1742872.

Yu, S., & Hu, G. (2017). Can higher-proficiency L2 learners benefit from working with lower-proficiency partners in peer feedback? *Teaching in Higher Education, 22*(2), 178–192. doi: 10.1080/13562517.2016.1221806

Yu, S., Zhang, Y., Zheng, Y., Yuan, K., & Zhang, L. (2019). Understanding student engagement with peer feedback on master's theses: A Macau study. *Assessment & Evaluation in Higher Education, 44*(1), 50–65. doi: 10.1080/02602938.2018.1467879

Yuan, T. (2015). *Children as multimodal composers: A case study of early elementary students' digital literacy practices.* PhD Dissertation, Columbia University, USA.

Zhang, H., Song, W., Shen, S., & Huang, R. (2014). The effects of blog-mediated peer feedback on learners' motivation, collaboration, and course satisfaction in a second language writing course. *Australasian Journal of Educational Technology, 30*, 670–685. doi:10.14742/ajet.860

Zimmerman, B., & Reisemberg, R. (1997). Becoming a self-regulated writer: A social cognitive perspective. *Contemporary Educational Psychology, 22*, 73–101. doi:10.1006/ceps.1997.0919

Zuercher, N. T. (1986). *Word processing and writing apprehension in freshman composition.* Doctoral dissertation, University of South Dakota, USA.

5 Motivating students to write
Some research-driven guidelines

5.1 Introduction

Having discussed the correlates and sources of writers' demotivation in chapter 3 and reviewed the relevant instructional studies in chapter 4, it is time now to provide key guidelines for how to motivate learners to write. In general language learning motivation research, some works have addressed the classroom motivational strategies of students. An oft-cited relevant work is Dörnyei's (2001) framework of motivational teaching practice. The framework is mainly based on an earlier model Dörnyei and Ottó (1998) developed and it was also reproduced and explicated by Dörnyei and Ushioda (2011). In this framework, Dörnyei provides a number of pedagogical motivational strategies organized under the following four main guidelines: a) creating a motivational learning environment and supportive atmosphere (through good teacher-student relationship and cohesive learner groups); b) generating learners' positive dispositions, goals, and realistic ability beliefs (by fostering students' language-related values and goals, increasing their success expectancy, and using instructional materials of interest and relevance to them); c) maintaining learners' motivation (by making learning enjoyable and motivating, setting achievable leaner goals, and protecting learners' self-confidence); and d) encouraging positive self-ability beliefs (through promoting students' effort attributions and providing motivational feedback).

The task of motivating students to write seems to be a much more complicated one than motivating them to learn a language. When learning a foreign language, students have many options to prioritize or select from. They may, for instance, prefer to allocate more efforts to learning receptive skills than to developing productive ones. Given that language learners attend various classes covering different language areas, it follows that the task of motivating them to learn a particular language is normally assumed by a number of teachers and is also stimulated by some out-of-school factors (such as integrative or extrinsic motives). In writing classes, the task of motivating learners to write is only assumed by the writing teacher(s). What makes this task more challenging for teachers is the fact that writing is the most cognitive of all the language skills. In other words, performing writing tasks requires much more time and involves more complex cognitive or thinking processes compared to listening, reading, or speaking tasks. Due to this cognitively demanding nature of writing tasks, many students may not feel motivated to write regularly. For example, Klassen, Krawchuk, and Rajani (2008) found that university students had higher procrastination on writing tasks than on reading, study, or research ones.

Not much has been written about how to motivate learners to write. Compared to the much measurement, descriptive and instructional writing motivation research conducted since the mid-1970s, very few works have focused on providing guidelines for fostering students' writing motivation or helping them overcome demotivation. These few works were reported by Abdel Latif (2019), Bruning and Horn (2000), Reeves (1997), Troia, Shankland, and Wolbers (2012), and Walker (2003). Apart from these works, some empirical research reports also end with brief pedagogical suggestions and recommendations for motivating student writers; many of these recommendations are often related only to one or two writing motivation constructs. For example, Limpo and Alves (2017) describe how students' writing self-ability beliefs and mastery goals can be nurtured in the following way:

> As teachers manage the learning context, decide on writing assignments, and react to students' behaviours and feelings, teachers are in a privileged position to nurture incremental views of ability particularly by creating mastery goal structures in the classroom as well as by fostering realistic and strong self-efficacy beliefs, particularly focused on self-regulation. There is now considerable evidence showing that this can be achieved by proposing challenging and meaningful assignments, providing frequent opportunities for success, emphasizing the process of learning, stressing self-improvement over social comparisons, giving regular progress feedback, praising for effort rather than for ability, and promoting students' sense of autonomy. (pp. 118-119)

With regard to the works concerned solely with providing guidelines for motivating students to write, these have varied orientations. For example, Reeves's (1997) guidelines are related to minimizing writers' apprehension, and include: getting them to write more, listening to fearful writers and conferring with them, varying writing modes, and preparing students for peer feedback activities. Walker (2003) discusses the cultivation of writers' self-efficacy, whereas Troia et al. (2012) focus on enhancing students' writing self-efficacy, goals, and task interest. As for the guidelines provided by Bruning and Horn (2000), they group them into the following four categories: cultivating learners' functional beliefs about writing, engaging them in performing authentic writing tasks, creating a supportive writing learning environment, and creating a motivating learning atmosphere. A gap in these guidelines, however, lies in how to meet L2 writers' motivational needs. This issue has been considered in the guidelines given by Abdel Latif (2019).

Arguably, there is a need for a more complete list of research-driven guidelines for motivating learners to write. In developing these guidelines, we need to consider students' motivational needs in both L1 and L2 writing contexts and the factors influencing their affective perceptions, beliefs, and goals. In the following sections, the author delineates six guidelines deemed necessary for reinforcing students' writing motivation. While some of these guidelines are based on Abdel Latif's (2019) work, they are further explained and explicated here. The six guidelines discussed in the following sections are:

Nurturing and fostering students' writing motivational perceptions, beliefs, and goals.
Using appropriate teaching materials and writing tasks.
Meeting students' language and writing performance needs.
Integrating technological tools in writing instruction.
Optimizing teacher feedback.
Orchestrating peer assessment activities.

5.2 Nurturing and fostering students' writing motivational perceptions, beliefs, and goals

From the beginning of any writing course or programme to the end of it, teachers need to nurture and enhance students' writing motivational perceptions, beliefs, and goals. Therefore, they should cultivate students' writing motivation at the beginning of the writing course/programme by developing their positive attitudes towards it, helping them recognize the importance and value of writing and set achievable writing learning goals, and changing any inappropriate writing ability beliefs they may have. Then, throughout the various stages of the course/programme, teachers can follow other procedures to foster their students' writing motivation.

In many cases, students get uninterested in improving their written skills because they are unaware of the value of writing. Many students start writing courses with the belief that writing is of no much value to them or their success. In this case, writing teachers need to intervene and correct these beliefs by raising their awareness of the importance of writing to their academic success and other life experiences. A number of motivational gains will be obtained from getting students to recognize the importance of writing. As Codling and Gambrell (1997) state:

> The value an individual places on a task or goal often determines whether or not the individual will expend the effort necessary to accomplish it. Perceptions of task value are based on an individual's beliefs

about both the importance of and interest in the task. With respect to motivation to write, it would appear that students who see writing as important and interesting are more likely to be motivated to initiate and engage in sustained writing behaviours. (p. 38).

As implied in Codling and Gambrell's explanation, students' recognition of the value of writing will enhance their positive attitudes towards it, and will lead them to show persistence and exert efforts to accomplish the mastery writing learning goals they have developed.

Students' recognition of the value of writing will need to be further enhanced during the course/programmme. This can be achieved by explaining the value of each set of learning activities to students' academic growth and personal achievement (Codling & Gambrell, 1997; Troia et al., 2012), and engaging them in various writing tasks of personal relevance (Codling & Gambrell, 1997). Needless to say, the good teacher-student relationship can play a key role in reinforcing students' perceived value of the writing course/programme and their writing motivation.

In other cases, some students may show rigid beliefs about the improvability of their writing performance. These students believe that they are not born talented in writing and that their writing skills are unchangeable no matter how much they may try to improve them. When discovering such negative beliefs, teachers have to correct students' perceptions and enhance their writing skill learnability and improveability beliefs (Troia et al., 2012). At this early stage, it is also important for teachers to help students set objective writing mastery goals (Bruning & Horn, 2000). Teachers can then monitor students' progress towards achieving their goals during the course taught. Students should be helped to prioritize their goals and modify them when needed in order to remain motivated (Troia et al., 2012). Teachers need also to monitor students' writing motivational levels during the course. This can be done though either getting students to complete a writing motivation measure during the several stages of the course/programme or listening to struggling students about their writing motivation problems in classroom time or office hours. In many classroom situations, teachers can easily notice demotivated students. In this case, they can individually meet these demotivated students in their office hour or writing centre time, help them in overcoming their demotivation symptoms, and provide them with suggestions for improving their writing performance. A relevant suggestion is given by Martinez, Kock, and Cass (2011) for alleviating students' writing apprehension:

> For students who demonstrate behavioral anxiety through avoidance, withdrawal, and procrastination [i.e., demonstrate writing apprehension], faculty support and mentoring may help to lower their levels of anxiety [i.e., apprehension] and increase self-efficacy....Faculty members can enhance their relationships with their students by encouraging

students to attend office hours outside of class, providing detailed feedback on students' papers, facilitating discussion on the challenges of writing, and mentoring and tutoring students who need additional writing support. If students' writing anxiety [i.e., apprehension] is rooted in their early experiences…, then perhaps the more positive writing experiences they have, the more they will realize that writing can be enjoyable and not something they wish to avoid. (p. 358)

As noted, Martinez and colleagues' suggestion is similar to the workshops Bloom (1982, 1985) organized for demotivated writers. While conferring with students, teachers should not only focus on discussing their writing dispositional perceptions, but also their ability beliefs and goals. Based on these discussions, they can suggest appropriate solutions for helping students become motivated. Teachers need then to monitor how demotivated students respond to their suggested solutions, and intervene when necessary by providing them with further guidance.

The suggestions given in this section aim at directly fostering students' writing motivation or helping them overcome their demotivation, i.e., they are concerned with nurturing students' writing motivational perceptions, beliefs, and goals through appropriate diagnosis and then raising their motivational consciousness and/or guiding them. The guidelines given in the following sections aim at enhancing students' writing motivation indirectly. This can be accomplished via enabling students to overcome their perceived and real performance deficiencies, and learn writing in a supportive and safe environment.

5.3 Using appropriate teaching materials and writing tasks

In many writing learning environments, students get demotivated because the instructional materials studied are not interesting enough. For example, these materials can be either too easy or too difficult. Likewise, demotivation can be caused by getting students to write about uninteresting or unfamiliar topics. This has been shown by some studies reviewed in chapters 3 and 4 (e.g., Albin, Benton, & Khramtsova, 1996; Behizadeh & Engelhard, 2014; Hidi & McLaren, 1990, 1991). Therefore, due attention should be given to using the writing materials and tasks students feel motivated with.

Writing teachers need to make sure their students interact optimally with the learning materials they use in the classroom. Research findings indicate that student writers get demotivated as a result of the uninteresting instructional materials (e.g., Abdel Latif, 2015; Lo & Hyland, 2007). Due to some institutional requirements in particular educational environments, some writing teachers may find themselves obliged to use a specific textbook whose activities do not properly match their students' needs. In this case, those teachers can supplement the basic textbook with more stimulating materials taken from other sources.

Topic interest is the first dimension teachers need to consider when choosing the writing assignments students have to complete. According to Boscolo and Cisotto (1999), students' writing motivation can be nurtured by getting them to write about authentic topics of interest to them. Teachers can accomplish this pedagogical task at the beginning of each course by surveying the writing topics and the types of tasks their students are likely to be interested in and familiar with. Based on the results of their survey, teachers can engage students in writing about a highly-rated set of writing topics they have chosen. Varying task types is also important for two reasons. First, performing different tasks and writing about different genres can help in maintaining students' motivation and avoid them task monotony. Second, engaging students in performing multiple and different tasks will likely foster their self-ability beliefs. As Oldfather and Shanahan (2007) explain:

> We recommend that students have numerous opportunities to write for different purposes and to different audiences. Students can write to themselves or their best friend, they can communicate to a group of peers or a larger audience. Students who engage in brainstorming, freewriting, writing constructive responses, and writing multiple drafts, students who write letters… and reports and critiques and advertisements for important purposes are gaining in writing competency and, in turn, are developing a sense of themselves as empowered. (p. 278)

Assigning students writing tasks of graded difficulty levels is another important dimension for maintaining their motivation. Therefore, writing teachers need to engage students in performing graded tasks by starting with the easiest tasks and ending with the most difficult ones. For example, students can be assigned guided writing topics before performing non-guided ones. They need also to practice writing narrative essays prior to writing argumentative ones, which require higher-order thinking skills. Engaging students in performing writing tasks of moderately challenging level is key to their motivation. As Rahimi and Zhang (2019) suggest:

> Pedagogically, teachers might need to consider aligning the degrees of the task complexity with their L2 learners' proficiency by adjusting the level of reasoning and the number of elements required for successful completion of the assigned tasks; teachers can increase the complexity of the tasks along the level of reasoning and the number of elements in order to improve the learners' syntactic complexity and also create opportunities for task-based and contextualised pedagogical mediations for the development of both complexity and accuracy. (p. 776)

It should be noted, however, that teachers need to provide students with adequate scaffolding when engaging them in performing newly challenging tasks (Troia et al., 2012).

5.4 Meeting students' language and writing performance needs

Students will not likely feel motivated to write without having a sense of possessing the required skills for performing a target task. As a result of their perceived language ability or writing skill deficiencies, many students may not be enthusiastic to show their texts to others or to participate in classroom activities where their poor writing capabilities are compared to those of their peers. Through meeting such needs, students will develop a sense of competence and empowerment (Oldfather & Shanahan, 2007). Given the research findings highlighted in chapters 3 and 4, developing students' language ability will in particular enhance their writing self-ability beliefs and attitudes towards writing. Meanwhile, meeting students' writing performance needs will interact positively with their dispositional and situational perceptions, self-ability beliefs, and goals (see chapter 3).

The degree of language instruction integration into writing classrooms depends on students' linguistic needs. In L2 writing contexts where students are expected to encounter many linguistic difficulties in text composing, teachers should be aware of their students' language problems. Therefore, they need to start teaching a given writing course by identifying students' vocabulary and grammar knowledge levels, and act accordingly. As Ryu (1997) explains:

> [T]he focus of EFL writing instruction should vary depending on the students' English-language proficiency. For low English-language proficiency students, the focus of EFL writing instruction should be on developing their English-language skills. For intermediate English learners whose English-language proficiency and native-language writing skills are significantly correlated with their EFL writing skills at the same time, the focus of the instruction should be on developing both English language and writing skills. For advanced English learners, the focus of the instruction should be on developing their writing skills rather than their English language skills. (pp. x-ix)

In writing classrooms, teachers can develop student writers' language ability and knowledge through using product and genre activities. Three main approaches have been used in teaching writing: the product, process, and genre approaches. The product approach to teaching writing focuses on improving students' language performance via using controlled, guided, and free writing activities. With the process approach, students learn how to write through collaborative activities of text planning, drafting, and revising. When using the genre approach, students are taught writing through providing examples of the target text (for more information, see section 4.5 in the previous chapter and also see Badger & White, 2000; Hyland, 2003, 2004). In light of Ryu's (1997) above view, writing instruction has to be more product-oriented until students reach a specific level of language proficiency. When students reach the target language ability level(s), writing instruction can then become more process-oriented.

Optimally, combining product and genre activities in writing instruction can help low language level students acquire particular lexical and grammatical features and become aware of the target rhetorical aspects and lead them to model the texts they are exposed to. While Badger and White (2000) call for using the process-genre approach, there is also room for a combined version of the product and genre approaches in writing instruction. The proposed product-genre approach resembles the process-genre one in exposing students to meaningful input for developing their writing knowledge, but the two approaches differ in the nature of their language activities and their expected impact on enhancing students' linguistic knowledge. Students' language ability is developed partially as a by-product through the genre approach, whereas the explicit linguistic activities of the product-genre approach directly fosters their grammatical and lexical knowledge.

Student writers' language ability can also be enhanced through engaging them in reading activities. Extracurricular reading activities have been found beneficial to improving students' writing performance (Janopoulos, 1986; Kaplan & Palhinda, 1981). Through reading texts, learners develop their language and text structure awareness. That is why writing teachers can draw their students' attention to the importance of out-of-classroom reading and provide them with appropriate list of reading sources. Developing student writers' language abilities directly through the product activities and indirectly through the genre and extracurricular reading activities will help them write fluently, produce better texts, and in turn overcome language and writing ability deficiency and belief problems. The expected result of such improvement in students' text production processes and outcomes is getting them more motivated to write.

Once students have reached a threshold language ability level, teachers can allocate more classroom time and efforts to writing strategy instruction. They specifically need to model the writing strategies deemed appropriate to students and to raise their awareness of how to plan and revise texts, regulate and monitor their cognitive processes, and use online resourcing tools while writing. It is important to regularly engage students in an adequate number of collaborative writing process activities (Harris & Graham, 2009). This will gradually help in alleviating students' writing demotivation symptoms.

Important also is employing various types of assessments in evaluating students' writing performance. For instance, in the early stage of a given writing course/programme, teachers can use rubrics assessing one or two aspects of students' texts only (e.g., content and organization versus language use and vocabulary). During this early stage, they also could depend on text planning and revision tasks in rating students' writing performance. At a later stage of the writing course/programme, teachers can then move to using rubrics assessing the various aspects of students' texts. Employing these multiple writing rubrics and assessment tasks can meet the motivational needs of students' writing performance.

5.5 Integrating technological tools into writing instruction

As indicated in the two related overviews given in chapters 3 and 4, technology has been increasingly integrated in writing instruction. The technological tools used in writing instruction so far include, among others, Word processors, computer-mediated communication applications, WebQuests, blogs, wikis, and automated writing evaluation programmes. Intuitively, future technological developments will bring us more applications that could be integrated into writing instruction.

Integrating technology into writing instruction helps in creating a supportive writing environment for students through enabling them to develop and (re)write texts easily and efficiently, check their writing errors using resourcing tools such as online dictionaries, and share their written texts with others. Thus, engaging students in technology-assisted writing tasks is likely to have a positive motivating impact on them. The studies reviewed in chapter 4 provide evidence for such positive impact on students' writing motivation (e.g., Li, Chu, & Ki, 2014; Mabrito, 2000; Wang, 2014; Yuan, 2015; Zhang, Song, Shen, & Huang, 2014). Given this, writing teachers need to make as much use of technology as they can in their classroom practices. In addition to Word processors, blogs, and wikis, student writers have also started to increasingly use automated writing evaluation programmes, which provide them with corrective feedback on their texts. Arguably, the easiness or complexity of the use of these applications in writing instruction varies from one technological application to another. Thus, before deciding upon using any application in their classes, teachers have to make sure that students feel comfortable with or have adequate knowledge of using it.

At the simplest level, writing teachers can start with replacing paper-and-pen or handwritten tasks with computer-based ones. This can be intriguing and motivating to students at all educational stages, and will also enable them to write in a supportive technology-assisted environment. Meanwhile, computer-based tasks will also help teachers provide learners with electronic feedback on their Word processor-composed texts, for example, by using the electronic commenting and/or tracked changes features. In a number of occasions during the writing course/programme, teachers can depend on electronic feedback (sent via email communication) as an alternative to giving students feedback in the classroom or office hours. This feedback alternative can alleviate students' writing apprehension in particular.

Automated writing evaluation software represents a type of technological tools that can be easily used in learning writing situations. At the moment, students can use a number of automated writing evaluation programmes to check the accuracy of their writing, including Criterion®, Grammarly®, Grammark, Grammarcheckme, MY Access, Spellchecker.net, and

SpellCheckPlus. Though little empirical evidence has been provided for the motivating effects of using automated writing evaluation programmes, it is hypothesized that they can potentially motivate students to produce better drafts due to the autonomous role they have in completing writing tasks and to enabling them to have a private window for evaluating their texts. Initial evidence for this was provided by Zhang (2017) who found that automated writing evaluation significantly increased students' engagement with writing behaviourally, emotionally, and cognitively. Writing teachers, therefore, need to draw their students' attention to some useful and efficient automated evaluation programmes which they will likely find motivating.

Integrating other applications (such as wikis, blogs, and multimodal composing tasks) into writing instruction is a multistep process and requires following some guidelines to positively influence students' writing motivation. For example, in their review work, Stoddart, Chan, and Liu (2016) synthesized some research-driven guidelines for successful and motivating wiki-based collaborative writing teaching. These guidelines include: familiarizing students with the concept of collaboration and the wiki application to be used, introducing the assignment component and breaking it into smaller units, establishing student-student feedback procedures, raising students' awareness of the appropriate feedback techniques, and obtaining students' evaluation. Likewise, McVee and Miller (2012) identified some action principles for integrating multimodal composing into teaching writing. These include: creating a social space for collaborative student work, identifying the learning task purpose, and explicitly explaining design features. Finally, Zhang et al. (2014) recommend that blog-mediated instruction can be effectively implemented in writing classes through choosing a reliably technical blog and making use of teacher's role in fostering the effectiveness of peer feedback.

Needless to say, teachers should consider students' age when trying to integrate a particular technological tool or application in their instruction. For example, wiki-mediated and blog-mediated instruction can be more appropriate to university students, whereas multimodal composing tasks will be likely engaging to young learners. Teachers may also slightly modify the instructional procedures related to technology integration into writing instruction depending on students' age and characteristics. At any rate, the basic rule for getting students to learn writing using a given technological tool or application is to tailor the instructional design in a way influencing their performance and motivation positively rather than negatively.

5.6 Optimizing teacher feedback

As indicated in chapters 3 and 4, research has congruently shown that teacher feedback influences students' engagement in writing and their motivational beliefs. Therefore, teacher feedback provision on students' writing should be optimized. Based on the relevant research reviewed in chapters 3 and 4, teacher feedback on students' texts is expected to be motivational if the following four principles are considered: interactivity, selectivity, mitigation, and improvement suggestion provision.

Interactivity refers to considering the timing of teacher feedback provision (i.e., initial text draft(s) versus a final one) and the student's characteristics. The amount of error corrections, and praise and criticism in teacher feedback on an initial text draft is not supposed to be the same when responding to a final one. As a motivating strategy to students, teachers could highlight more errors and give less praise when providing feedback on the initial text drafts; in contrast, they are supposed to give more praise and correct fewer errors when commenting on final text drafts. Moreover, the amount of praise and criticism given in teacher feedback should vary depending on the student's responsiveness (i.e., responsive versus low- or non-responsive learners) and their writing competence (i.e., proficient versus low-proficient learners). A greater amount of praise is supposed to be given on the texts written by responsive students than low or non-responsive ones. Likewise, teachers need to give a less amount of criticism to low-proficient writers than proficient ones. Varying teacher praise and criticism in such interactive way could keep students with different responsiveness and competence levels motivated to write and lead them to set reachable and/or higher goals for their writing performance. Pajares, Johnson, and Usher (2007) emphasize the need for using such interactive feedback approach as follows:

> To ensure that students approach writing with less anxiety and stress, it is wise for teachers to frame writing feedback in terms of gains rather than shortfalls… In other words, it pays dividends for a teacher to provide students with feedback focusing on how far they have come rather than how far they have yet to travel. When encouraged to reflect on their writing progress rather than their writing deficiencies, young people develop robust efficacy beliefs that lead to growth and perseverance. Conversely, students who are often reminded of the distance between their current and their ideal performance often lose heart and give up. In many cases, students' apprehension about their writing is a product of the type of feedback they receive in school. (p. 115)

Another interactive element in teacher feedback is related to outcome or achievement attribution which refers to ascribing the causes of success and failure to either students' effort or their ability. According to Troia et al. (2012), teachers need to foster effort attributions when motivating students' learning mastery goals and enhance ability attributions for reinforcing their self-efficacy beliefs.

As for selectivity in teacher feedback, it means focusing on the most important or salient errors or features in students' written texts and avoiding the overuse of corrective feedback. On the one hand, this will minimize the potential frustrating experience students may have from teacher feedback.

On the other hand, it will also contribute to raising students' consciousness of their own writing performance strengths and weaknesses. This will be particularly important for helping students pay attention to specific types of errors in their writing (Reeves, 1997). Such selectivity can be reinforced by giving students terminal comments or a rubric summarizing their overall evaluation of the written texts.

Teachers also need to consider mitigating or reducing the severity of the criticism or negative comments they give on students' texts. They can do this via using some strategies such as paired act patterns (combining criticism with praise or suggestions, or both), personal attribution (commenting on the text as an ordinary reader rather than as an expert), and hedges and interrogative syntax (see Hyland & Hyland, 2001). Mitigation can be also accomplished through using the progress feedback technique (Duijnhouwer, Prins, & Stokking, 2010). Students particularly value the suggestions given by the teacher for improving their performance on future writing tasks (e.g., Yu, Jiang, & Zhou, 2020). As shown by some instructional writing motivation studies (e.g., Duijnhouwer, Prins, & Stokking, 2012), these suggestion positively influence students' writing mastery goals.

5.7 Orchestrating peer assessment activities

As indicated in chapters 3 and 4, peer feedback activities do not always enhance students' writing motivation. Problematic issues in writing peer feedback activities are mainly related to their time-consuming nature and to students' potential individual differences and varied attitudes to the value of their classmates' comments. Therefore, there is a need for orchestrating these activities in writing classes to prevent their counterproductive effects.

Prior to implementing peer feedback activities in their writing classes, teachers should make sure that students are well-prepared enough for them, i.e., they have adequate peer feedback literacy. As Han and Xu (2019) explain:

> Teachers, curriculum developers, tutors and program administrators can make concerted efforts to develop student feedback literacy using various pedagogical strategies, not just at the beginning, but throughout a course or, ideally, a programme. Second, to promote student feedback literacy, teacher feedback on peer feedback needs to be tailored to individual students' needs, specifically their competence, beliefs and motivations. (p. 15)

If students are found unfamiliar with peer assessment dynamics, teachers need to follow some steps for training them and developing their peer feedback literacy. For example, they can model such processes to students and guide them to appropriate peer interactions (Hansen & Liu, 2005).

The counterproductive motivating effects of peer feedback can be also avoided by selecting the most appropriate peer response mode (i.e., oral, written, or computer-based feedback), involving students in grouping and organizing peer work, planning well for the teacher's role and for monitoring students' peer work, allocating adequate time to these activities, and using an appropriate peer feedback sheet (see more information about these issues in Hansen & Liu, 2005). Since some students may not like showing their own texts to peers, an alternative solution could be getting students to evaluate anonymous texts. This will allow implementing peer feedback activities in a more comfortable classroom atmosphere. Research generally indicates that orchestrating peer assessment activities in writing classes is a complex process (Hu & Lam, 2010; Wang, 2014; Yu & Hu, 2017; Yu, Zhang, Zheng, Yuan, & Zhang, 2019). Therefore, engaging student writers in peer feedback activities without considering the above prerequisites will likely cause some of them to become demotivated.

5.8 Conclusion

In the above sections, six main guidelines for motivating students to write have been discussed. The six guidelines cater for meeting students' motivational needs and optimizing the factors influencing their motivation. Table (5.1) provides a summary of the pedagogical procedures of these guidelines.

As indicated in the delineation of the six guidelines and their procedures, each guideline can promote some writing motivation aspects rather than others. For example, students' perceived value of writing and their attitudes towards it could be reinforced though using interesting and authentic writing topics and appropriate teaching materials. Meanwhile, meeting students' linguistic needs will likely promote their writing self-ability beliefs and learning mastery goals. Likewise, improving students' writing performance and getting them to use appropriate technological applications is expected to interact positively with their attitude towards writing, and writing self-ability beliefs and goals. Some feedback practices could foster student writers' attitudes while others may enhance their writing mastery goals. As for the treatment of situational perceptions and behaviours (i.e., writing anxiety and the motivational regulation of writing) in the above guidelines, it is expected that these will be shaped depending on the reinforcement of the other motivational beliefs and perceptions. For example, when students' writing self-ability beliefs and attitudes are fostered as a result of meeting their language and performance needs, they will unlikely demonstrate anxiety symptoms in writing classes. Besides, their motivational regulation of writing processes will be likely associated with strengthened mastery goals.

It is worth noting that writing teachers are not required to implement the procedures representing all these guidelines at one time. While some of these guidelines need to be followed during all the stages of a given writing course/programme, the implementation of others depends on students'

Table 5.1 Main guidelines and specific pedagogical procedures for motivating students to write

Main guidelines	Pedagogical procedures
Nurturing and fostering students' writing motivational perceptions, beliefs, and goals	• Help students recognize the value of writing to their academic success and personal life. • Explain the value of writing learning activities to students' academic and personal growth. • Help students set achievable writing mastery goals. • Help students believe that their writing skills are learnable and improvable. • Regularly diagnose students' writing motivational levels either through using measures or classroom discussion. • Confer with demotivated students and provide them with the appropriate guidance. • Monitor demotivated students' implementation of your suggested solutions and intervene when necessary.
Using appropriate teaching materials and writing tasks	• Make sure the teaching materials used are stimulating enough to students. • When necessary, supplement basic teaching materials with stimulating materials from other sources. • Engage students in writing about interesting and familiar topics. • Engage students in performing various writing task types. • Assign students writing tasks of graded difficulty levels. • Scaffold students' performance on challenging tasks.
Meeting students' language and writing performance needs	• Integrate language activities into writing instruction depending on students' linguistic needs. • Use product and genre activities to develop students' language knowledge. • Stimulate students to do extracurricular reading activities outside the classroom. • Once students reach the target language ability level(s), make writing instruction more process-oriented. • Engage students regularly in adequate number of collaborative writing process activities. • Use writing rubrics and assessment tasks reflecting various aspects in students' writing process and product performance.
Integrating technological tools into writing instruction	• Get students to perform technology-assisted writing tasks as much as you can. • In a number of times, replace face-to-face feedback with electronic feedback. • Guide students to use efficient automated writing evaluation programmes. • Make sure students are familiar and comfortable enough with using the target technological tool(s). • Consider the suitability of using a particular technological tool or application to students' age and maturity level. • Follow research-based guidelines when using some applications (e.g., wikis or blogs).

(Continued)

Table 5.1 Main guidelines and specific pedagogical procedures for motivating students to write (*Continued*)

Main guidelines	Pedagogical procedures
Optimizing teacher feedback	• Vary your feedback provision strategies depending on the draft type, student's responsiveness to your feedback, and their writing competence. • Highlight more errors and give less praise when providing feedback on initial text drafts than on final text drafts. • Give more positive comments on the texts written by responsive students. • Give little criticism to low-proficient writers. • Avoid overusing written corrective feedback and focus on the most salient errors or features in students' texts. • Mitigate your criticism or negative comments on students' texts. • Provide suggestions for improving students' performance on future writing tasks. • Enhance effort attributions for motivating students' learning mastery goals. • Foster ability attributions for reinforcing students' self-efficacy beliefs.
Orchestrating peer assessment activities	• Make sure students are prepared enough for peer feedback activities. • Choose the appropriate peer response mode (oral, written, or computer-based). • Involve students partially in grouping and organizing peer work. • Allocate adequate time to peer feedback activities. • Use an appropriate peer feedback sheet or rubric. • Get students to evaluate anonymous texts. • Monitor students' work in peer response activities. • Support peer feedback interactions at an appropriate time.

needs. The first, second, and fifth guidelines (i.e., nurturing and fostering students' writing motivation, using appropriate teaching materials and writing tasks, and optimizing teacher feedback) belong to the former type, whereas some of the procedures listed under the third, fourth, and sixth ones (i.e., meeting students' language and writing performance needs, integrating technological tools into writing instruction, and orchestrating peer assessment activities) can be only followed when needed. For example, if students' writing demotivation is caused by their low language ability levels and/ or beliefs, teachers can then focus more on integrating linguistic activities into writing instruction. Once students' language needs are met, teachers will need to focus more on writing process instruction. Likewise, at the beginning of the writing course/programme, students' inadequate peer feedback literacy may not allow teachers to implement peer response activities. Thus, these may be delayed to a later stage when students become prepared enough for them.

While following the pedagogical procedures representing the six guidelines, teachers need also to consider students' age, gender, and cultural backgrounds. For instance, the technological tools and applications that could motivate primary and middle school graders to write may not have the same motivating impact on high school and university students. Similarly, female and male students might react differently to some teacher and peer feedback procedures. Finally, culture-related issues may cause differences in students' responses to integrating language and strategy instruction into writing classes. Therefore, writing teachers need to cautiously consider these three factors when trying to foster students' writing motivation.

References

Abdel Latif, M. M. M. (2015). Sources of L2 writing apprehension: A study of Egyptian university students. *Journal of Research in Reading*, *38*(2), 194–212. doi: 10.1111/j.1467-9817.2012.01549.x

Abdel Latif, M. M. M. (2019). Helping L2 students overcome negative writing affect *Writing & Pedagogy*, *11*(1), 151–163. doi: https://doi.org/10.1558/wap.38569

Albin, M. L., Benton, S. L., & Khramtsova, I. (1996). Individual differences in interest and narrative writing. *Contemporary Educational Psychology*, *21*, 305–324. doi:10.1006/ceps.1996.0024

Badger, R., & White, G. (2000). A process genre approach to teaching writing. *ELT Journal*, *54*(2), 153–160. doi: 10.1093/elt/54.2.153

Behizadeh, N., & Engelhard, G., Jr. (2014). Development and validation of a scale to measure perceived authenticity in writing. *Assessing Writing*, *21*, 18–36. doi:10.1016/j.asw.2014.02.001

Bloom, L. (1982). Why graduate students can't write: Implications of research on writing anxiety for graduate education. *Journal of Advanced Composition*, *2*(1/2), 103–117.

Bloom, L. (1985). Anxious writers in context: Graduate school and beyond. In M. Ross (Ed.), *When a writer can't write*, (pp. 119–133). New York, NY: Guilford.

Boscolo, P., & Cisotto, L. (1999). *Making writing an interesting activity in elementary school*. Unpublished manuscript.

Bruning, R., & Horn, C. (2000). Developing motivation to write. *Educational Psychologist*, 35, 25–37. doi: 10.1207/S15326985EP3501_4

Codling, R. M., & Gambrell, L. B. (1997). *The motivation to write profile: An assessment tool for elementary teachers*. College Park: University of Maryland.

Dörnyei, Z. (2001). *Motivational strategies in the language classroom*. Cambridge: Cambridge University Press.

Dörnyei, Z., & Ottó, I. (1998). Motivation in action: A process model of L2 motivation. *Working papers in applied linguistics*, *4*, 43–69. London: Thames Valley University.

Dörnyei, Z., & Ushioda, E. (2011). *Teaching and researching motivation*. Edinburgh: Pearson Education Limited.

Duijnhouwer, H., Prins, F. J., & Stokking, K. M. (2012). Feedback providing improvement strategies and reflection on feedback use: Effects on students' writing motivation, process, and performance. *Learning and Instruction*, *22*, 171–184. doi: 10.1016/j.learninstruc.2011.10.003

Duijnhouwer, H., Prins, F. J., & Stokking, K. M. (2010). Progress feedback effects on students' writing mastery goal, self-efficacy beliefs, and performance. *Educational Research and Evaluation*, *16*(1), 53–74. doi: 10.1080/13803611003711393

Han, Y., & Xu, Y. (2019). The development of student feedback literacy: The influences of teacher feedback on peer feedback. *Assessment & Evaluation in Higher Education*. doi: 10.1080/02602938.2019.1689545

Hansen, J., & Liu, J. (2005). Guiding principles for effective peer response. *ELT Journal*, *59*(1), 31–38. doi: 10.1093/elt/cci004

Harris, K. R., & Graham, S. (2009). Self-regulated strategy development in writing: Premises, evolution, and the future. *British Journal of Educational Psychology*, *6*, 113–135. doi: 10.1348/978185409X422542

Hidi, S., & McLaren, J. (1990). The effect of topic and theme interestingness on the production of school expositions. In H. Mandl, E. De Corte, N. Bennett, & H. Freidrich (Eds.), *Learning and instruction: European research in an international context*, (Vol. 2.2, pp. 295–308). Oxford: Pergamon Press.

Hidi, S., & McLaren, J. (1991). Motivational factors and writing: The role of topic interestingness. *European Journal of Psychology of Education*, *6*, 187–197. doi: 10.1007/BF03191937

Hu, G., & Lam, S. T. E. (2010). Issues of cultural appropriateness and pedagogical efficacy: Exploring peer review in a second language writing class. *Instructional Science*, *38*(4), 371–394. doi: 10.1007/s11251-008-9086-1

Hyland, F., & Hyland, K. (2001). Sugaring the pill: Praise and criticism in written feedback. *Journal of Second Language Writing*, *10*, 185–212. doi: 10.1016/S1060-3743(01)00038-8

Hyland, K. (2003). Genre-based pedagogies: A social response to process. *Journal of Second Language Writing*, *12*, 17–29. doi: 10.1016/S1060-3743(02)00124-8

Hyland, K. (2004). *Genre and second language writing*. Ann Arbor, MI: University of Michigan Press.

Janopoulos, M. (1986). The relationship of pleasure reading and second language writing proficiency. *TESOL Quarterly*, *20*(4), 764–768. doi: 10.2307/3586526

Kaplan, J., & Palhinda, E. (1981). Non-native speakers of English and their composition abilities: A review and analysis. In W. Frawley (Ed.), *Linguistics and literacy*, (pp. 425–457). New York: Plenum.

Klassen, R. M., Krawchuk, L. L., & Rajani, S. (2008). Academic procrastination of undergraduates: Low self-efficacy to self-regulate predicts higher levels of procrastination. *Contemporary Educational Psychology*, *33*, 915–931. doi: 10.1016/j.cedpsych.2007.07.001

Li, X.-S., Chu, S. K. W., & Ki, W. W. (2014). The effects of a wiki-based collaborative process writing pedagogy on writing ability and attitudes among upper primary school students in mainland China. *Computers & Education*, *77*, 151–169. doi: 10.1016/j.compedu.2014.04.019

Limpo, T., & Alves, R. (2017). Relating beliefs in writing skill malleability to writing performance: The mediating role of achievement goals and self-efficacy. *Journal of Writing Research*, *9*(2), 97–125. doi: 10.17239/jowr-2017.09.02.01

Lo, J., & Hyland, F. (2007). Enhancing students' engagement and motivation in writing: The case of primary students in Hong Kong. *Journal of Second Language Writing*, *16*, 219–237. doi: 10.1016/j.jslw.2007.06.002

Mabrito, M. (2000). Computer conversations and writing apprehension. *Business Communication Quarterly*, *63*(1), 39–49. doi: 10.1177/108056990006300104

Martinez, C. T., Kock, N., & Cass, J. (2011). Pain and pleasure in short essay writing: Factors predicting university students' writing anxiety and self-efficacy. *Journal of Adolescent and Adult Literacy*, *54*, 351–360. doi: 10.1598/JA AL.54.5.5

McVee, M. B., & Miller, S. M. (2012). *Multimodal composing in classrooms: Learning and teaching for the digital world*. New York: Routledge.

Oldfather, P., & Shanahan, C. H. (2007). A cross-case study of writing motivation as empowerment. In P. Boscolo & S. Hidi (Eds.), *Writing and motivation*, (pp. 257–279). Oxford: Elsevier.

Ryu, H. (1997) *Threshold level of English language proficiency for EFL writing: Effect on the interaction between English language proficiency and writing skills on Korean college students' EFL writing*. PhD Dissertation, University of Florida, USA.

Pajares, F., Johnson, J., & Usher, E. (2007). Sources of writing self-efficacy beliefs of elementary, middle and high school students. *Research in the Teaching of English*, *42*(1), 104–120.

Rahimi, M., & Zhang, L. J. (2019). Writing task complexity, students' motivational beliefs, anxiety and their writing production in English as a second language. *Reading and Writing*, *32*, 761–786. doi: 10.1007/s11145-018-9887-9

Reeves, L. L. (1997). Minimizing writing apprehension in the learner centered classroom. *English Journal*, *86*(6), 38–45. doi: 10.2307/820367

Stoddart, A., Chan, J. Y., & Liu, G. (2016). Enhancing successful outcomes of wiki-based collaborative writing: A state-of-the-art review of facilitation frameworks. *Interactive Learning Environments*, *24*(1), 142–157. doi: 10.1080/10494820.2013.825810

Troia, G., Shankland, R., & Wolbers, K. (2012). Motivation research in writing: Theoretical and empirical considerations. *Reading & Writing Quarterly*, *28*, 5–28. doi: 10.1080/10573569.2012.632729

Walker, B. (2003). The cultivation of student self-efficacy in reading and writing. *Reading & Writing Quarterly*, *19*, 287–302. doi: 10.1080/10573560308217

Wang, W. (2014). Students' perceptions of rubric-referenced peer feedback on EFL writing: A longitudinal inquiry. *Assessing Writing*, *19*, 80–96. doi: 10.1016/j.asw.2013.11.008

Wang, Y.-C. (2014). Using wikis to facilitate interaction and collaboration among EFL learners: A social constructivist approach to language teaching. *System*, *42*, 383–390. doi: 10.1016/j.system.2014.01.007

Yu, S., & Hu, G. (2017). Can higher-proficiency L2 learners benefit from working with lower-proficiency partners in peer feedback? *Teaching in Higher Education*, *22*(2), 178–192. doi: 10.1080/13562517.2016.1221806

Yu, S., Jiang, L., & Zhou, N. (2020). Investigating what feedback practices contribute to students' writing motivation and engagement in Chinese EFL context: A large scale study. *Assessing Writing*, *44*, 1–15. doi: 10.1016/j.asw.2020.100451

Yu, S., Zhang, Y., Zheng, Y., Yuan, K., & Zhang, L. (2019). Understanding student engagement with peer feedback on master's theses: A Macau study. *Assessment & Evaluation in Higher Education*, *44*(1), 50–65. doi: 10.1080/02602938.2018.1467879

Yuan, T. (2015). *Children as multimodal composers: A case study of early elementary students' digital literacy practices*. PhD Dissertation, Columbia University, USA.

Zhang, H., Song, W., Shen, S., & Huang, R. (2014). The effects of blog-mediated peer feedback on learners' motivation, collaboration, and course satisfaction in a second language writing course. *Australasian Journal of Educational Technology*, *30*, 670–685. doi: 10.14742/ajet.860

Zhang, Z. (2017). Student engagement with computer-generated feedback: A case study. *ELT Journal*, *71*, 317–328. doi: 10.1093/elt/ccw089

6 Advancing writing motivation measurement, research and pedagogy

6.1 Introduction

As noted in the previous five chapters, there have been various measurement, research, and pedagogy orientations in the writing motivation area since the mid-1970s. During the last four decades, the area has gained the interest of an increasing number of researchers in different contexts worldwide. The writing motivation research reported so far has addressed a variety of issues related to measuring its constructs, identifying their predictors, and treating writers' demotivation or negative affect. However, other measurement and instruction research issues remain to be explored. Meanwhile, there is a need also for fostering effective writing motivation pedagogy practices.

In the following sections, the author summarizes the main conclusions drawn from the previous five chapters, highlights the gaps yet to be addressed in researching writing motivation, and the ways of promoting its effective pedagogy. Filling in the highlighted research voids could advance the theoretical, measurement, and instructional perspectives and practices related to writing motivation. As for the pedagogical issues raised, they are related to popularizing writing motivation pedagogy awareness and advancing related instructional practices.

6.2 Strengthening the conceptualizations and operationalizations of writing motivation constructs

Since the publication of the early and seminal works on it (e.g., Blake, 1976; Daly & Miller, 1975a, 1975b, 1975c; Daly & Shamo, 1976, 1978; Emig & King, 1979), writing motivation has been conceptualized and operationalized in varied ways. Apprehension and attitudes were the only writing motivation constructs researched in the 1970s and early 1980s. That is why the measures developed for assessing the two constructs during this early stage (Blake, 1976; Daly & Miller, 1975a; Emig & King, 1979; Thompson, 1978) reflect broad operationalizations. In other words, the items in these measures tap these two constructs along with other writing motivation ones, e.g., writing self-concept and anxiety, and the perceived value of writing. The frequently published research reports on writing self-efficacy in the 1990s led to operationalizing writers' apprehension/attitude in more accurate ways using short measures. This can be noted, for instance, in Graham, Schwartz, and MacArthur's (1993) attitude towards writing scale, and Pajares and his colleagues' modified writing apprehension scales (e.g., Pajares, Britner, & Valiante, 2000; Pajares, Valiante, & Cheong, 2007). The 1990s writing motivation research led also to characterizing two other different constructs; namely writing outcome expectancy (labelled in later studies as writing achievement goal orientation) (Pajares & Johnson, 1994, 1996; Shell, Colvin, & Bruning, 1995) and self-concept (Charney, Newman, & Palmquist, 1995; Palmquist & Young, 1992).

Accordingly, writing motivation has been historically represented in increasing numbers of constructs as a result of the growing research on it. In the 1970s and early 1980s, it was narrowly represented in apprehension/attitude only, and then in apprehension/attitude and self-efficacy constructs in the late 1980s. By the end of the 1990s, writing motivation was more broadly represented in these constructs along with outcome expectancy (i.e., writing achievement goals) and self-concept. With the other research developments that occurred in the last two decades, writing motivation is now viewed as an umbrella term composed of the following four main types of constructs: a) attitudinal/dispositional constructs: writing apprehension/attitude and the perceived value of writing; b) situational constructs: writing anxiety and the motivational regulation of writing; c) ability belief constructs: writing self-efficacy and self-concept; and d) learning goal constructs: writing achievement goal orientations.

Though much progress has generally been made with regard to characterizing these main writing motivation constructs, some of them still need to be conceptualized and operationalized in a better way. Specifically, we can build more robust conceptualizations of three constructs: writing apprehension/attitude, the perceived value of writing, and writing self-concept. The writing apprehension/attitude construct could be better represented by adding learners' disposition towards instructional materials, teaching and testing practices, and teacher or peer feedback to the dimensions already found in previous measures (i.e., interest in learning writing, liking and disliking of writing, and writing evaluation situations). The unclear place of the perceived value of writing construct in previous research has perhaps resulted from the terminological differences (i.e., writing interest, task value, beliefs about writing, and the perceived authenticity of writing) and from the scales used previously in assessing it. Therefore, the first step in overcoming this problem will be through terminological unification of the construct. The second step lies in expanding the construct through drawing on educational psychology literature pertinent to expectancy-value and learning task value, and including other dimensions in its conceptualizations, for example: the relevance of writing to learners' personal and academic interests and the perceived value of specific writing topics. At the operationalization level, this can be initially accomplished by synthesizing an adapted measure from the items found in the scale used by Behizadeh and Engelhard (2016), MacArthur, Philippakos, and Graham (2016), Pajares et al. (2007), and Wright, Hodges, and McTigue (2019). Meanwhile, there is also a good opportunity for broadening writing self-concept by conceptualizing it as a construct encompassing learners' writing ability self-esteem, writing teachability and performance improvability beliefs, and their social comparison, comparison deficiency, and social feedback perceptions. The items tapping these writing self-concept dimensions are found in the scales developed by Bottomley, Henk, and Melnick (1997), Ehm, Lindberg, and Hasselhorn (2014), Limpo and Alves (2014), Pajares and his colleagues (e.g., Pajares et al., 2000, 2007; Pajares & Valiante, 1999, 2001), Palmquist and Young (1992), and Waller and Papi (2017).

There is also need for purer measures of some other writing motivation constructs; specifically, writing anxiety and self-efficacy. With regard to writing anxiety, there has been an increasing tendency to address it as a construct of purely situational nature (e.g., Tsai, 2008; Tsao, Tseng, & Wang, 2017; Woodrow, 2011; Yao, 2019), and in turn to differentiate it from writing apprehension. In line with this orientation, there is a need for avoiding the conflation of the two constructs and for using situational measures of writing anxiety. In addition to the items included in previous writing anxiety scales (e.g., Cheng, 2004; Tsai, 2008), more items tapping writers' contextualized anxious feelings can be generated using qualitative data sources such as semi-structured interviews and reflective journals. The issue of construct validity should be also considered when designing future writing self-efficacy measures. Some previous writing self-efficacy measures include self-concept items (e.g., Graham et al., 1993; Wong, Butler, Ficzere, & Kuperis, 1997), whereas some supposedly unidemensional self-efficacy scales have items related to two dimensions (e.g., Prat-Sala & Redford, 2010; Zimmerman & Bandura, 1994). Thus, a given writing self-efficacy measure should include only the items tapping writers' task-specific beliefs and represent the dimension it claims assessing.

A final issue that is worth mentioning is designing writing motivation scales for children. As noted in chapter 2, the very vast majority of the scales used were developed for adult writers. Exceptional cases include the children's writing attitude scales developed by Graham, Berninger, and Fan (2007), Hogan (1980), Kear, Coffman, McKenna, and Ambrosio (2000), and Knudson (1991, 1992). Obviously, there is a scarcity of writing motivation scales designed specifically for young learners; a gap that needs to be filled in future research.

6.3 Researching writing motivation correlates and sources

Increasing research has addressed the various correlates and sources of writing motivation (i.e., personal variables, performance, belief and behaviour correlates, and the learning and instructional practices). As noted in chapter 3, this research reported consistent results on the direction of the relationship of writers' motivation with some of the variables (e.g., language ability level, writing performance, previous writing learning experiences, and teacher feedback) rather than others (e.g., gender and age, and interaction among writing motivation perceptions and beliefs). Besides, research on some other correlates is still scant. Therefore, future research addressing particular research voids will help in developing clearer profiles of the affective, behavioural, and performance characteristics of motivated and demotivated writers.

Future research needs to tackle particular issues related to the association between learners' writing motivation and their gender, age, and sociocultural background. Previous studies on gender-, age-, and culture-related differences in writing motivation were limited to some international contexts and motivational constructs (specifically writing apprehension, anxiety, and self-efficacy). As shown in chapter 3, the larger number of these gender and age studies was conducted in L1 contexts. Researchers could conduct future large-scale and cross-cultural studies examining how these variables correlate with all writing motivation constructs (i.e., apprehension/attitude, anxiety, motivational regulation of writing, perceived value of writing, self-efficacy, self-concept, and writing achievement goals). These large-scale and cross-cultural studies could show us how personal variables differ from one international context to another and how they relate to each writing motivation construct or type of constructs (i.e., dispositional, situational, self-ability belief, and goal constructs). It will be beneficial also to compare how writers' motivational constructs differ in L1 and L2 environments. From these large-scale and cross-cultural studies, we may gain important insights into how international cultures mediate the role of gender and age in writing motivation. The scarce research on graduate students and L2 young learners' writing motivation is also noteworthy. Only a few studies have addressed writing motivation in the graduate education context (e.g., Huerta, Goodson, Beigi, & Chlup, 2017; Yu, Zhang, Zheng, Yuan, & Zhang, 2019), whereas the studies on the latter age category (i.e., L2 young learners) are almost non-existent.

On the other hand, a number of issues are yet to be explored in the research addressing the performance and behavioural correlates of writing motivation. The little research correlating writers' motivation with their linguistic knowledge and perceived language ability beliefs has only addressed writing self-efficacy, apprehension, and anxiety constructs. Therefore, there is a need for exploring the relationship between these two factors and other writing motivation constructs (e.g., writing achievement goals and the perceived value of writing). These other constructs should also be addressed in the future research examining the process and product performance of writing motivation. Besides, some other writing process and product performance dimensions need to be considered in future writing motivation research. Better insights about writers' processes can be obtained by combining data sources, for example, the think-aloud method with retrospective interviews or keystroke logging with eye-tracking (see Abdel Latif, 2019a, 2019b). Enriching the writing process data in such a way and examining how it relates to various writing motivation constructs can add to the originality of future relevant studies. As for the future writing product studies, these can examine how writers' motivation correlates with the lexical richness features in their texts, a neglected dimension in previous research, along with the syntactic complexity and text quantity aspects.

With regard to the interaction among writing motivation constructs, their mediating influence on performance variables remains to be elucidated. This issue has been examined in very few studies (e.g., Goodman & Cirka, 2009; Pajares et al., 2007). Research dealing with such mediating influence issue can inform us about the relative contribution of each construct to writers' performance. More attention should be also given to exploring the behavioural correlates of writing motivation. The correlates dealt with in previous few studies only include: the nature of the writing courses attended, extracurricular activities, writing procrastination, and writing learning styles. More behavioural correlates can be explored in future research such as writing study habits, seeking feedback, and writing test preparation.

Some issues related to instructional practices also need due attention in writing motivation research. Little research evidence is available about how writers can be motivated or demotivated as a result of the topics assigned, and the nature of the instructional practices and learning materials used. Not much research is either available about the influence of peer feedback on writing motivation. Since motivation has been addressed as a peripheral variable in most teacher and peer feedback writing studies, there is a need for feedback research tackling writing motivation from an in-depth angle. The feedback studies reported by Yu and his colleagues (Yu et al., 2019; Yu & Hu, 2017; Yu, Jiang, & Zhou, 2020) are good examples of such in-depth research.

6.4 Developing writing motivation instructional research

As has been seen in chapter 4, the instructional research of writing motivation has experimented various types of teaching treatments and training, including technology-supported instruction, strategy instruction, feedback types, genre-based instruction, task interest-based instruction, and therapeutic training. Though these studies have deepened our understanding of the elements of instruction or training potentially reinforcing writing motivation, advancing future instructional research requires addressing a number of issues and gaps. In future instructional studies, there is a need for creating a prominent place of writing motivation, investigating a wider range of motivational constructs, using more accurate measures, and experimenting instructional treatments in different educational contexts.

In many of the previous instructional studies reviewed in chapter 4, writing motivation constructs have been peripherally addressed. Since the main focus in these studies was on writing performance, they investigated writing motivation constructs either as a secondary variable tackled quantitatively (e.g., Duijnhouwer, Prins, & Stokking, 2010, 2012; Garcia-Sanchez & Fidalgo-Redondo, 2006; Graham, Harris, & Mason, 2005) or an aspect elicited through qualitative data (e.g., Arslan & Şahin-Kızıl, 2010; Vurdien, 2013). Exceptional cases, in which the main research focus was on writing motivation constructs, include the therapeutic training studies and other few ones employing different instructional types (e.g., Jiang & Luk, 2016; Mahfoodh, 2017; Yao, 2019). Overall, it is concluded that writing motivation has a secondary place in the majority of the published instructional studies. Accordingly, there is a need for creating a prominent place for writing motivation in future instructional studies. Through the availability of much research of this type, we could gain far better insights about the impact of various instructional treatments on writers' motivation.

A main shortcoming in the previous instructional research is related to the writing motivation constructs it has addressed. As noted, the very vast majority of the studies focused on testing the effect of a particular instructional treatment on either students' writing dispositional perceptions or their self-ability beliefs. The situational- or goal-orientation constructs of writing motivation were almost neglected in these studies. Therefore, we need to have a clearer picture about the interaction between different instructional treatments and a wider range of writing motivation constructs. Filling this research gap requires moving beyond the writing apprehension/attitude/self-efficacy cycle noted in the reviewed instructional studies.

A clear weakness in many instructional studies reviewed in chapter 4 lies in the measurement of writing motivation constructs. A large number of these studies depended on short scales with items synthesized from different sources. In many cases, the items of these scales do not mirror the construct they claim assessing. A natural consequence of this is the terminological overlap, i.e., labelling the assessed constructs in a confusing way. We can note, for instance, that in many instructional studies, the term "writing motivation" has been used to refer to a specific attitudinal construct. As noted earlier in chapter 4, this seems to have resulted from the inadequate writing motivation research background. One way for overcoming this measurement weakness in future instructional research is collaborating with researchers with experience in assessing writing motivation and its constructs. Another way is to comprehensively review previously published measures of the target writing motivation construct(s) prior to deciding upon the assessment tools to be used.

A final gap noted in the previous instructional research of writing motivation is experimenting instructional treatments in different learning contexts. Chapter 4 shows that some types of instructional studies have been experimented in L1 writing contexts only (i.e., writing strategy and therapeutic training studies), whereas other types have been more frequently employed in L2 ones (i.e., feedback instructional treatments and genre-based writing instruction studies). Likewise, the writing strategy instruction studies have been commonly used with school students, contrarily to the genre-based instruction and therapeutic training studies, which have been only experimented in university settings. Noted also is the lack of instructional writing motivation studies in some international contexts. The studies reported so far have been mainly concerned with writing learning environments in Western and South-East Asian countries. Given this, there is a need for filling these contextual research gaps in future instructional studies.

6.5 Promoting effective writing motivation instructional practices

At the pedagogical level, we can advance the instructional practices of writing motivation through two main approaches to popularizing its pedagogy awareness. The first approach lies in publishing more works for prescribing writing motivation enhancement. The second one is raising teachers' awareness of writing motivation pedagogy.

Many teachers may not be interested in reading empirical writing motivation research reports which are full of jargon terms and statistical formulas. Instead, they normally look for the works synthesizing research findings in the form of guidelines for motivating students to write. As mentioned in chapter 5, the works prescribing how writing motivation can be fostered are very scarce (e.g., Bruning & Horn, 2000; Reeves, 1997; Walker, 2003; see also chapter 5 in this book). In the future, there is a need for publishing regular papers providing different guidelines for how to reinforce students' writing motivation. These guidelines should depend on the accumulated evidence gained from the increasing relevant research. International journals of writing (such as *Journal of Second Language Writing*, *Reading and Writing*, *Reading & Writing Quarterly*, and *Writing & Pedagogy*) could assume a leading role in this area by publishing these motivational-oriented instruction tailoring papers. Publishing an increasing number of these works could greatly lead to disseminating writing motivation pedagogy culture among teachers, and their educators.

Language teacher education and educators also have an important role to play in popularizing writing motivation pedagogy awareness. In the education programmes tailored to pre-service or in-service teachers, educators could allocate a part to raising trainees' awareness of what causes student writers to be motivated or demotivated, and how to help them overcome their writing demotivation. These issues could also be highlighted in the writing instructional scenarios given in the teacher guides designed for textbooks. At the school level, teaching supervisors may also draw teachers' attention to how to optimize their practices to meet students' writing motivation needs. Popularizing writing motivation pedagogy awareness in such ways will result in significant gains for all stakeholders. Junior and senior teachers and their educators will discuss and employ important writing instruction guidelines. Students will learn writing in more positive and supportive environments. Ultimately, this will be reflected in short- and long-term gains in their performance and engagement in writing.

References

Abdel Latif, M. M. M. (2019a). Using think-aloud protocols and interviews in investigating writers' composing processes: Combining concurrent and retrospective data. *International Journal of Research & Method in Education*, *42*(2), 111–123. doi: 10.1080/1743727X.2018.1439003

Abdel Latif, M. M. M. (2019b). Eye-tracking in recent L2 learner process research: A review of areas, issues, and methodological approaches. *System*, *83*, 25–35. doi: 10.1016/j.system.2019.02.008

Arslan, R. Ş., & Şahin-Kızıl, A. (2010). How can the use of blog software facilitate the writing process of English language learners? *Computer-Assisted Language Learning*, *23*(3), 183–197. doi: 10.1080/09588221.2010.486575

Behizadeh, N., & Engelhard, G., Jr. (2016). Examining the psychometric quality of a modified Perceived Authenticity in Writing Scale with Rasch measurement theory. In Q. Zhang (Ed.). Pacific Rim Objective Measurement Symposium (PROMS) 2015. Conference Proceedings, pp. 71–87. Singapore: Springer. doi: 10.1007/978-981-10-1687-5_5

Blake, R. W. (1976). Assessing English and language arts teachers' attitudes toward writers and writing. *The English Record*, *27*, 87–97.

Bottomley, D. M., Henk, W. A., & Melnick, S. A. (1997). Assessing children's views about themselves as writers using the writer self-perception scale. *The Reading Teacher*, *51*, 286–296.

Bruning, R., & Horn, C. (2000). Developing motivation to write. *Educational Psychologist*, *35*, 25–37. doi: 10.1207/S15326985EP3501_4

Charney, D., Newman, J. H., & Palmquist, M. (1995). "I'm just no good at writing": Epistemological style and attitudes toward writing. *Written Communication*, *12*(3), 298–329. doi: 10.1177/0741088395012003004

Cheng, Y. S. (2004). A measure of second language writing anxiety: Scale development and preliminary validation. *Journal of Second Language Writing*, *13*(4), 313–335. doi: 10.1016/j.jslw.2004.07.001

Daly, J. A., & Miller, M. D. (1975a). The empirical development of an instrument to measure writing apprehension. *Research in the Teaching of English*, *9*(3), 242–249.

Daly, J. A., & Miller, M. D. (1975b). Further attitudes in writing apprehension: SAT scores, success expectations, willingness to take advanced courses and sex differences. *Research in the Teaching of English*, *9*, 250–256.

Daly, J. A., & Miller, M. D. (1975c). Apprehension of writing as a predictor of message intensity. *Journal of Psychology*, *89*, 175–177. doi: 10.1080/00223980.1975.9915748

Daly, J. A., & Shamo, W. G. (1976). Writing apprehension and occupational choice. *Journal of Occupational Psychology*, *49*, 55–56. doi: 10.1111/j.2044-8325.1976.tb00329.x

Daly, J. A., & Shamo, W. G. (1978). Academic decisions as a function of writing apprehension. *Research in the Teaching of English*, *12*, 119–126.

Duijnhouwer, H., Prins, F. J., & Stokking, K. M. (2010). Progress feedback effects on students' writing mastery goal, self-efficacy beliefs, and performance. *Educational Research and Evaluation, 16*(1), 53–74. doi: 10.1080/13803611003711393

Duijnhouwer, H., Prins, F. J., & Stokking, K. M. (2012). Feedback providing improvement strategies and reflection on feedback use: Effects on students' writing motivation, process, and performance. *Learning and Instruction, 22*, 171–184. doi: 10.1016/j.learninstruc.2011.10.003

Ehm, J., Lindberg, S., & Hasselhorn, M. (2014). Reading, writing, and math self-concept in elementary school children: Influence of dimensional comparison processes. *European Journal of Psychology of Education, 29*(2), 277–294. doi: 10.1007/s10212-013-0198-x

Emig, J., & King, B. (1979). *Emig-King attitude scale for teachers*. ERIC Document, ED 236 629.

Garcia-Sanchez, J., & Fidalgo-Redondo, R. (2006). Effects of two types of self-regulatory instruction programs on students with learning disabilities in writing products, processes, and self-efficacy. *Learning Disability Quarterly, 29*, 181–211. doi: 10.2307/30035506

Graham, S., Berninger, V., & Fan, W. (2007). The structural relationship between writing attitude and writing achievement in first and third grade students. *Contemporary Educational Psychology, 32*, 516–536. doi: 10.1016/j.cedpsych.2007.01.002

Graham, S., Harris, K. R., & Mason, L. (2005). Improving the writing performance, knowledge, and self-efficacy of struggling young writers: The effects of self-regulated strategy development. *Contemporary Educational Psychology, 30*, 207–241. doi: 10.1016/j.cedpsych.2004.08.001

Graham, S., Schwartz, S., & MacArthur, C. (1993). Learning disabled and normally achieving students' knowledge of writing and the composing process, attitude toward writing, and self-efficacy. *Journal of Learning Disabilities, 26*, 237–249. doi: 10.1177/002221949302600404

Goodman, S. B., & Cirka, C. C. (2009). Efficacy and anxiety: An examination of writing attitudes in a first-year seminar. *Journal on Excellence in College Teaching, 20*, 5–28.

Hogan, T. P. (1980). Students' interests in writing activities. *Research in the Teaching of English, 14*(2), 119–125.

Huerta, M., Goodson, P., Beigi, M., & Chlup, D. (2017). Graduate students as academic writers: Writing anxiety, self-efficacy and emotional intelligence. *Higher Education Research & Development, 36*(4), 716–729. doi: 10.1080/07294360.2016.1238881

Jiang, L., & Luk, J. (2016). Multimodal composing as a learning activity in English classrooms: Inquiring into the sources of its motivational capacity. *System, 59*(1), 1–11. doi: 10.1016/j.system.2016.04.00

Kear, D., Coffman, G., McKenna, M., & Ambrosio, A. (2000). Measuring attitude toward writing: A new tool for teachers. *The Reading Teacher, 54*(1), 10–23.

Knudson, R. E. (1991). Development and use of a writing attitude survey in grades 4 to 8. *Psychological Reports, 68*(3), 807–816. doi: 10.2466/pr0.1991.68.3.807

Knudson, R. E. (1992). Development and application of a writing attitude survey for grades 1 to 3. *Psychological reports, 70*(3), 711–720. doi: 10.2466/PR0.70.3.711-720

Limpo, T., & Alves, R. (2014). Implicit theories of writing and their impact on students' response to a SRSD intervention. *British Journal of Educational Psychology, 84*, 571–590. doi: 10.1111/bjep.12042

MacArthur, C., Philippakos, Z., & Graham, S. (2016). A multicomponent measure of writing motivation with basic college writers. *Learning Disability Quarterly*, *39*(1), 31–43. doi: 10.1177/0731948715583115

Mahfoodh, O. H. (2017). "I feel disappointed": EFL university students' emotional responses towards teacher written feedback. *Assessing Writing*, *31*, 53–72. doi: 10.1016/j.asw.2016.07.001

Pajares, F., Britner, S., & Valiante, G. (2000). Relation between achievement goals and self-beliefs of middle school students in writing and science. *Contemporary Educational Psychology*, *25*, 406–422. doi: 10.1006/ceps.1999.1027

Pajares, F., & Johnson, M. J. (1994). Confidence and competence in writing: The role of writing self-efficacy, outcome expectancy, and apprehension. *Research in the Teaching of English*, *28*, 313–331.

Pajares, F., & Johnson, M. J. (1996). Self-efficacy beliefs and the writing performance of entering high school students. *Psychology in the Schools*, *33*, 163–175. doi: 10.1002/(SICI)1520-6807(199604)33:2<163::AID-PITS10>3.0.CO;2-C

Pajares, F., & Valiante, G. (1999). Grade level and gender differences in the writing self-beliefs of middle school students. *Contemporary Educational Psychology*, *24*(4), 390–405. doi: 10.1006/ceps.1998.0995

Pajares, F., & Valiante, G. (2001). Gender differences in writing motivation and achievement of middle school students: A function of gender orientation? *Contemporary Educational Psychology*, *26*, 366–381. doi: 10.1006/ceps.2000.1069

Pajares, F., Valiante, G., & Cheong, Y. F. (2007). Writing self-efficacy and its relation to gender, writing motivation, and writing competence: A developmental perspective. In S. Hidi, & P. Boscolo (Eds.). *Motivation and writing: Research and school practice*, (pp. 141–162). Dordrecht, The Netherlands: Kluwer.

Palmquist, M., & Young, R. (1992). The notion of giftedness and student expectations about writing. *Written Communication*, *9*(1), 137–169. doi: 10.1177/0741088392009001004

Prat-Sala, M., & Redford, P. (2010). The interplay between motivation, self-efficacy, and approaches to studying. *The British Journal of Educational Psychology*, *80*(2), 283–305. doi: 10.1348/000709909x480563

Reeves, L. L. (1997). Minimizing writing apprehension in the learner centered classroom. *English Journal*, *86*(6), 38–45. doi: 10.2307/820367

Shell, D., Colvin, C., & Bruning, R. (1995). Self-efficacy, attributions, and outcome expectancy mechanisms in reading and writing achievement: Grade-level and achievement-level differences. *Journal of Educational Psychology*, *87*, 386–398. doi: 10.1037/0022-0663.87.3.386

Thompson, M. O. (1978). *The development and evaluation of a language study approach to a college course in freshman composition*. PhD dissertation, The American University, Washington D.C., USA.

Tsao, J., Tseng, W., & Wang, W. (2017). The effects of writing anxiety and motivation on EFL college students' self-evaluative judgments of corrective feedback. *Psychological Reports*, *120*(2), 219–241. doi: 10.1177/0033294116687123

Tsai, H. M. (2008). The development of an English writing anxiety scale for Institute of Technology English Majors. *Journal of Education and Psychology*, *31*(3), 81–107. doi: 10.1177/0033294116687123

Vurdien, R. (2013). Enhancing writing skills through blogging in an advanced English as a foreign language class in Spain. *Computer-Assisted Language Learning*, *26*(2), 126–143. doi: 10.1080/09588221.2011.639784

Waller, L., & Papi, M. (2017). Motivation and feedback: How implicit theories of intelligence predict L2 writers' motivation and feedback orientation. *Journal of Second Language Writing*, *35*, 54–65. doi: 10.1016/j.jslw.2017.01.004

Walker, B. (2003). The cultivation of student self-efficacy in reading and writing. *Reading & Writing Quarterly*, 19, 287–302. doi: 10.1080/10573560308217

Wong, B. Y. L., Butler, D. L., Ficzere, S. A., & Kuperis, S. (1997). Teaching adolescents with learning disabilities and low achievers to plan, write, and revise compare-and-contrast essays. *Learning Disabilities Research and Practice*, *12*(1), 2–15.

Woodrow, L. (2011). College English writing affect: Self-efficacy and anxiety. *System*, *39*, 510–522. doi: 10.1016/j.system.2011.10.017

Wright, K. L., Hodges, T. S., & McTigue, E. M. (2019). A validation program for the self-beliefs, writing-beliefs, and attitude survey: A measure of adolescents' motivation toward writing. *Assessing Writing*, *39*, 64–78. doi: 10.1016/j.asw.2018.12.004

Yao, Q. (2019). Direct and indirect feedback: How do they impact on secondary school learners' writing anxiety and how do learners perceive them? *The Asian Conference on Language Learning 2019, Official Conference Proceedings*, 1–12.

Yu, S., & Hu, G. (2017). Can higher-proficiency L2 learners benefit from working with lower-proficiency partners in peer feedback? *Teaching in Higher Education*, *22*(2), 178–192. doi: 10.1080/13562517.2016.1221806

Yu, S., Jiang, L., & Zhou, N. (2020). Investigating what feedback practices contribute to students' writing motivation and engagement in Chinese EFL context: A large scale study. *Assessing Writing*, *44*, 1–15. doi: 10.1016/j.asw.2020.100451

Yu, S., Zhang, Y., Zheng, Y., Yuan, K., & Zhang, L. (2019). Understanding student engagement with peer feedback on master's theses: A Macau study. *Assessment & Evaluation in Higher Education*, *44*(1), 50–65. doi: 10.1080/02602938.2018.1467879

Yu, S., Zhou, N., Zheng, Y., Zhang, L., Cao, H., & Li, X. (2019). Evaluating student motivation and engagement in Chinese EFL writing context. *Studies in Educational Evaluation*, *62*, 129–141. doi: 10.1016/j.stueduc.2019.06.002

Zimmerman, B., & Bandura, A. (1994). Impact of self-regulatory influences on writing course attainment. *American Educational Research Journal*, *31*, 845–862. doi: 10.2307/1163397

Glossary

Attitude towards writing: One's liking or disliking of writing and writing evaluation situations.
Blog-mediated writing instruction: A type of writing instruction that engages students in creating their personal pages and sharing blog posts with their peers so as to exchange feedback on writing performance.
Comparison deficiency of writing ability: One's belief that their writing ability is deficient when compared to what it should be.
Construct validity: The extent to which a measure assesses what it claims.
Construct under-representation: A case in which a given measure assesses a construct from a narrow angle, and thus fails to cover its dimensions.
Descriptive writing motivation research: The research concerned with describing and identifying the correlates, predictors, or sources of writers' de-/motivation. See also *Instructional writing motivation research* and *Writing motivation measurement research*.
Entity theory of writing intelligence: The belief that one's writing ability is unimprovable and unlearnable. This belief is viewed as a dimension of writing self-concept.
Feedback provision treatments: The different feedback instructional treatments used in writing studies to explore their impact on students' performance and/or emotional responses and engagement in writing. These treatments may include using a particular type of teacher written corrective feedback or comments, or may also involve learners in providing feedback to their peers.
Genre approach: An instructional approach through which writing is taught by exposing students to model texts in the target genre.
Genre-based writing instruction: A type of writing instruction that focuses on raising learners' awareness of the linguistic and structural features in the target genre.
Ideal writing self: A writing achievement goal orientation construct close to intrinsic motivation. It reflects learners' desired goals of their writing ability/competence mastery.

Implicit theories of writing: One's beliefs about the improvability or learnability of writing skills. These beliefs are viewed as a dimension of writing self-concept.

Incremental theory of writing: The belief that one's writing ability is improvable and learnable. This belief is viewed as a dimension of writing self-concept.

Instructional writing motivation research: The research concerned with experimenting particular instructional treatments and examining their impact on learners' writing motivation. See also *Descriptive writing motivation research* and *Writing motivation measurement research*.

Learning writing self-efficacy: A writing self-efficacy type which means one's perceived ability to complete specific writing classroom activities or learn particular writing course contents; for example, understanding course materials, doing good assignments, and performing well in writing courses.

Motivational regulation of writing: The self-talk or verbalized thoughts writers use to foster their engagement in task performance, avoid anxiety and frustration, and encourage themselves while performing the task.

Multidimensional writing self-efficacy: Conceptualizing and assessing writing self-efficacy as a construct composed of more than one dimension. See also *Unidimensional writing self-efficacy*.

Multidimensional writing self-efficacy scales: The scales assessing more than one dimension of writers' self-efficacy. For example, they may include subscales assessing learners' confidence in producing particular textual features, possessing writing process regulation skills, and their perceived ability to study and understand specific writing learning materials. See also *Unidimensional writing self-efficacy scales*.

Multimodal composing: The process of communicating ideas through using written words along with visual and audio elements.

Ought-to writing self: An achievement goal orientation construct close to extrinsic writing motivation.

Perceived value of writing (also known as task value and task interest): The perceived enjoyment, usefulness, or importance of writing or writing tasks.

Perceived authenticity of writing: The belief that a writing task is associated with or relevant to one's life situations.

Process approach: An instructional approach through which students learn how to write in collaborative activities of text planning, drafting, and revising.

Process-genre approach: An instructional approach which combines the activities of both the process and genre ones in teaching writing. See also *Process approach* and *Genre approach*.

168 *Glossary*

Product approach: An instructional approach which focuses on improving students' language performance via using controlled, guided, and free writing activities.

Process-focused writing self-efficacy (also known as text composing process self-efficacy): A writing self-efficacy conceptualization and assessment perspective concerned with one's perceived ability to regulate and use particular composing processes; for example, generating ideas, planning essay writing, and evaluating and monitoring text production.

Product-focused writing self-efficacy (also known as written convention self-efficacy): A self-efficacy conceptualization and assessment perspective concerned with one's perceived ability to produce certain written text features; for example, writing grammatically correct sentences or good paragraphs with appropriate topic sentences.

Product-genre approach: A proposed instructional approach that combines the activities of both the product and genre ones in teaching writing. See also *Genre approach* and *Product approach*.

Progress feedback: An approach to feedback provision through which the teacher focuses mainly on the performance aspects which have been improved as compared to previous performances.

Social feedback on writing performance (also known as social persuasion): The feedback received from others (e.g., teacher, peers, or family members) on one's writing performance. This feedback plays a role in forming writers' self-concept.

Social or observational comparison of writing performance (also known as vicarious experiences): Observing others' writing performances and comparing theirs to one's performance. These observational experiences lead the learner to develop writing self-concept beliefs.

Task interest-based instruction: A type of writing instruction that aims at enhancing students' writing performance and motivation via getting them to write about the topics relevant to their life experiences and of interest to them.

Therapeutic training of writing motivation: The training that aims at optimizing learners' writing motivation through using particular psychotherapy-based techniques or procedures. Examples of these training procedures include: visualization (i.e., stimulating learners' positive thinking about performing writing tasks) and the writing anxiety group (involving learners in guided free writing and group discussions of their writing motivation problems).

Unidimensional writing self-efficacy: Conceptualizing and assessing writing self-efficacy as a construct composed of one dimension only. See also *Multidimensional writing self-efficacy*.

Unidimensional writing self-efficacy scales: The scales assessing one dimension in writers' self-efficacy. This dimension can be related to either the writing product (i.e., learners' confidence in either producing particular textual features) or the writing process (i.e., learners' confidence in possessing writing process regulation skills). See also *Multidimensional writing self-efficacy scales*.

Wiki-mediated writing instruction: A type of writing instruction through which students are engaged in collaboratively writing multiple drafts with collective content about certain topics.

Writing achievement goal orientations: Learners' reasons, purposes, or desired outcomes for doing a specific writing activity. See also *Writing mastery achievement goals*, *Writing performance avoidance goals*, and *Writing performance approach goals*.

Writing anxiety: The negative feelings experienced while performing a writing task or doing a writing activity.

Writing apprehension: One's avoidance of writing and writing evaluation situations.

Writing mastery achievement goals: Learning writing or performing its tasks for the purpose of developing one's writing ability as an ultimate goal.

Writing mastery experience: The interpreted outcome of one's previous writing performance and the improvement made in it.

Writing motivation: An umbrella term which includes learners' liking or disliking of writing situations and the perceived value of writing, the situational feelings they experience while writing and the way they regulate them, beliefs about their writing ability and skills, and their desired goals for learning to write.

Writing motivation and engagement: A broad multidimensional construct that refers to some behavioural actions and motivational aspects associated with engaging in performing writing tasks and activities.

Writing motivation measurement research: The research concerned with developing and validating measures of particular writing motivation constructs. See also *Descriptive writing motivation research* and *Instructional writing motivation research*.

Writing outcome expectancy: The outcome expected from learning writing or performing writing tasks.

Writing performance avoidance goals: Learning writing or performing writing tasks for the purpose of concealing any incompetence symptoms before others.

Writing performance approach goals: Learning writing or performing writing tasks for the purpose of demonstrating one's ability, obtaining teacher praise, or receiving social recognition.

Writing procrastination: Frequently delaying one's performance of writing tasks as a result of experiencing some kind of discomfort.

Writing self-concept: Beliefs about one's general writing ability and learnability of writing skills.

Writing self-efficacy: One's perceived ability to perform or demonstrate task-specific writing skills and processes. See also *Learning writing self-efficacy*, *Process-focused writing self-efficacy*, and *Product-focused writing self-efficacy*.

Writing self-perceptions: A broad term that may refer to one's writing ability beliefs, writing interest, or anxiety.

Writing self-regulation strategy instruction (also known as writing self-regulated strategy development): A type of writing strategy instruction that focuses on helping learners manage and monitor their text production processes. See also *Writing strategy instruction.*

Writing strategy instruction: A type of writing instruction that focuses on helping learners use effective strategies or processes for planning, monitoring, and revising texts. See also *Writing self-regulation strategy instruction.*

Writing styles (also writing approaches): The general approaches writers follow in composing their texts (e.g., the deep or reflective composing style versus the surface composing style).

Writer's block: One's inability to proceed with writing or to find what to write.

Index

Abdel Latif, Muhammad M. M. 3–4, 12, 16, 19, 37–38, 48, 52, 63–64, 80, 82, 85–86, 95–96, 138–139, 141, 159
ability attributions 147, 151
age 22, 38, 77–78, 96, 98, 146, 150, 152, 158
attitude towards writing 5, 6, 10–11, 33–38, 55, 58, 60, 87, 125, 129, 149, 156, 166
attitudinal/dispositional constructs 21, 33, 156
automated writing evaluation 145, 146, 150

Bandura, Albert 4, 11–12, 15, 47–48, 51, 157
Behizadeh, Nadia 7, 18, 40, 93, 125, 141, 157
beliefs about writing 3, 18, 39, 40, 138, 156
blog-mediated writing instruction 111–112, 166
Bloom, Lynn 78, 126–127, 141
Bong, Mimi 6, 13, 55
Boscolo, Pietro 1, 3, 93, 125, 142
Bottomley, Diane M. 13, 19, 53, 55–56, 157
Bruning, Roger 5–6, 10–12, 14, 34–35, 37, 46, 48–50, 77, 138, 140
Burgoon, Judee K. 5, 35

Charney, Davida 6, 34, 36, 53, 55, 156
Cheng, Yuh-show 8–9, 11, 35, 37, 41–43, 61, 64, 81, 86, 157
comparison deficiency 55–56, 157, 166
Conradi, Kristin 17, 18
construct under-representation 35, 37, 57, 166
construct validity 7, 33, 35–37, 66, 157, 166

corrective feedback 118–119, 122, 129, 145, 149, 151, 166
Csizér, Kata 9–12, 41–42, 46, 62, 76–77

Daly, John A. 3–6, 8–11, 34–37, 53, 55, 82, 85, 89, 92, 126, 128, 155
Demotivated writers 22, 75, 83–85, 89–90, 96–97, 141, 158
Dörnyei, Zoltan 2, 18, 44, 61, 64, 76, 78, 90, 93, 137
Duijnhouwer, Hendrien 46, 118–120, 129–130, 148, 160
Dweck, Carol 14, 54

Eccles, Jacquelynne 4, 17
effort attributions 137, 147, 151
Elliot, Andrew J. 16
Emig, Janet 5, 34–36, 155
entity theory of writing intelligence 14, 21, 53–54, 166
extrinsic motivation 2, 15–16, 57, 78

factor analysis 35, 60, 66
Faigley, Lester 5, 8, 85
feedback instructional treatment 117, 128–129, 161, 166
feedback seeking 90; seeking feedback 97, 159
Ferris, Dana 95
focus group interviews 61–62, 125
free writing 89, 126, 128, 143, 168
Fritzsche, Barbara A. 3, 9–10, 41–42, 89

Gardner, Robert 2, 4
gender 22, 75–78, 96, 98, 117, 152, 158
genre approach 143–144, 166–168
genre-based writing instruction 122, 124, 128, 129, 161, 166

Index

Graham, Steve 4–5, 7, 10, 12, 34, 47–38, 40, 46–48, 53, 55, 55–66, 78, 86, 111, 115–117, 156–157, 160
guidelines 22, 33, 64, 112, 124, 137–141, 146, 149–152

Hansen, Jette, G. 148–189
Harris, Karen 5, 37, 46, 115–116, 144, 160
Hayes, John 1, 3
Hidi, Suzanne 1, 3, 76, 124–125, 129
Hiver, Philip 5, 7, 10, 12, 16, 41–42, 46, 58, 63, 122–124, 129
Hyland, Ken 62, 94, 118–119, 122, 125, 129, 141, 143, 148

ideal writing self 21, 166; ideal L2 writing self 5, 7, 16, 58)
implicit theories of writing 14–15, 21, 52–54, 66, 84, 116, 167
incremental theory of writing 15, 21, 53–54; incremental and entity theories of writing 6, 15, 26, 52
instructional practices 90, 94, 98, 155, 158–159, 161
instructional treatments 110, 117–118, 122, 128–130, 159–160, 166–167
instrumental motivation 2, 77
integrative motivation 2, 57, 77
intervention 60, 62, 110, 115–116, 124, 127–129
intrinsic motivation 2, 16, 57, 76, 112, 116, 166
item generation 61, 64

Jones, Ed 12, 46–48, 50, 52

Kaplan, Avi 7, 56–58
Klassen, Robert 47, 138
Knudson, Ruth E. 34–36, 38, 157

language ability level 79, 144, 150–151, 158
language learning motivation 1–2, 4, 75–78, 90, 127; L2 learning motivation 1–4, 15, 18, 75, 78, 93
language needs 151
Lavelle, Ellen 20
learners' journals 61; student journals 62
learning styles 159
learning writing self-efficacy 13, 167
Lee, Icy 5, 7, 12, 16, 58, 76, 78, 94–96
Lee, Sy-ying 89, 85
Li, Xuanxi 113
Likert scale 35, 38, 44, 64
Limpo, Teresa 6–7, 14–15, 34, 36, 53–54, 56, 85, 87–88, 116, 129, 138, 157

MacArthur 7, 12, 18, 34, 40, 46, 48–52, 56, 57–58, 88, 111, 156–157
MALL 92
malleability beliefs 87–88, 116
Marsh, Herbert 14, 53, 55
Martin, Andrew J. 20
McCarthy, Patricia 4–6, 11, 37, 49
medium of writing 91, 99
Meier, Scott 5, 9, 11, 37, 41–42, 46, 64
Middleton, Michael J. 4, 16, 57
mindful breathing 26–127, 129
motivated writers 75, 83–84, 96–99
motivational regulation of writing 4–5, 18, 21, 41–42, 66,67, 149, 156, 158, 167
multidimensional writing self-efficacy 46, 48, 167–168
multimodal composing 92, 111, 114, 129, 146, 167

notion of writing giftedness 6, 14, 21, 52–54, 86

observational comparison 19, 52, 55, 59, 168
Onwuegbuzie, Anthony J. 3, 86, 89–90
ought-to writing self 21, 66, 167; ought-to L2 writing self 5, 7, 16, 58
Oxford, Rebecca 18, 90

Pajares, Frank 1, 4, 6–7, 11–12, 14–18, 34–35, 37, 39, 46–47, 49, 53, 56–57, 59, 65, 77–78, 85–88, 147, 156–157, 159
Palmquist 6, 14, 34, 53–54, 86, 156–157
Papi, Mostafa 6, 14–15, 53, 54, 90, 157
peer feedback 39, 91, 96, 112, 117–118, 120–121, 129–130, 138, 146, 148–149, 151–152, 156, 159
peer feedback literacy 148, 151
perceived authenticity of writing 18, 39, 156, 167
perceived language ability beliefs 80–81, 158
perceived value of writing 3–4, 7, 17, 18, 20–21, 36, 39–41, 67, 81, 87–88, 97, 129, 149, 155, 158, 167, 169
personal variables 75, 78, 158
Phinney, Marianne 36, 91, 111
Pintrich, Paul 16, 18
pre-/post-testing 110, 112, 115, 117, 126–127
previous writing learning experiences 85, 158
process-focused writing self-efficacy 13, 46, 65, 168–169

process-genre approach 144, 167
product-genre approach 144, 168
process approach 143, 167
product approach 143, 167
product-focused writing self-efficacy 13, 46, 168–169
progress feedback 119–120, 129, 138, 148, 168

qualitative approach 33, 60–61
qualitative assessment 64, 67
qualitative data 60–63, 81, 110, 113, 117, 118, 124, 157, 160

reflective essays 61, 121
reflective journals 63, 157
response format 57, 64
Riffe, Daniel 5, 34–46, 76, 89
Rose, Mike 19, 34–36, 60

Sanders-Reio, Joanne 10, 34–35, 80, 85
Selfe, Cynthia 3, 5, 82, 83
semi-structured interviews 61, 63–64, 121, 157
Shaver, James 6, 10, 37
Shell, Duane 4–6, 11–12, 15, 17, 37, 46–47, 49, 56–57, 77, 156
situational constructs 21, 41–42, 156
social comparison 13, 53, 56, 138, 157
social feedback 19, 55–56, 157, 168
social persuasion 52, 59, 76, 78, 87, 168
socio-cultural background 22, 78, 98
strategy instruction 110–111, 114–117, 128–130, 144, 152, 159, 161, 170; writing Strategy instruction 114, 116–117, 129, 144, 161, 170
Spielberger Charles D. 9, 41–42

task interest 17, 125, 129, 138, 167
task interest-based instruction 110, 124, 128, 159, 168
task value 17–18, 39, 41, 112, 139, 156, 167
teacher feedback 39–40, 61, 91, 94–96, 99, 118–122, 129, 146–148, 151
technological tools 91–92, 111, 139, 145, 150–152
Teng, Lin S. 5, 7, 12, 18, 38–39, 41, 44–46, 48–52, 61, 64, 82, 84
terminological overlap 7–9, 21, 160
texts 4, 14, 50, 54, 79, 80, 81, 83–85, 88, 90–95, 97–98, 110, 112, 114, 115, 117–119, 122–123, 125, 143–149, 151, 159, 166, 170

therapeutic training 110, 125–126, 128–130, 159–161, 168
Troia, Gary A. 7, 17, 39, 56, 58, 89, 138, 140, 142, 147

unidimensional 46, 48, 67
unidimensional writing self-efficacy 168
Ushioda, Ema 2, 78, 137

Valiante, Gio 1, 6–7, 11–12, 14–18, 37, 39, 47, 49, 53, 56–57, 65, 76–77, 88, 156–157
validate 36, 45
validating 22, 64
validation 66
vicarious experience 59, 76, 87, 168
visualization 126, 129, 168

Warschauer, Mark 111, 113
Wiki-mediated writing instruction 113, 169
Wong, Bernice 46, 53, 55, 117, 157
Woodrow, Lindy 9–12, 41–42, 44, 46–48, 157
Word processors 91–92, 111, 145
Wright, Katherine 1, 3, 7, 13–14, 18, 40, 157
writer's block 19, 21, 170, 36, 51, 60
writing ability belief 21, 55, 61, 84–87, 139, 170
writing ability belief constructs 21, 45
writing achievement goal 6–7, 16–17, 20–21, 56–59, 84, 156, 158, 166, 168
writing affect 1, 22
writing anxiety 5, 8–11, 20–21, 35, 41–44, 61–62, 77–78, 81, 87, 94, 118, 126–127, 129–130, 141, 149, 156–157, 168–169
writing anxiety group 126–127, 129, 168
writing anxiety workshop 126–127, 129
writing apprehension 63–65, 67, 76–76, 80–83, 85–86, 88–90, 98, 111, 122, 124, 126–129, 140, 145, 152, 156–158, 160, 169
writing interest 18, 39, 114, 156, 170
writing learning goal constructs 21, 56, 58
writing mastery experience 79, 85, 124, 169
writing mastery goals 58, 90, 97, 120, 129, 140, 148–150; writing mastery achievement goals 169
writing motivation and engagement 20–21, 60, 94–95, 169
writing motivation pedagogy 155, 161
writing motivation sources 33, 59–60

writing outcome expectancy 6, 15–16, 21, 56–57, 156, 169
writing performance approach goals 16, 169 (performance approach goals 16, 57, 87–89)
writing performance avoidance goals 16, 169; performance avoidance goals 57, 87, 88
writing process 3, 13, 36, 48, 50–51, 61, 81–84, 87–88, 98, 114–115, 120, 128, 144, 149–151, 158–159, 169
writing procrastination 19, 21, 89, 97, 159, 169
writing product 49, 84, 159, 168
writing self-concept 6, 13, 15, 19–21, 35–37, 52–53, 55–56, 64, 67, 86, 88, 116, 155–157, 166–169
writing self-efficacy 4–6, 11–13, 20–21, 35, 37, 45–48, 51–52, 59, 64–67, 76–78, 80–81, 86–88, 112–113, 116, 120, 122–125, 129, 138, 156–158, 167–169
writing self-regulation strategy instruction 114–115, 170
writing self-regulated strategy development 114–115
writing self-perceptions 1, 19, 21, 170
writing styles 20, 170
writing topics 39, 41, 62, 91, 93, 142, 149, 156
written convention self-efficacy 45, 47, 168; writing convention self-efficacy 13, 87
written corrective feedback 90, 94–95, 118, 151, 166
Wynne, Craig 8, 126–129

Yilmaz Soylu, Meryem 7, 16, 56–58, 87
Yu, Shulin 5, 20, 58, 60, 76–77, 94–96, 120–121, 148–149, 158–159

Zimmerman, Barry 6, 12–13, 17–18, 46–48, 50–51, 60, 115, 157